About the author

Milford Bateman is a freelance consultant
specialising in local economic development policy,
particularly in relation to the western Balkans.
From 1991 to 2000, he was based at the University
of Wolverhampton in the UK, first as a lecturer in
East European economics, and then in 1996 he was
appointed senior research fellow in local economic
development. In 2000, he moved into the business
sector to become a full-time consultant. Since 1993,
he has worked as a consultant for most of the major
international development agencies, for a number
of local governments in Eastern Europe, and for
several of the major international NGOs. He is also
currently a visiting professor of economics at the
University of Juraj Dobrila at Pula, Croatia.

WHY DOESN'T MICROFINANCE WORK?

the destructive rise of local neoliberalism

Milford Bateman

Zed Books

LONDON · NEW YORK

Why Doesn't Microfinance Work? The destructive rise of local neoliberalism was first published in 2010 by Zed Books Ltd, 7 Cynthia Street, London N1 7JF, UK and Room 400, 175 Fifth Avenue, New York, NY 10010, USA

www.zedbooks.co.uk

Set in Monotype Sabon and Gill Sans Heavy by Ewan Smith, London
Index: ed.emery@thefreeuniversity.net
Cover designed by Rogue Four Design
Printed and bound in Great Britain by the MPG Books Group, Bodmin and King's Lynn

Distributed in the USA exclusively by Palgrave Macmillan, a division of St Martin's Press, LLC, 175 Fifth Avenue, New York, NY 10010, USA

A catalogue record for this book is available from the British Library
Library of Congress Cataloging in Publication Data available

ISBN 978 1 84813 331 0 hb
ISBN 978 1 84813 332 7 pb
ISBN 978 1 84813 333 4 eb

Contents

Preface | vi
Acronyms | x

1 Introduction 1

2 The rise of microfinance 6

3 Microfinance myths and realities 28

4 Microfinance as poverty trap 60

5 Commercialization: the death of microfinance 112

6 The politics of microfinance 154

7 Alternatives to conventional microfinance . 166

8 Conclusion: the need for a new beginning . . 201

Notes | 213
Bibliography | 233
Index | 253

Preface

This book has its roots in my frustration with the huge disconnect
that exists between the heady claims made for microfinance and
the everyday reality I have witnessed for many years now. Like
many others, I was initially intrigued and then very excited by this
innovation. It seemed to offer so much to so many – employment
generation, poverty reduction, additional income, sustainable
'bottom-up' development, empowerment of the poor, and rising
community solidarity. These were important economic and social
development outcomes. So if it really was the case that microfinance
was behind them, then it could certainly count on my full support.
Very early on in my PhD research at the University of Bradford,
starting in late 1986, and then over the course of more than two
years spent in the former Yugoslavia collecting material for my thesis
('Local economic strategies and new small firm entry: the case of
Yugoslavia'), I was steered towards microfinance. It seemed to be one
of the most obvious financial support policies I should think about.
On becoming a UK-based university lecturer in economics in 1990,
and also active in local economic development policy consulting
soon after, my contact with microfinance greatly increased. For
teaching purposes, I began to delve into the growing amount of
research on microfinance and microenterprises. I was able to access
the published outputs arising from many microfinance programmes.
And as part of my growing engagement in policy consulting work,
I also began to come across many microfinance programmes in the
field. Whenever I looked a little closer at microfinance policy and
programmes, however, nothing seemed to add up. It was a brilliantly
marketed and politically vital concept, but it was actually an empty
vessel.

The 1990s were an incredibly exciting time for those of us
involved in teaching, research and consulting in the area of local
economic development. Economists were coming to a much greater
understanding of the key development 'triggers' in any local economy, and the various ways many countries, regions and localities
have been successful in 'pressing them'. All the academic talk was

of the importance of supporting institutions, 'industrial districts', networks, local industrial policy, clusters, the Italian 'third way' model, commodity chains, technology development, and so on and so forth. I began to realize, however, that the microfinance model was an almost perfectly designed foil with regard to these important development policies, institutions and trajectories. It was soon clear, too, that microfinance programmes were starting to absorb the valuable financial resources that might otherwise have been channelled into precisely these areas. And not just international donor funds and government spending, but also – crucially – local savings, which were increasingly being locked into microfinance. If poor African, Latin American and South-East Asian countries seriously wanted to emulate the rich Western economies or the newer East Asian 'Tiger' economies, and so also patiently build relatively sophisticated and scaled-up industrial and agricultural sectors from the 'bottom up', I remember thinking, the growing emphasis on microfinance as development policy was leading them in completely the wrong direction.

Consulting assignments in the western Balkans and wider eastern Europe from the mid-1990s onwards amply confirmed my deep unease with microfinance, now in the context of post-communist restructuring. Working and living in the western Balkans from 2002 onwards brought me into much greater everyday contact with life and ordinary people in countries undergoing quite fundamental change. Almost right away I came across a local language term, *Africanizacija* (Africanization). This was a tragicomic reference to the massive proliferation everywhere across the region of the very simplest informal microenterprises, almost all engaged in some form of petty trade or services. In previously quite advanced countries, there was understandable resentment at what appeared to be a programmed return to nineteenth-century ways of living and working. This was not at all what most people thought capitalism and the market economy would deliver for them. Meanwhile, it quickly became apparent that the far more productive small and medium-sized enterprise (SME) sector was being left to wither on the vine: the private commercial banks (now mainly foreign owned) were simply not interested. Yet because all this activity was 'market-driven', as they say, the international development agencies and their key advisers argued that *by definition* an optimum development trajectory was under way, so there was no need to worry. But just in case, governments in the region were effectively prohibited from saying or doing anything to the contrary, not least by being threatened with losing important international financial aid flows if they did. It was all beginning to look really unhealthy to me.

I first started to publicly register my unease with microfinance in the mid-1990s. I attended a couple of seminars and conferences in order to formally express my fear that, for a number of reasons, microfinance was very likely going to undermine the post-war reconstruction effort in the western Balkans. I argued instead for a solid local industrial policy response to the accelerating economic collapse in the region, something not unlike that pioneered in equally devastated northern Italy after 1945. I got a rough ride at first. Since the key international development bodies were vigorously selling 'market-driven' microfinance to the new post-communist governments in the region, this was perhaps not surprising. I well remember receiving a pretty angry reception speaking at one event in Sarajevo in February 1999, organized by the Warsaw-based Microfinance Centre (MFC). Nevertheless, my interest in microfinance continued. In fact, I probably became keener than ever to put something much longer down on paper. But for the next five years this notion was put to one side. Now employed by a large UK-based consulting company, I was pretty much fully tied up with work and travel right across the region. Moving on in 2006 to a much less stressful life as a freelance consultant, however, finally made it possible to think about carving out some serious free time for writing. Fortuitously, too, right at this time an article on microfinance I was working on came to the attention of Ha-Joon Chang, who was then co-editing for Zed Books a series on new approaches to key economic issues. He got in touch and, after some discussion, a book contract with Zed was raised as a possibility. Things began to fall into place. Eventually, I managed to free up most of the summer and autumn of 2009, and this book is the result.

Over the years, a number of individuals have stimulated my critical interest in microfinance and have helped me by providing material and 'inside' commentary on many of the most important issues. For obvious reasons, many of these informants prefer to remain anonymous, but I publicly offer them my thanks now. Even though we disagree in a number of areas, Malcolm Harper has nevertheless been extremely supportive of my academic work and ideas, including with regard to this book on microfinance (as well as a good friend, along with Uschi Kraus-Harper), for which I offer my warm thanks. Others who have also provided me with useful insights, data and/or comments on draft sections of this book include Bina Agarwal, Hanns Pichler, Tom Dichter, Dave Richardson, David Ellerman and Hans Dieter Seibel, to whom I also offer my thanks. Elizabeth Hughes-Komljen very kindly provided important editorial help at a time when I really needed it. I am grateful to my good friend Alistair Nolan for taking time away from his annual holiday to discuss with me some of the key issues I raise in the book, and for his editorial and technical comments on some early chapter drafts. Zed Books' commissioning editor Ken Barlow made many useful suggestions and comments, for which I am especially appreciative. I need to thank also the anonymous reviewers of the early book proposal, who between them provided many useful comments and suggestions that helped kick-start the project. Vicky, Neil, Joe and Greg Walsh helped me immensely by providing an extremely congenial atmosphere in Halifax (UK) over the 2009 Christmas holiday season, effectively allowing me to complete the manuscript with only a minor delay. Finally, the biggest thank-you is to Ha-Joon Chang for his constant encouragement and support, right from what was an awkward book proposal stage (many thought that critically addressing such a 'feel-good' subject was risky), through to the processing of his extensive comments on each of the draft chapters. Of course, it must be stressed that none of the above bears any responsibility whatsoever for the misinterpretations and errors contained in this work, which are mine alone.

Milford Bateman
January 2010

Acronyms

BDP	Banco de Desarrollo Productivo (SME development bank)
CCT	conditional cash transfer
CGAP	Consultative Group to Assist the Poor
DfID	Department for International Development
FDI	foreign direct investment
HIID	Harvard Institute for International Development
IFC	International Finance Corporation
ILO	International Labour Organization
IPO	initial public offering
MFI	microfinance institution
MNC	multinational corporation
SHG	self-help group
SME	small and medium-sized enterprise

ONE
Introduction

This book is about one component of the global financial sector – microfinance – that in just thirty years has risen to become one of the most important policy and programme interventions in the international development community. As originally conceived, microfinance is the provision of tiny loans to poor individuals who establish or expand a simple income-generating activity, thereby supposedly facilitating their eventual escape from poverty.[1] Its advocates claim that microfinance has been critical to the fate of the poor in many developing countries, creating jobs and raising incomes in the poorest communities, helping to empower the poor (especially women), and generally kick-starting a 'bottom-up' economic and social development process. The person most associated with the 'discovery' of microfinance in the 1970s is the Bangladeshi economist and 2006 Nobel Peace Prize co-recipient, Dr Muhammad Yunus. With his vision of rapid and affordable poverty reduction being achieved through microfinance, Yunus was able to convince virtually everyone in the international development community to support his efforts. Indeed, the next generation, he famously said in the 1980s, would be able to understand the concept of poverty only after having visited a 'poverty museum'. Here, surely, was the poverty reduction concept that all developing countries had been waiting for.

The central argument that I will develop in this book, however, is that microfinance is largely *antagonistic* to sustainable economic and social development, and so also to sustainable poverty reduction. Put simply, microfinance does not work. I fully accept that there are some minor benefits to be derived from the widespread provision of microfinance to the poor. An intervention that puts a little extra cash into the hands of the poor in any community – and especially if that cash is brought in from *outside* the local community in question – could hardly do otherwise. But I argue that these benefits are very minimal indeed, and anyway wholly insignificant when set alongside the huge longer-term downsides and opportunity costs inherent in the operation of the microfinance model. To focus upon these few minor shorter-term benefits is to deliberately focus on the few trees left standing after having helped the entire forest to burn down. In truth, once we go beyond the fabulous 'feel-good' PR and marketing effort undertaken on behalf of the microfinance model, no more so than by Muhammad Yunus himself, we find a completely different reality. Sustainable local economic development trajectories are actually undermined and blocked. Local communities are structurally weakened and destroyed. Important reserves of solidarity, mutuality and cooperation are trashed thanks to the internecine competition between desperate individuals 'poverty-pushed' into establishing the very simplest of microenterprises. Human dignity and self-respect are lost as the poor in developing countries are increasingly forced to accept their permanent engagement with the most primitive, illegal, dangerous and demeaning business activities imaginable. Overall, those developing countries awash with microfinance – and the prime example, of course, is Bangladesh itself – are increasingly being left behind by other developing countries, those that have proved far sighted enough to channel investment into the type of enterprises, infrastructures and institutions that, when combined, have far more potential to produce a substantive and sustainable growth and development payback. All the while the various ways in which the poor have in recent history been able to successfully escape grinding poverty and achieve tolerable living standards and opportunities – by exercising their collective capabilities through pro-poor political parties, social movements, supportive state structures, trade unions, associations, single-issue pressure groups, and the like – are now ruled to be completely off the agenda. The poor are instead increasingly thrown back on to their old, and largely unsuccessful, historical mission; to attempt vainly to rescue themselves from their own poverty and suffering solely through their own individual actions and meagre resources.

Another core argument I make in this book is that the increasing commercialization of microfinance is responsible for greatly amplifying the destructive impact registered by the basic Grameen Bank microfinance model. A central development within the world of microfinance was the schism that took place in the 1990s, when the subsidized Grameen Bank model was effectively abandoned and a completely new commercialized microfinance model – what I term the 'new wave' microfinance model – was ushered in as its replacement. From now on, a microfinance institution was to be a business, and its primary objective was to attain full financial self-sustainability and profits as quickly as possible. Even if the poor would greatly benefit from low interest rates and the additional net income that would then result from any simple income-generating project, an outcome that might in turn necessitate subsidies from the wider (richer) community, tough. Reconstituting microfinance as a for-profit business model, however, has had quite disastrous consequences. Just as on Wall Street, we now find 'new wave' microfinance increasingly defined by unethical profiteering, greed, irresponsible risk-taking, speculation and 'microcredit bubbles'. PR efforts to the contrary notwithstanding, that microfinance largely exists to promote poverty reduction is a concept that lost any traction many years ago.

The arguments made here also have considerable implications for theories of financial systems, and particularly how a financial system influences economic growth, as well as its impact upon the distinct process of sustainable economic development (where growth is based on respect for economic, social and environmental outcomes). If we accept that it is not simply the quantity of finance available which determines the rate of growth and sustainable development, but also how, where, when and in what form financial resources are deployed, then we have here a very useful case study indeed. Many developing-country financial systems have been very significantly restructured towards microfinance, with the corollary being the progressive abandonment of lending to the small and medium-sized enterprise (SME) sector. So how does a microfinance-dominated financial sector work, and is it good for growth and sustainable development? With Bangladesh, the most famous example of a financial system structured around microfinance, later joined by Bolivia, Mexico, Cambodia, Uganda, Mongolia, Bosnia, Peru, Nicaragua, and many parts of southern India, we now have important real-life country and regional examples of microfinance 'saturation' to examine. While we still await the definitive large-scale empirical work on the topic, the evidence that has emerged so far seems to suggest that the growing presence of microfinance within a local financial system has been quite destructive of sustainable development and poverty reduction objectives.

Going beyond theory, I hope this book will also, finally, help to outline important practical lessons for local communities, and why alternatives to microfinance must be urgently fashioned. Local communities in most developing countries have been under stress for far too long, with the global financial crisis beginning in late

2008 adding massively to their existing woes. I firmly believe that in conjunction with sympathetic and proactive higher government structures, poor local communities could achieve far better things than at present under microfinance. To do this we need to study and learn from the notable successes enjoyed by other local financial systems and heterodox local microfinance models. I outline in Chapter 7 a number of the most interesting examples from recent history. Of course, these examples have their problems. And replication and adaptation of policy models are never easy: historical, economic, cultural and political context can be crucial. But the many successes of post-1945 European countries and regions, and then of the East Asian 'Tiger' economies from the 1960s onwards, help to show just what an appropriately designed 'development-driven' local financial system can accomplish. It is far better that developing countries learn from and adapt these positive 'on the ground' experiences, rather than look to neoclassical economics textbooks pointing to the theoretically possible development benefits of microfinance, benefits that I argue in this book simply don't exist in practice to any meaningful extent.

Bringing reality back in

This book was largely put together as the most serious economic crisis since the 1930s was unfolding right across the globe. Now officially defined as 'The Great Recession', this latest economic crisis meted out a very severe beating to the idea that free market capitalism is the answer to the growing economic, social, cultural and environmental problems confronting humankind. To be more accurate, we have just seen the most recent and most fundamentalist variant of capitalism – neoliberalism – explode before our eyes. An ideology premised on the infallibility of self-regulated financial markets, private ownership and unrestrained individual self-interest collapsed in late 2008 just as spectacularly as the Berlin Wall and communism fell at the end of 1989. And it could even have been much worse than this – the end of the entire global capitalist system no less, according to the *Financial Times*[2] – had it not been for unprecedented levels of state intervention and company rescues, subsidies to the financial sector running into the trillions of dollars, and Keynesian-inspired stimulus packages propping up consumer demand right across the globe. Even the reflexively anti-state *Economist* magazine had to come clean and admit that a second and even deeper Great Depression was only very narrowly avoided, thanks to the 'biggest, broadest and fastest government response in history'.[3]

So we are – or, at least, *should be*[4] – in the middle of a major episode of rewriting economic theory and policy to take into account the sheer enormity of the destruction that has just happened, and the human suffering now left in its wake. If the Great Recession has a silver lining to it, then, it will come in the shape of much greater freedom to challenge and discard the core neoliberal policies that have patently failed not just today's generation, but also future generations as well (thanks to truly astonishing levels of debt now bequeathed to them). Today, there are no more 'sacred cows' in economic policy.

Accordingly, in this book I take the opportunity to provide my own critical take on perhaps the most popular 'sacred cow' in the international development policy field – microfinance. I will show why it is not the solution to poverty and underdevelopment that we were originally led to believe it would be. In fact, I suggest that microfinance is actually a 'poverty trap', an 'anti-development policy' that ultimately destroys the potential for sustainable local economic and social development, and so also for sustainable poverty reduction.

TWO
The rise of microfinance

'I strongly believe that we can create a poverty-free world, if we want to … In that kind of world, [the] only place you can see poverty is in the museum. When school children will be on a tour of the poverty museum, they will be horrified to see the misery and indignity of human beings. They will blame their forefathers for tolerating this inhuman condition to continue in a massive way …' Muhammad Yunus[1]

Largely thanks to the pioneering work of Muhammad Yunus and the Grameen Bank that he established in Bangladesh a little under thirty years ago, a new concept of small-scale finance was added to the financial lexicon: microfinance. In a short space of time, the microfinance model became the international development community's poverty reduction policy and programme of choice. The award of the 2006 Nobel Peace Prize jointly to Muhammad Yunus and to the Grameen Bank he founded in 1983, followed in August 2009 by the award of the US Presidential Medal of Freedom, are just the most high-profile in a long line of awards and glowing tributes to the individual most closely associated with microfinance. Having pioneered such an important new financial sector innovation, one that has supposedly proved to be of enormous importance to the world's poor, such personal awards and celebrity are widely seen as richly deserved.

This chapter will chart the 'discovery' of microfinance by Muhammad Yunus in 1970s Bangladesh. I will show how an idea designed to help Yunus's local village was turned into an international development policy and programme behemoth. What is so extraordinary about the Grameen Bank story is that it was based on a flawed understanding of basic economic principles (as we shall see), and initially it could offer nothing more than hope and good intentions to convince the international development community to offer its support. But it nevertheless rapidly prospered and went on to become the enormous power and influence that it is today in international development circles, if not – judging by the number of ordinary people who have rallied to its cause – in everyday life too.[2] Moreover, it is even more extraordinary to find that in the course of three decades lifting Muhammad Yunus up almost to sainthood, the international development community actually had to insist in the meantime that he abandon almost all of the core principles upon which he had established the original Grameen Bank model! Yunus overwhelmingly remains the public 'face' of microfinance right across the globe, but the 'new wave' microfinance model that dominates today is a radically different local financial model to the one he pioneered in Bangladesh in the 1970s.

Birth of an idea

The 'discovery' of what we commonly refer to today as micro-finance is by now a well-told story.[3] It starts in Bangladesh, a country that in the 1970s was recovering from a bloody conflict associated with its independence from Pakistan in 1971. In the early 1970s, Muhammad Yunus was chairman of the Economics Faculty at Chitta-gong University. He obtained this position after returning from a long sojourn in the USA, where he had been first a doctoral student and then a university lecturer. Shocked at the appalling poverty and human suffering he found on his return, Yunus began to think about what might be done to improve the situation.

Immediately Yunus made himself more familiar with a number of the credit-based projects under way in the poorest communities in Bangladesh. As he set about thinking what he was going to do next, Yunus was able to draw inspiration and important lessons from these projects. Perhaps the most important of the credit-based projects under way in the early 1970s was a form of microcredit directed towards the poor. This project had been pioneered in the 1950s in East Pakistan (later to become Bangladesh) by Akhtar Hameed Khan.[4] In Khan's 'Comilla Model', microcredit was disbursed to poor rural communities through village- and sector-based cooperatives. The basis for Khan's experiment was the urgent need for an alternative to the rich local moneylenders and traders, who were widely seen as holding back the rural poor through the usurious interest rates they charged. There were many positive aspects to the Comilla Model, such as the solidarity generated within the cooperatives, a feature that was also projected out into the community. The Comilla Model failed to flour-ish as much as had been hoped, however. Analysts identified several reasons for this. One was that the Pakistani government continually interfered in the project, hoping to use it as a vehicle for rebuilding local physical infrastructure. Another problem was that of 'elite capture'. This occurred when the richer and more articulate members of the cooperatives began to manipulate themselves into positions of power in order to appropriate most of the project's benefits.[5] Still, the Comilla Model provided an obvious reference point for Yunus and the direction he was about to take.[6]

At the same time, Yunus was struck by the creativity of the poor in his district in figuring out how to survive. This was especially so in the case of poor women. On regular visits to the nearby village of Jobra he saw that, alongside traditional farming activities on the family plot, almost all poor women were engaged in some form of tiny income-generating activity – rice-husking, raising chickens for eggs and meat, net-making, street food preparation, petty trading, and so on. Yunus immediately thought that if these poor individuals could be encouraged to expand their existing income-generating activities, or start a new line of work, their lives, and the lives of those around them, would be improved considerably.

Expanding and establishing such income-generating activities, however, was not easy. The returns were generally so irregular and so small that most income-generating activities simply did not generate enough spare cash to kick-start the next economic cycle. Most cash earned simply had to be used to fund present consumption. By default, therefore, the economic cycle only kept going thanks to new or rolled-over small loans from local moneylenders. The women returned to the moneylender knowing that they would be in the very same situation in the near future, but with no other obvious way out. The end result was that most women barely survived from one wretched day of toil to the next. In other words, the women in Jobra were in a classic 'poverty trap'.

Many free market economists have argued that the persistent demand for informal moneylenders effectively confirms how much the poor value such services. Moneylenders cannot therefore be viewed as exploitative.[7] But Yunus thought differently, at least on this issue. For a start, the turbulent rural history of his own native land, and of neighbouring India, was steeped in class-based antagonisms. This centrally involved poor farmers losing out to the local class of rich moneylenders. Among other things, moneylenders traditionally used defaults, some of which they deliberately prearranged,[8] as the pretext for seizing land owned by the poor. This dynamic partly explains why, across the entire Indian subcontinent, the local moneylenders typically evolved into important local landowners as well.

More importantly, Yunus's personal experience began to extend to the influence of the moneylenders. In several of his books Yunus vividly recounts his shock at seeing the 'near enslavement' of the poor to local moneylenders in Jobra village.[9] On the spur of the moment, Yunus asked whether he could make a quick list of all the women in Jobra in debt to local moneylenders. He came away with a list of forty-two names, and a collective debt of just $US27. He decided to cancel this debt out of his own pocket, and was embarrassed to be almost royally feted for such a small service to the community.[10]

Liberation from the moneylender Soon Yunus's core idea began to take shape. He had come to the conclusion that if the poor were to ever stand a chance of benefiting from their labour and escaping poverty, they needed to be freed from the local moneylender. The poor needed instead a *microcredit*: a small low-interest loan to establish or expand an income-generating activity. Low interest rates were important because they would liberate more cash for the poor, which would put more food on the table, help educate any children, permit some savings, and so on. With more cash free to be invested in the microenterprise, the poor also had a much better chance of really making their way out of their poverty. Yunus started to believe that microcredit could form the core of a policy and programme to actively promote poverty reduction and local development in Bangladesh.

Using his own money once again, in 1976 Yunus began an action research experiment providing microcredit in Jobra. His initial clients included both men and women. When it quickly became apparent that women were far better at repaying than men, he made the important decision to work mainly with local women. Yunus then managed to persuade a local bank in Jobra to start offering microcredit as part of its business in the community. In this scaled-up exercise, the poor proved again to be exceptionally good clients. And again, women proved to be the very best at repayment.

Further investigation shed light on why repayment was surprisingly high in such poor communities and among women borrowers. Poor borrowers first hoped to find their regular repayment from the results of the income-generating activities supported by the microcredit. But often this was not possible. The returns were not large enough, or else the project had actually failed. In this case, the client would tap into traditional family and community support networks to meet the required repayment. Being able to access low-cost finance in future was a benefit that clients did not want to lose. But it was largely the fear of damage to one's family's reputation in the community which drove clients to repay their microloan, howsoever they had to do it. Moreover, women had a relatively heightened sensitivity to and fear of bringing shame and disrepute upon their male partner and the wider family. This accounted for the fact that women clients were by far the most determined to avoid defaulting on any microcredit.

The existence of these family and community support structures, and their positive impact on repayment suggested to Yunus an additional innovation – 'solidarity circles' (or *Kendra*). 'Solidarity circles' were groups of a minimum of five women. If an individual member was having difficulty repaying their own microcredit, the solidarity circle was supposed to provide an environment within which the potentially errant member could be helped to repay. Although it appears that Yunus himself never suggested that these solidarity circles should cover the repayments of any member unable to do so (i.e. joint liability), still less expel errant members for their inability to repay their microcredit, no real action was taken to stop this gradually becoming the common practice.[11] The solidarity circle acted as a form of 'social collateral' that substituted for the traditional formal collateral usually expected of a potential client (and which the poorest often did not have). If not exactly operating as Yunus had envisaged, at any rate this innovation seemed to work very well in securing a high repayment rate.

The Grameen Bank was formally established by Muhammad Yunus in 1983. It was set up as an NGO owned by its member-clients, but controlled by Yunus and senior managers. The authorized capital base was contributed 40 per cent by members, 40 per cent by the government of Bangladesh and 10 per cent each by two state banks (within a few years it became majority owned by members). Its formally stated ambition was to provide microcredits to the poor at affordable rates of interest, especially to poor women, which were intended to be used to help establish or expand an income-generating microenterprise. It was particularly important to Yunus that this new institution reach the *very* poor. Grameen therefore started off with a stipulation that eligible members were those with less than a half-hectare of land, or assets worth less than a half-hectare of land.

The Grameen Bank took off and the number of clients grew rapidly.

As Yunus had hoped, repayment rates were extremely high. Compared to the 40 to 60 per cent repayment rates achieved by the government banks in Bangladesh,[12] the 98 per cent repayment rates said to have been achieved by Grameen seemed impressive. The Grameen Bank idea appeared to work, at least so far as the repayment rate angle was concerned. Yunus had helped to show that the poor were 'bankable'.

The Grameen Bank idea begins to catch on The Grameen Bank was not the only experiment in microcredit getting under way in Bangladesh in the early 1980s. Alongside the ongoing experiments with microcredit promoted by Akhtar Hameed Khan, two other important institutions were also getting established alongside the Grameen Bank, both of which soon followed Grameen by offering microcredit to the poor. The first of these organizations was the Bangladesh Rural Advancement Committee (BRAC), founded in 1972 by Fazle Hasan Abed, followed in 1978 by ASA, which was founded by Shafiqual Haque Choudhury. Elsewhere in Asia, similar microcredit operations were also under way. The state-owned Bank Rakyat Indonesia (BRI) (People's Bank of Indonesia) was somewhat in advance of the Grameen Bank. Established as early as 1972, it provided microloans to rural families for non-farm productive activities. In 1986 Yunus himself helped to start a Grameen-type microcredit institution in Malaysia. In the early 1990s in India, an important variant of the Grameen Bank model emerged, the self-help group (SHG) movement.[13] Combining microcredit with social empowerment, outreach and capacity-building activity, SHGs allow small groups of women (generally no more than twenty) to come together as a 'solidarity group' and, among other things, obtain a low-cost microloan through funds passed down to them from the formal banking sector. Meanwhile, in Latin America microcredit operations were also being established with rapidity and enormous enthusiasm. Microcredit quickly assumed as much importance in Bolivia as in Bangladesh, thanks to pioneering microcredit institutions like PRODEM, established in 1986 to provide microloans in the capital city of La Paz. By the late 1980s, microcredit and microenterprise development had become the international development community's anti-poverty intervention of choice.[14]

In addition, new types of micro-services (micro-insurance, micro-savings) were being added to the simple microcredit offer provided to the poor by most microfinance institutions (hereafter MFIs). Among other things, this eventually resulted in the coining of the now generic term *microfinance*[15] (which we will revert back to from now on), a term which better describes the evolving complex reality of very small-scale finance. The microfinance experiment and Grameen Bank began to enter the popular imagination too. Yunus and the Grameen Bank became increasingly regular features on TV and radio, in business magazines, and in major newspaper articles and editorials.

Most of the MFIs established in the immediate wake of the Grameen Bank experiment were deliberately structured to operate as NGOs with non-profit status. In addition, the vast majority of MFIs were initially capitalized by government and/or international donor funding. The thinking at the time was that, since Grameen had apparently shown high repayment rates to be a real possibility, this should mean that little ongoing funding was required to maintain an MFI. Moreover, if Grameen was actually going to reduce poverty as much as Yunus maintained that it would, then the initial government and international donor 'pump-priming' support should be quite easily justifiable on the basis of standard cost–benefit analysis. The initial cost would be seen as a fantastic investment rather than a subsidy. A key issue within Grameen was the importance of maintaining affordable interest rates for the poor clients. Yunus had been quite unequivocal in wanting interest rates to be kept as low as possible, in order to allow the maximum financial space for the poor to benefit from their hard work, and to help them reinvest if they could. Most new MFIs naturally wanted to follow Grameen practice in this important respect, not become the despised moneylenders that Yunus had been so keen to displace. Market-based interest rates were not on the agenda, at least not at this stage.

The 'problem' of subsidies In order to maintain low interest rates for its poor clients, however, it gradually became clear that it was not always possible for an MFI to remain financially self-sufficient. Even with very high repayment rates, providing lots of tiny microloans to the poor is a complicated, and thus sometimes an expensive, business. This became manifestly clear when it transpired that the Grameen Bank itself was actually heavily dependent upon external financial support in order to keep its interest rates low. Because its repayment rates were not anywhere near as high as Muhammad Yunus had been claiming, the Grameen Bank had been in receipt of government and international donor funds pretty much right from its establishment.[16]

To many in the international development community applauding the Grameen Bank model on the basis of its financial self-sustainability, this information apparently came as something of a surprise. The Grameen Bank microfinance model had been promoted throughout the 1980s on the basis not just of its individual entrepreneurship and self-help attributes, but also – wrongly it now turned out – on the basis of its financial viability as well.[17] To some 'insiders' in the microfinance industry, however, it was generally no secret that, because of its weaker than advertised repayment rate, the Grameen Bank was always in receipt of subsidies.[18] But this was a fact that was largely kept quiet. As leading microfinance advocate Jonathan Morduch admitted, 'Grameen's repayment rates have never been as good as they've claimed [but] because Grameen has been so well-known, nobody has wanted to risk undermining the reputation of the idea'.[19]

But it was not just the Grameen Bank which was finding it difficult to survive without constant external financial support. Many other MFIs were in exactly the same boat. They too found that repayment rates were generally high, but still insufficient to ensure complete financial self-sustainability. The upshot was that the majority of the MFIs that immediately followed in the wake of Grameen were therefore forced, like Grameen itself, to effectively base their operations on regular financial injections. But also, again like Grameen, most MFIs figured that their strong desire to promote poverty reduction in the poorest communities would more than justify any subsidy forthcoming from the international development community or from their own governments.

The international development community soon began to disabuse the microfinance industry of this notion, however. The rejection of subsidies was essentially rooted in changing politics: specifically, the rapid ascendance of the neoliberal political project that began in the mid-1970s. One of the core imperatives of neoliberalism is a firm belief in the financial self-sustainability of *all* institutions that operate in the economy and society. This belief applies not just to private business enterprises, of course, but also to state enterprises, government departments, local public services (e.g. health, education), and virtually everything else in between (e.g. NGOs, voluntary associations, clubs). Government financial support should neither be sought nor offered, no matter what, because it will ultimately weaken any financial institution, as well as lead to higher taxes on other members of the community. The way to achieve this financial self-sustainability imperative was through a combination of liberalization, commercialization and privatization. Centrally this meant market-based interest rates had to apply, rather than below-market interest rates requiring a subsidy. Great efforts were made to commission as much supporting evidence as possible in favour of the chosen trajectory. Famously stepping up to the plate here was a group of mainly agricultural economists based at Ohio State University in the USA, who very conveniently provided a stream of arguments discrediting the notion of subsidies in rural finance and state involvement overall.[20] As neoliberalism rapidly emerged to become the dominant political philosophy, the restructuring of all international development community interventions naturally began to reflect this belief as well. The microfinance industry was to be no exception.

The 'neoliberalization' of microfinance begins The ideologically driven requirement to fully commercialize and privatize microfinance began in earnest towards the end of the 1980s. The stated aim was to ensure large-scale outreach without the need for subsidization. The core methodology of commercialization was equally clear. As much as possible, MFIs had to become conventional profit-maximizing private financial businesses. Introducing market-based interest rates would be paramount, cutting the need for subsidies as well as helping to mobilize savings (through the introduction of higher interest rates on deposits). The drive to maximize profits would also ensure that an MFI would automatically push hard to increase the number of clients, since it would wish to spread its fixed costs across as large a number of microloans as possible. It was also felt important to fully incentivize an MFI's senior managers, which called for greater tolerance of Wall Street-style financial reward programmes – that is, high salaries and bonuses. It also suggested that senior staff should eventually be offered the opportunity to obtain a significant ownership stake in their own MFI, if not eventually to take over full ownership.

By the early 1990s, the 'new wave' microfinance model was firmly established in practice. It was formally termed the 'financial systems' approach, in contradistinction to the 'poverty lending' approach that described the Grameen Bank. One of the very first financial institutions to move in this radical new direction was the Bank Rakyat Indonesia (BRI) mentioned earlier. BRI appeared to be a prime candidate for commercialization. The results of its state-subsidized credit programmes, mainly working in the rice sector, were apparently pretty weak. The poor only marginally benefited, and savings were not encouraged. Most of all, BRI's arrears and losses were quite high, which meant the need for constant subsidies. Advisers associated with Harvard University's Harvard Institute for International Development (HIID) offered to help. Importantly, HIID in the 1980s was becoming a recognized font of neoliberal policy wisdom,[21] not least through the troubleshooting international policy advisory work of its then director and arch-neoliberal, Jeffrey Sachs.[22] Given its strong neoliberal approach to policy work, it was therefore only to be expected that HIID would strongly push for the commercialization of BRI. The result was the establishment in 1984 of Unit-Desa (BRI-UD), an independent profit centre wholly owned by BRI. BRI-UD was designed to offer so-called 'Kupedes' microloans based on market interest rates. Alongside a variety of savings programmes, 'Kupedes' microloans were to be provided through its own network of nearly 3,500 village bank branches. BRI-UD rapidly grew and by the end of 2004 it had 30 million savers and 3.1 million borrowers.[23] All the time under state ownership,[24] BRI-UD became the largest microfinance operation in the world, and a leading example of a financially sustainable rural microfinance programme.

Importantly, the first major transformation of a not-for-profit NGO into a fully state-regulated for-profit financial institution (in this case, a commercial bank) had taken place in Bolivia in 1992 with BancoSol. The origins of BancoSol lie in PRODEM, an NGO that was originally established in 1986 with support from the US government's aid arm, USAID, plus other development agency and private sector funding. Because PRODEM felt constrained by its inability to mobilize savings among its members and in the wider community, it was decided to establish a separate private commercial microfinance bank that would focus on urban clients. In return for part (18 per cent) of BancoSol's equity, PRODEM's loan portfolio and staff were transferred over to the new entity. BancoSol's success in quickly becoming the most profitable bank in Bolivia appeared to demonstrate that microfinance could be a very profitable business area indeed. Meanwhile, PRODEM did not end its involvement with microfinance, but very much continued to service its rural clients (in 2007 PRODEM's employees-turned-owners became wealthy individuals when they sold PRODEM to a Venezuelan government bank). Other such transformations from NGO to commercial bank soon followed.[25] Advising on the BancoSol transformation was the US-based NGO ACCIÓN, then working on many microfinance programmes in South and Central America under contract to USAID. ACCIÓN was one of the first and most important of the US-based NGOs to stand four-square behind the commercialized 'new wave' MFI model. Indeed, as ACCIÓN's then president and CEO, Maria Otero,[26] boldly stated,[27] 'ACCIÓN created the commercial model, and the commercial model is the one that works'.

The early experience of BRI-UD, BancoSol and of some other MFIs having successfully moved towards commercialization was crucially important in giving real impetus to the 'new wave' microfinance concept. Supporters of the 'new wave' commercialization approach argued that it was indeed better practice than subsidized programmes. Many microfinance advocates began to write about an exciting 'new world' of commercialized microfinance opening up.[28] The international development institutions and their key supporters needed no further proof than this. Already committed to the 'new wave' microfinance concept because of its focus upon individual self-help, these additional financial sustainability features were exactly what they were looking for. Efforts to promote the concept and to establish 'new wave' MFIs were rapidly stepped up.

As just noted, USAID was one of the main very early supporters of the 'new wave' microfinance model. It had jumped in to provide technical advice to developing-country governments, as well as helping mobilize financial support for a large number of 'new wave' microfinance programmes. Now a core driving force behind the 'new wave' microfinance model, the World Bank was a little late getting into the field. Its initial fear was that microfinance was a little 'too amateurish and touchy-feely',[29] and anyway too close to international NGOs largely critical of its neoliberal policies. In the World Bank's eyes, this made microfinance ineligible for support. But it soon realized, as USAID had done, that 'new wave' microfinance was actually perfectly consonant with its overall mandate to address poverty while also enforcing neoliberal policies within developing countries. Accordingly, in the early 1990s the World Bank moved into the microfinance field, especially through its International Finance Corporation (IFC) arm. In fact, the World Bank soon took the lead in aggressively pushing for the 'new wave' microfinance model. One way it found to do this was to establish the Consultative Group to Assist the Poor (CGAP), an institution physically located within the World Bank but with a multi-stakeholder structure. CGAP was mandated to 'coordinate' international donor policy towards microfinance. As in most World Bank activities, we must remember, 'coordinate' is simply coded language for ensuring that the other international agencies fall into line behind World Bank policy. Among other things, CGAP produced the so-called 'Pink Book',[30] a concise explanation of the core 'new wave' principles that all microfinance programmes now had to be built around.[31] Taking their cue from USAID and the World Bank, most developed-country governments, bilateral development agencies and international NGOs quickly began to shift their microfinance support policy and programmes towards the favoured 'new wave' approach.

By the mid-1990s, it was possible to say that the 'new wave' microfinance model had pretty much established itself as the 'best practice' microfinance model.[32] The international donor community now signalled to the microfinance industry that it would not help establish any other model of an MFI, and it would also seek to transform all existing MFIs into 'new wave' MFIs if at all possible. Commercial funding bodies also began to take a look at microfinance, thinking it might be an attractive location for profitable investment. Pretty soon, too, profit-seeking commercial banks began their first tentative steps towards 'downscaling' their lending activities into microfinance, and so out of traditional SME lending. Importantly, even though many MFIs still operated (and wanted to operate) as not-for-profit NGOs, they were still encouraged to at least *try* to move in the direction of 'new wave' respectability if they possibly could, particularly by using market-based interest rates. In terms of 'new start' MFIs, a 'fallback' argument along 'infant industry' lines was deployed to justify any initial capitalization by the government or the international development community.[33]

Finally, and essentially coming full circle, the original 'old paradigm' MFI – the Grameen Bank – was itself forced to bow to the inevitable. The Grameen Bank had no other option but to accede to its transformation into a regular profit-driven financial institution. Under intense pressure for a long time to adopt the 'new wave' approach, thereby to finally attain the reality of financial self-sustainability, and with further financial pressure thanks to a major flood that hit Bangladesh in 1998, major change would clearly have to come. More prosaically, it hurt Yunus and those around him that the Grameen Bank was becoming marginalized within the microfinance industry that it had played the decisive role in actually establishing. As those close to the Grameen Bank saw it, 'Internationally, Grameen fell out of fashion as industry observers, particularly in North America, shifted their attention to other forms of microfinance' (i.e. 'new wave' microfinance).[34]

Accordingly, in 2001 the Grameen Bank began a move to completely relaunch itself in full 'new wave' mode. The 'Grameen II' project, as it came to be known, introduced all the required commercializing changes.[35] The advertised annual interest rate was set at 20 per cent, but a number of devices were used to quietly hike up this advertised interest rate to as near the free market rate as possible. One way to do this was through the use of an obligatory savings account, wherein a small percentage of any microloan (2.5 per cent) had to remain deposited at Grameen for at least three years.[36] Given that moving towards market-based interest rates was an idea that Yunus had originally very strongly resisted when establishing Grameen, arguing then that what was most important was the *repayment rate* not the *interest rate*,[37] this was an important break with the original Grameen Bank model.

Second, in order to substitute for international donor and Bangladesh government funds, Grameen II also began to give savings a much higher emphasis. Alongside the obligatory savings account just noted was a voluntary savings plan,[38] plus various other programmes strongly encouraging the poor to deposit their savings with Grameen, such as a pension plan. Moreover, with the poor desperate simply for a safe place to keep their money, there was no shortage of savings. With very little risk and low administrative costs, within a few years Grameen was largely lending back to its poor clients the bulk of their own obligatory and voluntary savings deposits. Importantly, with such savings deposits attracting an average 9 per cent rate of interest and microloans provided at the advertised rate of 20 per cent,[39] the margins achieved by recycling savings in this way were very healthy indeed. (Among other things, this helps to account for why Grameen clients soon began to come under pressure to continually 'top up' their microloan, irrespective of whether they needed the cash or not.[40])

Another key development associated with Grameen II concerned the issue of joint liability within the solidarity circles. Joint liability was an outcome that was actually not planned by Yunus, but it nevertheless emerged semi-spontaneously in most Grameen Bank units. Joint liability was now formally banned, however. In future, one potentially defaulting member could no longer hold back other members keen to expand their lending, and who would otherwise go to Grameen's competitors. One result was that the solidarity circles quickly began to fall into disuse.[41]

In short, the original Grameen Bank microfinance model was effectively consigned to history. Grameen Bank was now no different from most other for-profit commercial banks. Its continued existence was now predicated not upon the pursuit of poverty reduction, but upon its own expansion and the profitable provision of financial services to anyone willing to use them. The initial Grameen Bank goals of working only with the very poorest, and promoting poverty reduction, gender empowerment and sustainable development within this specific community, have quietly been dropped in practice. PR personnel are now largely responsible for upholding the notion that the Grameen Bank still primarily exists to promote poverty reduction. Yunus has helped matters by retrospectively moving the goalposts himself, dropping all his earlier references to eradicating poverty by individual self-help and 'sending it to a museum', claiming now that all along he had been interested only in the much more modest goal of simply 'bringing financial services to poor women in Bangladesh'.[42]

The results of the Grameen II transformation so far as the international development community was concerned, however, were just perfect. The Grameen Bank was apparently turned into a very solid for-profit private financial organization, with no further need for it to seek out Bangladesh government or international donor community support (i.e. subsidies). By the end of 2005, as David Hulme explains,[43] Grameen's client base had grown to more than five million, adding the last 2.5 million clients in just the three years since Grameen II was launched. Savings deposits were three times their 2001 figure. The portfolio of outstanding loans had doubled. It had expanded its branch network by some five hundred new branches. And, finally, Grameen was now making a healthy profit. The commercialized for-profit future being mapped out for the microfinance industry was now perfectly clear to all, including to Muhammad Yunus.

'New wave' microfinance becomes 'best practice' By the end of the 1990s, 'new wave' microfinance had reached a position of unparalleled power and influence within the international development community. 'New wave' microfinance was now *the* definition of microfinance, not just one of a number of possibilities.[44] Now that most of the awkward Grameen Bank 'old paradigm' innovations had been stripped from the microfinance model, Western governments, media outlets and the microfinance industry, paradoxically, began to raise the profile of Muhammad Yunus and the Grameen Bank to even dizzier heights than before. Yunus remained in huge demand as an adviser and as a high-level speaker right across the world, and he was increasingly active in fronting and participating in high-profile microfinance campaigns everywhere. Funding was also in full flow to help capitalize 'new wave' MFIs right around the globe. Western universities began to incorporate microfinance into most business, economics and management courses. MBAs with a major microfinance component became commonplace. Western charitable NGOs and foundations wishing to 'help the poor' could do no better than establish or help an MFI to operate in the geographical location of their choice. High-profile private initiatives were established to popularize and lobby for microfinance. One such initiative was the Microcredit Summit Campaign launched in 1997 with the active participation of Muhammad Yunus. Bringing together nearly three thousand people from 137 countries, it kicked off a nine-year campaign to make microcredit available for 100 million of the poorest families across the developing world, and especially to women, with the aim of helping them get involved in self-employment. Music industry icons, Hollywood stars, world sports personalities, well-known entrepreneurs, European and Middle Eastern royalty, current and former politicians (notably former US president Bill Clinton) and many other high-profile individuals began to campaign very publicly around the world in favour of microfinance. With a genuine desire to want to ameliorate poverty and human suffering, they acted in the belief that microfinance was a great way to do this. In recognition of its supposed achievements in addressing poverty and underdevelopment, the UN agreed to designate 2005 as the International Year of Microcredit. Finally, 2006 saw microfinance reach its apotheosis, when the Nobel Peace Prize was jointly awarded to Muhammad Yunus and to the Grameen Bank he had founded.

As the new millennium dawned, moreover, two new factors emerged with the potential to radically transform the dynamics of the microfinance industry in the years to come. The first was a product of the boom years of the 1990s, which saw the rise of a generation of mega-rich 'new money philanthropists' keen to use their huge personal fortunes to leave their mark on humanity and history. One way to do this was to support what everyone seemed to be saying was a brilliant way of reducing poverty and suffering everywhere – microfinance. Very significant sums of philanthropic cash soon began to find their way into microfinance programmes. Probably the most high-profile and generous supporter of microfinance is the $US32 billion Bill and Melinda Gates Foundation. Other notable supporters include eBay founder Pierre Omidyar and Dell Computers founder Michael Dell. In fact, it almost became convention for any self-respecting billionaire to have established some link with microfinance. At the same time, as Smith and Furman report,[45] a growing number of the just moderately wealthy were also becoming convinced that they could do no better for humanity than support microfinance. These individuals were encouraged to donate cash and their time to help the microfinance movement, or simply leave a bequest in their will. Internet-based institutions, such as Kiva, also greatly helped to encourage ordinary people to make a financial contribution towards microfinance and the poor. Claiming to directly connect relatively well-off individuals in developed countries with poor individuals in developing countries urgently seeking a microloan, Kiva has been able to use this 'person-to-person' link concept to raise several tens of millions of dollars for microfinance.[46]

The second major change to affect the 'new wave' microfinance industry has been the quite dramatic rise in commercial funding since the turn of the millennium. As noted above, to all intents and purposes the desired end-state of the 'new wave' MFI is to operate as a private for-profit financial company or bank. This very much includes a role for private investment, which would naturally expect to generate attractive dividends and profits. One obvious attraction of microfinance was its safety, reduced volatility and high returns compared to other sectors. In addition, funders liked the positive PR spin-off associated with microfinance, which also helped to motivate staff. Potential investors thought they were not just making money, but also helping humanity – a classic 'win-win' situation. Estimates of the amount of commercial funding that has been channelled into microfinance in recent years vary wildly. Some analysts suggest that possibly as much as $US30 billion of commercial funding has been directed its way since the turn of the millennium.[47] At any rate, it is possible to say that the amount of commercial funding is certainly very large and – at least until the global financial crisis erupted in 2008 – it was growing at a very fast rate. Microfinance has clearly emerged as one of the most important forms of investment around.

With these two major new sources of funding for the 'new wave' microfinance model now coming on stream, it became increasingly clear that the 'holy grail' of microfinance – total 'saturation' – was becoming a realistic possibility in just about every developing and transition country. In the very near future, virtually every poor individual wishing to access a microloan will be able to do so. The current group of microfinance 'saturated' countries noted in Chapter 1 will be joined by a good many more.

The 'new wave' microfinance model trips up But just when it looked as though the 'new wave' microfinance paradigm had conquered all before it, it ran into the proverbial brick wall. This was the dramatic 2007 initial public offering (IPO)[48] of Compartamos, Mexico's largest microfinance bank. The IPO led to the exposure of almost the complete inner workings of Compartamos. While a number of Compartamos's most disturbing developments were long known to the microfinance industry, and obviously to its long-standing advisers CGAP and ACCIÓN, the IPO exposed to the full glare of publicity quite dramatic Wall Street-style excess, greed and inefficiency. As a result, a fundamental challenge to the legitimacy and direction of the chosen 'new wave' microfinance model was set in motion.

The Compartamos IPO and the implications it has for microfinance will be covered in some detail in Chapter 5. For now it is important just to point out that the Compartamos episode centrally involved charging its poor women borrowers very high interest rates (at times over 100 per cent). This naturally translated into very high profits indeed, which, among other things, from the late 1990s onwards, allowed for a small group of directors and senior managers to pay themselves Wall Street-style salaries and bonuses. These same individuals then came into a truly massive personal financial windfall through the IPO that took place in 2007, a couple of key individuals netting several tens of millions of dollars each. Not surprisingly, the Compartamos IPO sparked an intense debate within the microfinance industry, and not a little acrimony too. Supporters of the 'new wave' microfinance model, centrally including both CGAP and ACCIÓN, initially cheered the Compartamos IPO to the rooftops, arguing that it proved commercialization was the best way to provide microfinance to just about all of Mexico's poor citizens. Others, however, said that the Compartamos episode demonstrated pretty convincingly that the 'new wave' microfinance model was actually a disaster in waiting. The IPO exposed to the public almost exactly the same sort of Wall Street savvy insiders who, in the USA, had proved so adept at manoeuvring their way into huge fortunes at the expense of an ill-informed client base. Pointedly, the most immediate and piqued response to the Compartamos IPO came from Muhammad Yunus. He called the developments at Compartamos 'the end of microfinance', and argued that Compartamos had effectively metamorphosed into the very same type of loan-sharking operation that he and others in the microfinance industry had originally set out to close down.

Arguments raging over the Compartamos IPO were soon overshadowed in 2008, however, when the global economy began to descend into the worst economic trough since the Great Depression. The 'new wave' microfinance model was hit particularly hard. As with virtually every form of investment, commercial funding for microfinance began to dry up. Several private commercial banks dismantled microfinance units established just a few years before. Crucially, it also meant that the huge growth in consumer microloans went into reverse. Local economies artificially inflated thanks to easily available consumer microloans then also began to go into reverse as the level of local demand rapidly declined. Repayment rates on microloans also began to decline, once clients found that the difficult economic situation had reduced their income and/or remittances. Recognizing the difficulties to be faced in 2010 and beyond, the international donor community has already established a $US500 million global fund to bail out the sector, and much more appears to be on its way.

The crux of the problem the 'new wave' microfinance model now faces in the aftermath of the collapse of Wall Street, however, is not simply impending shortfalls (possibly just temporary) in financial support for MFIs. Even if this was overwhelmingly what the microfinance industry itself preferred to focus upon as the global crisis began to hit home, the real problem lies elsewhere. 'New wave' microfinance is not just increasingly producing manifestly adverse Wall Street-style outcomes, it has still largely failed to produce any concrete evidence to show that it actually works to sustainably reduce poverty. In fact, 2009 saw two important adverse developments for the microfinance industry. First, two teams of internationally respected impact assessors were forced to report almost zero impact with regard to two major microcredit programmes they had been looking at.[49] Second, as we shall recount in more detail in Chapter 4, the positive results of an earlier and hugely influential study in Bangladesh were very awk-wardly overturned.[50] Thanks to 'the Compartamos affair', the hitherto robust narrative supporting and protecting microfinance increasingly began to come under much more serious critical scrutiny.

Before I go on to critically appraise the actual operations and de-velopment impact of the microfinance sector in the chapters to come, in the final section of this chapter I feel I need to briefly summarize the basic ideas that the microfinance industry and other supporters portray as 'what microfinance is all about'.

The case for microfinance

In general, the most important impact of microfinance is said to be the additional income and employment that are assumed to arise in poor communities. This is particularly the case when it has been possible to direct these benefits towards the most marginalized and 'at-risk' of the poor in the community. These benefits are obtained through the establishment of new, and the extension of existing, income-generating activities. This idea is very much the core of the original Grameen Bank philosophy. Small additions to income are valuable for immediate consumption purposes, while also opening up the possibility of some modest reinvestment. In some income-generating activities, new jobs are also created. Also, even where most successful clients do not include too many of the very poor, successful individuals using microfinance might nevertheless help to create waged employment opportunities for the very poor and the less entrepreneurial. Overall, some contend that microfinance is of major importance because it gives everyone an opportunity to escape poverty if they really want to.

A second important microfinance impact comes from the fact that formally constituted MFIs help the poor to avoid seeking re-course to the traditional moneylender or local 'loan shark'. Once again, this argument is very much Grameen Bank-inspired. The lower interest rates generally associated with microfinance compared to moneylenders create the space for additional earnings in small income-generating activities. In addition, as Davis vividly illustrates,[51] moneylenders are all too often associated with the 'dark underside' of economic and social life, so coming into regular contact with this world is risky for the poor. Also, many moneylending operations are extremely profitable, but only because they use 'high-pressure' tactics, if not outright violence, in order to enforce repayment on ultra-high-interest microloans. So, helping the poor to develop a relationship with an organization (an MFI) that has been specifically established to *assist* them with lower-interest microloans and sympathetic forms of support, rather than *exploit* them through ultra-high-interest microloans, must be a good thing.

Third, microfinance is very widely seen as important in helping to promote gender 'empowerment'. This principally arises through the increased involvement of women in the local business sector, thanks to the opportunity to access a microloan and to establish themselves in their own microenterprise. Many developing countries have a history of patriarchal control and very few have significant numbers of women actively involved in business. Microfinance therefore allows women the opportunity to begin to take part in business sector activities, albeit the very simplest of businesses to start off with. But with growing evidence of success, and suitable 'role models' to point to, it is said that women can begin to play a much larger and more creative role in the business economy. 'Empowerment' is also said to arise from the basic fact that when women receive a microloan they see it as their responsibility to manage and repay it, which improves confidence and business acumen.

Fourth, microfinance is also seen as useful in helping the poor in terms of consumption smoothing. Indeed, as we shall see, most microfinance is now used for simple consumption smoothing. Poverty is not simply a lack of income; it is also a lack of income at the time it is needed. By making it possible for poor individuals to borrow small sums of money when they most require it, and repay it when income comes in, microfinance helps the poor to compensate for the ups and downs of economic life as they see fit. Some important financial outlays, such as for health and education, are made increasingly possible because microfinance allows the cost to be spread over a longer time period. Access to such items via microfinance greatly helps the poor to improve their value on the labour market, thereby making a sustainable escape from poverty much more likely than had they forgone such expenditure.

Fifth, microfinance is seen as playing a role in building important reserves of social solidarity in poor communities. Notably, it has been argued, this is the case with regard to the famous solidarity circles pioneered by the Grameen Bank. These solidarity circles are said to extend the bonds of solidarity that exist in the family and community, thanks to the constant interaction and contact between poor individuals. Importantly, banks and MFIs are willing to accept such social solidarity as a substitute for formal collateral, which the poor simply do not have. The poor are therefore able to use their social interaction and mutual responsibility, rather than prior reserves of wealth, to obtain as much microfinance as they want.

These basic reasons represent the essential underpinnings to the case that has been made for microfinance since the 1980s. Of course, there are many other reasons advanced to justify microfinance as a development policy, as a quick look around the hundreds of books on the subject will show. Moreover, the importance of each of these reasons has shifted around as priorities have changed. For example, as unemployment has risen, the value of the employment-generating capacity of microfinance has been emphasized. And in some post-conflict scenarios, the solidarity-(re)building aspect of microfinance has come to the fore. I think, however, that I have provided the gist of the arguments made in support of the basic microfinance model.

Conclusion

From its apparent 'discovery' in Bangladesh in the mid-1970s by Muhammad Yunus right up to its very latest 'new wave' manifestation, events have moved with breathtaking speed in the world of microfinance. I emphasized how the initial Grameen Bank idea was very much centred on Muhammad Yunus's idea that the poor en masse should be encouraged to engage in tiny income-generating activities in order to escape their poverty. The international development community found Yunus's simple idea compelling. The politics and ideology of the Grameen Bank microfinance model, especially its stress on individual entrepreneurship, self-help and financial responsibility shown by the poor, were just what the international development community had been looking for. And at least in terms of its narrow objective of providing microloans to the poor at a relatively low cost, thanks to high repayment rates, the Grameen Bank appeared to work. The poor were found to be 'bankable'. But then the international development community fell out with the Grameen Bank-inspired microfinance model, and the 'new wave' microfinance variant was ushered in as its replacement. The fiscal austerity and commercialization imperatives associated with neoliberalism meant subsidies for Grameen Bank-style MFIs simply had to come to an end, and the more aggressive business posture of 'new wave' MFIs would soon make microfinance available to just about any poor individual.

As I have shown, a very large part of the argument put forward for microfinance actually concerns successes registered on the operational side, such as achieving high repayment rates, financial self-sustainability, increasing the number of clients, expanding the volume of microfinance disbursed (especially to women), and so on. None of this is to say, however, that microfinance therefore automatically functions as a sustainable development and poverty reduction instrument. I will argue in what follows, in fact, that we actually have very little evidence to support the contention that microfinance makes a genuine and substantive economic and social impact in the local economy. To start to make my case, it helps to first explore the wider narrative that arose to project microfinance into the very heart of the international development community's operations and strategies, as well as to justify microfinance in the public eye. To what extent is this public narrative based on solid evidence, or simply assumption? I attempt to provide an answer to this important question in the next chapter.

THREE
Microfinance myths and realities

'The aide said that guys like me were "in what we call the reality-based community," which he defined as people who "believe that solutions emerge from your judicious study of discernible reality." I nodded and murmured something about enlightenment principles and empiricism. He cut me off. "That's not the way the world really works anymore," he continued. "We're an empire now, and when we act, we create our own reality ..."' Ron Suskind[1]

'It is a far, far better thing to have a firm anchor in nonsense than to put out on the troubled seas of thought.' John Kenneth Galbraith[2]

'[the] current practices and ways of thinking in the (virtual) world of microfinance, [are] in many respects a world of make-believe.' Otto Hospes and Hotze Lont[3]

Helping to promote the microfinance model within the international development community, and also to popularize microfinance within the wider community, has been a distinct set of ideas. This is the public narrative. Explaining the basics of microfinance in layman's terms, the public narrative that began to emerge in the 1980s turned out to be a brilliant success. In terms of projecting the microfinance model as the logical, humane and 'best practice' response to poverty, unemployment, exclusion and human suffering, it could not have done a better job. The world rallied to support this thing called 'microfinance'.

Even a cursory investigation of this public narrative, however, exposes a very awkward problem for the microfinance industry: almost all of the most basic assumptions that underpin the microfinance model today are wrong. Many microfinance advocates are privately becoming very uncomfortable with this growing disconnect. Some have even gone on record with their concerns.[4] The purpose of this chapter is to point out that virtually *all* of the core assumptions that underpin microfinance today should more accurately be described as myths. This demonstrates just how dramatically weak the public explanation and justification for microfinance actually is in practice.

The basic myths behind the microfinance model

Microfinance supports income-generating activities The original motivation for the Grameen Bank, and still the overwhelming public justification for microfinance programmes today, is that microfinance helps start or expand an income-generating microenterprise. The PR material, publications and websites of MFIs and microfinance support organizations everywhere routinely highlight a poor individual having escaped grinding poverty with some new business line, one that allows her to become financially self-sufficient, feed her family, and send her children to school.

As Thomas Dichter has explained,[5] however, this uplifting picture is largely a mirage. Rather, the evidence shows that for a long time the bulk of microfinance has not actually been accessed in order to establish or expand an income-generating activity, but has been used instead simply to facilitate consumption spending that cannot be financed out of current income. By the early 1990s, the wealth of evidence in support of this trend was overpowering. For example, one of the earliest studies of Grameen Bank was undertaken in the mid-1990s by anthropologist Aminur Rahman. He found that between 1994 and 1995 up to 70 per cent of microloans in a sample of 217 in the study village were being used for purposes other than the income-generating activities originally specified.[6] Reporting in 2007 on its work in Bangladesh, the Goldin Institute came to a similar result, finding that most individuals took out microloans simply to see them through the *monga* season, a period of food insecurity between harvests.[7] Most recently, Collins, Morduch, Rutherford and Ruthven also found from their work in Bangladesh that business entry or expansion was not the most common use of microloans.[8] Estimates in India suggest a similar situation, with some studies demonstrating that only between one fifth and one third of microcredit disbursed is used to underpin an income-generating activity, with the bulk going into consumer loans.[9] In sub-Saharan Africa, the Finscope country studies all point to quite a small percentage of the clients using microcredit for microenterprise establishment and expansion purposes. In Uganda (where microfinance is now ubiquitous) it was only 15 per cent, and in Tanzania virtually the same.[10] The overview study concludes that 'The main reason for borrowing money is to buy food. Thereafter, funerals, school fees and medical expenses become the most pressing needs.'[11] A whole host of studies have shown exactly the same thing in most other countries (see also Chapter 5).

Looking back, the evolution of the separate terms 'microcredit' and 'microfinance' was largely a reflection of the general trend under way. The new term microfinance was introduced because it was no longer possible to argue that microcredit was disbursed mainly for business purposes. This purpose was now a comparatively minor one compared to the other financial products offered by MFIs in the field, including micro-insurance, savings services and microloans for consumption purposes.

Nevertheless, some within the microfinance industry are not completely reconciled to openly admitting this significant change. They see it as a threat to the entire legitimacy and appeal of microfinance to the international development community, which was always very centrally based upon the illusion of helping the poor into business and self-sufficiency. If it becomes clear that most MFIs have effectively turned into simple for-profit consumer lending operations, the fear is that the whole microfinance concept will inevitably become tainted by association with the sort of payday/doorstep consumer lending operations that are routinely vilified in the developed countries. For this reason, many MFIs seek to underplay their growing engagement with simple consumer loans. As long-time poverty researcher Stuart Rutherford notes, many MFIs prefer to keep quiet about this change within the microfinance industry, 'pragmatically realizing that the rags-to-riches-through-microenterprises story was valuable to the industry as a whole'.[12] Today, however, and if still only discreetly, the majority of microfinance industry analysts concede that consumption lending represents the vast bulk of their lending activity. What may have started as a movement to fund microenterprise development has clearly transmogrified into something else. As Beck and Ogden summarized in the *Harvard Business Review* in 2007, 'Many heads of microfinance programs now privately acknowledge what John Hatch, the founder of FINCA International (one of the largest microfinance institutions), has said publicly: 90% of microloans are used to finance current consumption rather than to fuel enterprise.'

I will leave it until Chapter 5 to discuss the implications of the microfinance industry's massive shift into consumption lending. What we can say here right away, however, is that a central assumption of really quite crucial importance to the establishment and continued growth of the microfinance model – that microloans are overwhelmingly used to support income-generating activities – is very largely a myth.

Microfinance 'empowers' the poor Another core assumption built into the microfinance model is that the poor are 'empowered' through microenterprises. Indeed, microenterprises are said to open the way towards a qualitative transformation in the life of the poor. Peruvian economist Hernando de Soto has lauded the way that a microenterprise can apparently empower an individual and release the 'heroic entrepreneur' that supposedly lies within us all.[13] Freed from bureaucratic structures and the boss, microenterprises are also said to represent a new form of personal and business freedom. Perhaps most of all, microfinance is supposed to represent a magnificent chance to promote 'gender empowerment' within society. This narrative is an extremely powerful and seductive one. Empowerment is such an emotionally loaded concept that everyone simply must be in favour of any policy or programme intervention that seemingly extends it.

Insofar as it is claimed to be a core impact of the microfinance concept, however, it is a wrong assumption to make. While historical experience is generally not always directly transferable, there are nevertheless some very interesting parallels with earlier historical episodes that help explain matters today. In particular, a careful reading of the evidence from economic history indisputably shows that self-employment and microenterprises have most often been promoted as part of the programmed *disempowerment* of the poor. Let us first recall a little of the early history of industrial capitalism, beginning with the passing of the Poor Law Reform of 1834 in England. As the economic historian Karl Polanyi shows in his classic study of economic history,[14] this was the crucial intervention that introduced the modern institution of the *labour market*. Prior to this, the 'right to live', if necessary with the help of local charitable support for those unable to find gainful employment (the so-called 'Speenhamland system'), was guaranteed by society. The Poor Law Reform did away with this albeit minimal security. From then on, poor individuals would have to confront labour market forces on their own and survive in any way they could. For the majority in the 1830s and 1840s, as intended, this meant quickly adapting to the rigours of wage employment within England's rapidly expanding industries and factories. For those unable to manage either wage labour in the new factories, or else continue to live as they had done before (for example, as home-based weavers or peasant farmers), the only remaining option to avoid complete penury was to move into a range of 'survivalist' individual activities – what we would now call 'micro-enterprises'. This 'new world' of survivalist microenterprises was exhaustively documented at the time by Henry Mayhew in his classic work *London Labour and the London Poor*.[15] Mayhew showed in graphic detail how mid-nineteenth-century England had very rapidly become a cornucopia of informal microenterprise 'survivalist' activity.

Both the old established aristocracy and the new industrial capitalist elites, as well as Henry Mayhew himself,[16] were very supportive of the rapid rise of these new informal 'survivalist' activities. The proliferation of such activities would, for a start, justify reducing the charitable burden then placed on the rich. Also, with more family members contributing to the family income through such activity, including any young children, there was likely to be much less upward pressure on factory wages. Perhaps the most important survival aspect so far as business elites in nineteenth-century England were concerned, however, was their own. Supporting the expansion of petty survivalist activities helped to steer the poor away from more transformational activities that risked upsetting the social order. Wrapped up in the act of merely surviving from one day to the next, the poor tended to have very little time, energy or knowledge to get involved in anything else. They therefore offered very little participation in the great number of popular movements getting under way at that time – trade unionism, cooperativism, communism-socialism, anarcho-syndicalism and those seeking the universal franchise (the Chartists) – even though these movements held up the very real prospect of an eventual exit from extreme poverty and degradation. The poor were thus contained thanks to microenterprise activity: that is, *they were disempowered*. Life was made a lot safer both for the new industrial capitalists and the old aristocracy they were in the process of displacing.

One individual who very quickly recognized the significance of this disempowerment was Karl Marx. The lumpenproletariat, Marx regretfully intoned – the term he coined for this class of desperately poor individuals[17] – were so docile and downtrodden, so self-absorbed in their own immediate survival, and so thoroughly lacking in hope for the longer term, that they could not be counted upon to play a major role in the revolutionary dismantling of capitalism. Largely thanks to the many new social movements just mentioned, which led to the growing 'collective capability' to bring about the required changes of most benefit to the poor, things did begin to change for the better; but through successful evolution, not revolution.

But perhaps history has turned a corner. If not in the past, then maybe today microenterprises are instruments leading to the empowerment of the poor? This proposition, however, does not seem to be backed up by any evidence either. As nineteenth-century economic liberalism was famously reborn in the 1980s under the contemporary rubric of neoliberalism, important elements of this disempowerment approach quickly resurfaced in the developed countries. As David Harvey sums up in his 2006 book *A Brief History of Neoliberalism*, even neoliberals are in pretty much full agreement on what was the central aim of the UK and US governments' labour market policy thrust in the 1980s and 1990s: to promote self-employment as a way of disempowering organized labour in particular, and the lower classes in general, thereby to (re-)empower the narrow business class.[18] And such policies were very successful too, as many noted labour economists reported.[19] Moreover, the US and UK governments naturally took steps to ensure that such favoured neoliberal labour market policies were also projected into the developing and transition countries too. Given the US government's effective control over policy development in the key international development agencies, notably with regard to the World Bank and the IMF, this was not too difficult. It should come as no surprise to find that similar disempowering outcomes as in the US and UK economies have thus been the overwhelming result in almost every developing and transition country.[20]

So there would appear to be very little evidence of a change of heart in relation to the historically assigned role for microenterprises, and so also for microfinance. The huge and growing microenterprise sector in developing countries today is, very much as in the past, the proximate working location for the vast bulk of the most thoroughly disempowered individuals imaginable. And as in the case of the long-term prisoner who is incrementally provided with a few privileges as a way of controlling any possible intention to reject the entire experience of prison life (say, by escaping or by suicide), even if the average poor micro-entrepreneur is afforded some minimal 'control' over a few trivial matters concerning her working life – when to start work, what clothes to wear, when to take lunch, and so on – this does not alter the bare fact that her overwhelming life situation is effectively marked out by pretty much complete powerlessness. You can control only what you are permitted to control. It is therefore quite wrong to suggest that microfinance is associated with either a genuine *intention* to empower the poor or any meaningful *outcome* having been achieved in this direction.

Microfinance impact assessments 'prove' that microfinance works

As microfinance evolved into a generously funded development policy, microfinance advocates began to realize the limitations of the anecdotal and individual case study approach to assessing impact. Though often heart-warming and extremely persuasive, generalizing sustainable impact from isolated cases is an unsatisfactory, and very often manipulative, methodology at best. The eventual result was the introduction of various impact assessment methodologies that would supposedly provide a more robust analysis of microfinance impact. USAID has been in the forefront of helping design and implement new impact assessment methodologies based on the evaluation of client impact versus non-client impact, with the difference attributable to microfinance.

Does impact assessment produce a genuine reflection of what microfinance can achieve economically and socially? Former World Bank staff member David Ellerman thinks not. He believes the current impact assessment methodologies are quite fundamentally mistaken. Ellerman essentially argues that the impact of microfinance cannot be assessed correctly by comparing microfinance to the alternative of 'doing nothing'. Without some reference to the real counterfactual or opportunity cost, which would be a similar programme with the same clients using the same resources, we inevitably come to quite erroneous conclusions as to development effectiveness. Where one local 'treatment' community receives a major new injection of funds via an MFI, while a counterpart 'control' community receives nothing, the typical gains registered in the 'treatment' community – more microenterprises, higher incomes, and so on – prove very little indeed about the power of microfinance. Generally *any* injection of outside cash will improve things, even if just dropped from a helicopter.

A further important problem regarding impact assessments, as I will discuss at some length in the next chapter, relates to lack of concern for two key issues – displacement and client microenterprise failure. These issues have in the past been very important counter-trends associated with small-enterprise programme impact, yet they are very largely ignored by the microfinance industry. Even the very latest type of impact assessment, those incorporating Randomized Control Trials (RCTs),[21] largely fail to account for these two issues.

Importantly, Ellerman thinks it is not a coincidence that the current preferred impact assessment methodologies tend to very seriously exaggerate the potential benefits and impact of microfinance. This arises, Ellerman claims, because a positive impact assessment – howsoever concocted – can help to justify an intervention favoured on political grounds, but which might have no justification on economic impact grounds. Calling them 'the ultimate low hurdle for aid agencies', he concludes that most impact assessments[22] 'have become a fad in their own right, and are now entwined with microfinance as a means to help sustain programmes that have little if any development effectiveness'.

In a similar vein, it is not unimportant to consider *who* actually undertakes most impact assessments. It is an awkward fact that the vast majority of impact assessments have been undertaken not by reasonably independent (but still committed, skilled and knowledgeable) evaluators, but by committed microfinance 'insiders'. That is, by a like-minded community of microfinance practitioners, academic researchers, policy advisers, boutique consultancy firms, and career staff working within the international development agencies and key NGOs. A growing trend is for the larger MFIs and high-profile microfinance advocacy NGOs to co-opt senior academics and researchers as board members, the better to ensure that favourable research outputs are forthcoming and potentially critical voices can be silenced. Inevitably, the likelihood of a comprehensively negative impact assessment emerging from within this network of dedicated microfinance supporters is negligible, still less a serious challenge to the fundamentals of the microfinance model. Among other things, you do not bite the hand (or the microfinance model or the international development agency or your own boss) that feeds you.

Predictably, the arrival of the 'new wave' microfinance model in the 1990s then made matters worse. Under pressure to raise commercial and international development agency funds in order to survive and expand, many MFIs have been only too willing to exaggerate and distort important aspects of their operational performance and ultimate impact. The Wall Street foundations of 'new wave' microfinance have, quite predictably, led to Wall Street-style results. In some countries, the main MFIs and their lobby groups help in preparing the industry evaluations of the microfinance sector. This cosy arrangement is designed to ensure that nothing disturbs the carefully created upbeat image of the microfinance sector. It also helps that many of the largest and wealthiest MFIs, especially the new generation of microfinance banks, are now in a position to offer extremely lucrative contracts and valuable ongoing research and advisory work to individual and institutional evaluators. Just as on Wall Street past and present,[23] it is unlikely that any of today's high-profile MFIs will find it too difficult to secure a broadly favourable impact assessment.

Microfinance is what the poor 'want' and 'need' The poor everywhere are attempting to survive. Against a background of steadily worsening economic opportunities around the globe for probably the majority of the poor, especially in the world's mega-city slums,[24] it has been getting harder and harder in recent years. The global economic crisis that began in 2008 has not helped matters here. It is therefore natural that the poor will try to survive by using whatever resources they find at their disposal, including microfinance. It is quite wrong, however, to extrapolate from the widespread use of microfinance by the poor to conclude that they actually 'want' and 'need' microfinance, and so fully agree with microfinance as the main or only way out of their poverty predicament.

Consider first the widespread idea within the microfinance industry that the demand for microloans simply must equate with their being able to enhance the welfare of the client, otherwise the poor would simply not wish to access one. The logic deployed here is quite seriously flawed. Many products and services are demanded, often aggressively demanded. But we also know that consumption of some products and services ultimately destroys human welfare: class-A drugs, tobacco, strong alcohol, images of violence and certain categories of junk food are obvious examples. Few would argue here that the demand for such products justifies ensuring a completely uninterrupted supply (if necessary facilitated by microfinance!). More specifically, what if it turns out – as is often the case, we should add – that demand for microfinance is actually a function of a downward spiral into deep poverty, with the poor effectively addicted to it because they hope to stave off complete destitution. Rather like the compulsive gambler forlornly hoping to gamble his way out of debt by enjoying 'one last big win at the horse races', the poor are often powerless to stop their descent into a nightmare world of debt. This is why, Mike Davis notes, it is no coincidence to find that rising poverty in many developing countries closely correlates with the rising popularity of various forms of gambling, lotteries and pyramid schemes, all promising the chance of an instant exit from grinding poverty.[25] The demand for microloans thus very often reflects some seriously debilitating social dynamics. Microfinance specialist Paul Rippey calls it right, then, when he concludes, 'Microcredit may or may not be of net social benefit, but the fact that people keep taking loans provides absolutely no evidence that microcredit does more good than harm.'[26] If this were otherwise, inveterate gamblers, substance abusers and alcoholics would be most pleased.

More importantly, whenever the poor are directly asked what they would like to see in terms of financial support, they invariably reply that they would like something *other* than microfinance. There is absolutely no debate about this. Thousands of studies, questionnaires and surveys actually point to what the poor really want – much lower interest rates on microloans, much longer repayment periods, much larger loans in fact (i.e. not microloans, but small business loans) and grace periods (especially if in agriculture, because of the agricultural cycle). Take just the very latest evidence for this, contained in a 2009 publication by the World Bank, *The Moving out of Poverty Study*. This study was undertaken across fifteen countries in Africa, East Asia, South Asia and Latin America, and included more than sixty thousand interviews with the poor. A major conclusion of the study was that 'Microcredit can help the poor subsist from day to day, but in order to lift them out of poverty, larger loans are needed so that the poor can expand their productive activities and thereby increase their assets.'[27]

This is quite compelling evidence that the poor are registering a strong desire for traditional small business loans, *not microfinance*.

Going farther, one must also point out that if what the poor really want are *lower-cost* loans, and this can only be made possible through extensive subsidization of a financial institution, then what is wrong with this? It is an entirely possible reality. As in the USA, the EU states and many other countries, it is a legitimate wish that requires only a political decision for it to come true. And there is much evidence to show that poor communities actually *do* hold the opinion that favourable financial support can and should be provided to them, because they believe that there is no other way of facilitating their escape from poverty. Referring once more to the World Bank's *Moving out of Poverty* study,[28] the poor consulted in the study called for their 'financial isolation' to come to an end, and for solidarity linkages to be formed with other groups in society, especially with the state and wealthy elite groups. The poor feel these solidarity linkages are crucial in helping them escape poverty because:[29]

> Poor people as a group lack cash, assets, education, market know-how, and connections with the rich and powerful. When poor people associate only with each other, they bring only their own meager resources to the table. Poor people understand these constraints and affirm that 'there is a limit to how much one hungry man can feed another.' The challenge is to extend these positive local traditions of mutual help so that they reach across social lines to involve those who can bring in new resources, ideas, and skills.

This is a powerful and eloquent statement by the poor in favour of elite groups and the state providing them with additional financial support over and above simple market provision. And particularly in times of economic crisis, when we know that mutual help and support networks are most prone to breaking down among the poor,[30] such cross-class and public–private solidarity linkages are even more valuable.

Support for the idea that the poor need and want microfinance also very often arises from the misguided romanticizing of the activities undertaken by the poor. Microfinance advocates are routinely guilty of this. The poor prefer individual microenterprise activity over all other possibilities, so the argument runs, because it supposedly meets their demands for self-respect, and their determination not to demean themselves by relying on the 'nanny state' or 'handouts'. Along these lines, for example, Getubig, Gibbons and Remenyi make the argument that 'The poor need the respect and dignity that flows from identifying and creating their own livelihood sources.'[31] This is a serious misunderstanding, as well as patronizing and offensive. Such blithe statements sit very uncomfortably alongside the routinely horrendous realities of enforced engagement with the informal sector in developing countries today, and the debilitating impact of brute market forces vectored upon the poor and most disadvantaged members of society. We should note that both the World Bank's *Moving out of Poverty* study just mentioned, as well as the forerunner *Voices of the Poor* study,[32] report that the poor actually see the routine lack of self-respect and humiliation to be important negative aspects associated with attempting to survive in the informal sector.

Finally, we should also add that the poor very often understand that the best way to secure real dignity and respect is actually *collectively*, using their most important asset – their numbers. This is why, historically, social movements, pro-poor political parties, trade unions, pressure groups and other forms of collective and popular action, and latterly state activism under democratic mandate, have proved to be the decisive factors in reducing generalized poverty and human suffering. In more recent times, of course, social mobilization and state activism helped a large section of the working class in the developed countries to become 'embourgeoisified', thereby to constitute a new middle class.[33] It is therefore hugely instructive of the real objectives and motives in play here to find that such historically decisive pro-poor strategies and methodologies are so often met with opposition and ridicule, not just from neoliberal policy-makers, but from many microfinance advocates too.[34] Concerned individuals and institutions that proclaim they have a 'burning passion' to help the poor, but just so long as the poor confine themselves to the world of individual entrepreneurship and microfinance, are clearly (if unwittingly) of real service to those seeking to *disempower* the poor.

In short, it is a myth that microfinance has very much to do with what the poor genuinely want or need, or that it automatically confers dignity or respect through microenterprise activity. For a variety of the reasons adumbrated above, the poor simply get what they are given.

Microfinance availability is increased by formal property titles One of the most high-profile advocates of microfinance and microenterprises is Hernando de Soto. De Soto first came to prominence in the late 1980s with his view that the microenterprise sector contained the seeds of sustainable development in Latin America and elsewhere.[35] The rather awkward failure of his signature idea was pretty clear by the late 1990s, however: poverty, inequality and human suffering actually increased in Latin America in the 1980s and 1990s in line with, and (as Chapters 4 and 5 will show) *at least partly thanks to*, the unrestrained growth of the informal microenterprise sector. Nevertheless, De Soto managed to maintain his international prominence in the new millennium thanks to another 'big idea'. In his best-selling book of 2000, *The Mystery of Capital*, De Soto put forward a novel concept concerning property rights and so-called 'dead capital'. By helping the poor to secure full legal property rights to the informal land and buildings upon and in which they live and work, De Soto argued, the poor can bring to life a very valuable asset, an asset that they can use as collateral in order to access almost unlimited quantities of microfinance. This additional microfinance would then support a massive step-up in microenterprise development, which, in spite of all the evidence to the contrary in his native Latin America, De Soto doggedly continues to claim is the ultimate solution to poverty.

Perhaps not surprisingly, De Soto's latest idea regarding property rights was also very warmly welcomed by the international development community. Right away the World Bank took a special interest in the land titling issue, wholeheartedly agreeing that an additional supply of credit will supposedly be forthcoming and that it will usefully underpin further microenterprise development.[36] Accordingly, large sums of money have been directed into formalizing property rights in many developing countries, starting with De Soto's native country, Peru. Peru attracted a major World Bank-funded project to establish land titles – the Peru Urban Property Rights Project (PUPRP). Most recently, the idea received a major fillip in 2006 with the establishment of the Commission on the Legal Empowerment of the Poor, a high-profile initiative hosted by UNDP, funded by a range of international donors, and co-chaired by De Soto himself and former US secretary of state Madeleine Albright.[37]

De Soto's ideas linking property rights to microfinance, however, stand on very shaky ground indeed. First of all, recall that one of the core Grameen Bank innovations was precisely that it largely did away with the need for the poor to present *any* formal collateral. In Peru, as in most other countries in Latin America, there has been a rapid expansion of the microfinance sector in the last two decades, and Peru is now regarded as one of the countries most 'saturated' with microfinance. But Peru's 'saturation' with microfinance, as in most other developing countries, has been arrived at almost exclusively thanks to collateral-free models. In most developing countries poor individuals are pretty much able to access as much microcredit as they want, and without any need for land titles (see 'Myths behind the "new wave" microfinance model' below). Moreover, if the poor in some place are *not* able to access as much microfinance as they want, then it is usually because of reasons quite unconnected to the land titling issue: their business idea is too risky, they are already too heavily indebted, and so on. In Peru, for example, Pait's study shows that the main factor stopping women accessing even more microfinance than at present is 'related to their inability to demonstrate sufficient steady cash flow or regular income'.[38]

Second, and quite logical in view of the previous point, to date there has been almost no independently verified empirical evidence to confirm that access to credit becomes far more widely available to those holding new land titles. Thanks to PUPRP, Peru is the most obvious first place to look for concrete evidence of a link. Carefully following up on PUPRP, however, Kagawa found little evidence of any link between land title consolidation and access to microcredit for those otherwise credit constrained, concluding that 'land titles have not been sufficient to open doors to access to credit'.[39] Nor could Calderon or Field and Torero find evidence of any link between land titles and credit in Peruvian practice.[40] Many years of field research by leading Latin American scholar Alan Gilbert left him similarly unimpressed by De Soto's claims here.[41] Going farther, Manji and also Nyamu-Musembi could find no evidence of any such link emerging in Africa either,[42] while Durand-Lasserve and Selod suggest there is little evidence to support such a link anywhere.[43]

In truth, just like his earlier miscalculation concerning the 'power' of the microenterprise sector to address poverty and human suffering, De Soto's ideologically driven notions concerning property rights have been brilliantly marketed and sold to his international development community supporters, even though they largely don't add up in practice.

Microfinance directly helps the very poorest The microfinance model is largely seen as helping the very poorest in developing countries; those who typically have received little help in the past and are in increasingly dire straits. Deliberately targeted at the very poor, microfinance is there to help them more than anyone else. Microfinance analysts universally accept that in practice, however, most MFIs now work with the less poor, and even with the moderately wealthy. Hulme and Mosely began to point this out in the mid-1990s.[44] Thereafter, the gradual establishment of the 'new wave' MFI model was associated with accelerating this exclusion process. Moreover, as we noted above, the massive shift into consumption lending by most MFIs means that in some countries the middle classes (who make the least risky and most profitable clients) actually benefit the most from the increased supply of microfinance.

One reason for the exclusion of the very poor as clients is because they tend to generate low profits and are also more risky to work with. Recall from Chapter 2, for example, the conversion of the Grameen Bank over to 'new wave' principles in 2001. One of the most worrying outcomes of Grameen II was that the proportion of very poor people serviced by Grameen – its original target group back in the 1970s – looked set to seriously decline. Since the new for-profit emphasis meant developing a client base composed of those most able to successfully repay a microloan, the non-poor and moderately poor now appear to be the focus of Grameen's growth.[45] Concerned at the PR implications for such an iconic MFI, however, and for microfinance in general, Grameen felt it had no choice but to introduce a special programme for the very poorest. This was its 'struggling members programme', which Grameen Bank quickly began to trail as a major aspect of its overall operations.[46] But in spite of much fanfare, with just over 55,000 members by 2005 compared to more than 5 million clients overall in the same year, even microfinance advocates recognize that the programme is no more than a token gesture at best.[47]

Microfinance empowers women A central thread running throughout the microfinance industry narrative right from its establishment in Bangladesh is that it promotes the empowerment of women. On awarding the 2006 Nobel Peace Prize jointly to Muhammad Yunus and Grameen Bank, the Nobel Prize Committee noted that[48] 'Microcredit has proved to be an important liberating force in societies where women in particular have to struggle against repressive social and economic conditions. Economic growth and political democracy can not achieve their full potential unless the female half of humanity participates on an equal footing with the male.'

Starting with the Grameen Bank, many MFIs and microfinance programmes took to prioritizing women as clients. To many, the mere act of putting a microcredit into the hands of poor women signified the huge potential that microfinance has opened up for gender empowerment. The idea quickly caught on. For example, the high-profile MicroCredit Summit Campaign made 'gender empowerment' one of its core aims, arguing that to achieve this objective microfinance had to be made available far more to women than to men.[49] Such is the widely presumed positive impact of microfinance on women that in

2008 *Time* magazine denoted it to be one of the 'ten ideas that are changing the world'.[50] But how robust is this hugely influential gender empowerment argument in practice?

Unfortunately, the idea of gender empowerment does not stand up well to independent scrutiny. In fact, a distinct mythology of gender empowerment has been created by the microfinance industry, based upon a number of questionable assertions, critical misunderstandings and deliberately created confusions. First of all, recall from what I have said above that there is a lack of historical evidence to suggest that petty microenterprise activity will substantively empower *anyone*, regardless of their gender. Nor do contemporary policy-makers seem to have changed their tune either. Especially in the USA and the UK, neoliberal social policy models are very clearly contingent upon the expansion of self-employment and microenterprises in order to facilitate the 'flexibilization' and disempowerment of the labour force. This is *especially* the case with regard to low-skilled and un-skilled women.[51] A good example of this trend is the dramatic rise in home-based work and 'contracting out' to self-employed women for services they previously undertook as a formal employee within the same private company or public body that now contracts out to them.[52] This is an innovative and now widely adopted scheme that arose specifically in order to exclude trade unions, thereby to extend working hours and trim labour costs as much as possible. Sectors felt to be particularly ripe for such treatment included textiles, healthcare and social services. Such microenterprise development schemes were certainly *not* adopted in order to improve things for those women now forcibly recast as self-employed subcontractors. Increasingly dependent upon ill-paid contracts regularly up for renewal, many women have been deliberately shifted into a far weaker and less remunerative self-employment position than hitherto – that is, they have been disempowered.[53] This, then, is a clear trend in the developed economies following the turn to neoliberalism in the 1980s. Is the trend likely to be any different in developing and transition countries falling under exactly the same doctrinal influences?

Consider, first, the obvious example of Bangladesh. If we leave aside the largely self-serving PR and hype produced by the Grameen Bank and its international donor supporters, we actually find a thriving subculture of academic and NGO work providing a quite different narrative. In a widely cited paper, Goetz and Sen Gupta showed that women most often lost control to their male partner of any microloan obtained, but they nevertheless retained the responsibility of repaying the microloan through an increasing workload of odd jobs.[54] Elsewhere, the typical Bangladeshi woman's gradual entrapment in a web of microdebt was poignantly captured in a major consultation exercise undertaken in 2007,[55] with one individual keen to point out that 'We did not have so many loans in the past; our children and wives could lead a comfortable life; they did only household chores under Purdah. But now they [also] have to work out in the field to collect money for repaying instalments.' To many independent researchers, then, microfinance seems most likely to have circumscribed the freedom of women in the typical Bangladeshi community, not advanced it. These awkward results were also backed up by Aminur Rahman's major study of the Grameen Bank itself. Rahman pointed out that women were good clients mainly because of their sociocultural vulnerability, which was expressed, among other things, by their willingness to agree to an onerous schedule of weekly meetings.[56]

Most recently, Lamia Karim has bravely reported on the growing extent of social violence and public humiliation deployed to enforce high repayment rates in Bangladesh's main MFIs, especially in Grameen Bank.[57] She concludes from her extensive fieldwork that Grameen Bank and other MFIs have essentially been constructed upon the routine use and abuse of Bangladeshi women's honour and shame. High repayment rates are therefore not surprising under such pressure. Karim describes 'a local economy of shame', and she shows how local norms of gender cohesion and community are undermined by the juggernaut that is microfinance. Such widespread practice mainly leads to the subjugation of women, rather than to their emancipation or empowerment. Importantly, Karim shows that the ongoing commercialization of the microfinance sector has markedly intensified these aggressive tactics, including routine pressure on the male partner and his wider kinfolk to repay a microloan. At least one of the major MFIs in Bangladesh, ASA, quite freely admits to using pressure on borrowers' husbands and male relatives to enforce its high repayment levels on microloans taken out by women (see below).

Such a negative interpretation of microfinance in Bangladesh strongly resonates in equally microfinance-saturated Bolivia. Many years of fieldwork in Bolivia have led anthropologist Lesley Gill to conclude that masculine hegemony has been *strengthened* by the restructuring of local society through (among other things) microcredit.[58] For example, she found that many MFIs choose to hire and train male employees to ensure that high repayment is maintained. As Gill sees it, the use of males in high-status jobs tends to reinforce the position of higher-gendered-status males compared to the lower-gendered-status females in local society. Moreover, in the 1980s, the Bolivian state saw microfinance as a way of smoothing the path towards dismantling important state capacities, in line with the international development community's instructions to cut costs and restore fiscal balance. In particular, key social infrastructures of most value to poor women were pointedly included in the institutions slated for closure, downsizing and/or privatization. As it set about dismantling many of Bolivia's most important social, health and educational capacities from the 1980s onwards, the Bolivian government simultaneously began to enjoin Bolivian women to petition the private sector to supply these support services instead. Poor women were told not to worry, because the rising supply of microfinance could now be used to facilitate the purchase of the most important services that had been withdrawn by the state. In other words, suitably lubricated by microfinance, responsibility for the provision of support services of most importance to women in poverty was increasingly being thrown back on to those very women. This is disempowerment of the first order. Overall, Gill found that the proliferation of microfinance was crucially important to the Bolivian state in the 1980s and 1990s, because it provided the important political 'cover' behind which it could deliberately withdraw from meeting its obligations to the poor, and especially to women in poverty. In no uncertain terms, with the help of microfinance Bolivia's women in poverty were disadvantaged and effectively disempowered.

The perspective from a previously well-developed transition economy is also very relevant here. Vanessa Pupavac argues that the microfinance concept in Bosnia represents a major setback in terms of the empowerment of women, and she finds that microfinance in Bosnia is actually quite widely resented by Bosnian women. In general terms, for many Bosnian women microfinance appears to represent the triumph of the West's very limited and externally imposed 'vision' for Bosnia's post-war future, one that is marked out by the Bosnian population's enforced (re-)engagement with primitive forms of informal sector employment thought to have been left behind in the early part of the twentieth century.[59] With many qualified and highly skilled Bosnian women forced into the most primitive of microenterprise activities simply in order to survive – petty cross-border trade, street selling, primitive agriculture (keeping a cow in the back garden), running a basement shop – resentment is perhaps inevitable. Many Bosnian women and NGO advocacy groups also point out another conundrum. Why was it possible to make hugely important empowerment advances for women within the former Yugoslavia[60] – following a viciously destructive war (1941–44), when human capital, technology and institutions were underdeveloped, and when the country was comparatively much less wealthy – but yet today Bosnian women are told such advances are simply no longer possible. Seen in this context, it is not surprising that contemporary microfinance-driven outcomes in Bosnia are increasingly viewed as a fundamentally backward step in terms of sustainable development and gender empowerment.

Moreover, there seems to be no getting away from the fact that the increasing commercial orientation of microfinance everywhere jars with any supposed concern to empower women. This is why leading microfinance advocate Linda Mayoux argues that microfinance programmes need to move far beyond the mere provision of microloans, and start to include and financially support specific gender empowerment components as standard. As she succinctly remarks,[61] 'Unless microfinance is conceived as part of a broader strategy for transformation of gender inequality, *it risks becoming yet one more means of shifting the costs and responsibilities for development onto very poor women*' (my italics).

Exactly. But Mayoux herself then goes on to admit that implementing this 'broader strategy' approach will be a very difficult task indeed. This is particularly the case, she argues, in view of the fact that the 'new wave' microfinance model's primary concern lies with profitability and financial self-sustainability, and not with ensuring gender empowerment.[62] For example, consider the hundreds of private MFIs set up in Bangladesh, India and Pakistan this last decade, virtually all promising gender empowerment. Most, if not all, actually have very little genuine concern for this issue. These new MFIs are overwhelmingly straightforward profit-maximizing institutions, and were established with the primary concern of enriching their investor-owner(s). Most operate only under the cover of gender empowerment because this is the coded language needed to ensure 'respectability' within the microfinance industry, thereby to increase the chances of unlocking some additional government and international donor financial and technical support.

Further evidence to back up the fears expressed by Linda Mayoux in the quotation cited above comes from Africa, where the international development community has developed a fascination with using microfinance to promote subsistence farms. In many parts of Africa, the World Bank has been pushing hard for MFIs to work with quite inefficient subsistence farms, as opposed to them offering affordable financial products suitable for small family farms that are a far more efficient agricultural structure (this important distinction is discussed in Chapter 4). As Ambreena Manji points out,[63] however, there is a disturbing reason for this otherwise somewhat puzzling trend. Promoting rural microfinance is premised on a subsistence farm realizing a competitive advantage through the extensive use of 'non-contractable labour', which in practice, she argues, effectively boils down to 'unpaid female labour'. This 'advantage', the World Bank hopes,[64] will offset the many disadvantages of a tiny farming unit otherwise operating well below minimum efficient scale. The intended result is that the average subsistence farm can now be made sustainable/profitable thanks to unpaid female labour, backed up by growing quantities of microfinance. Subsistence farms will help to provide a little extra food, maintain rural employment, deter rural–urban migration and so also help to ensure political stability. Importantly, because financially self-sustaining ('new wave') microfinance can be made to substitute for subsidy-dependent agricultural support regimes, these benefits can be achieved at no cost to governments or to the international development community. Working with small family farms and their related infrastructures would involve far more complicated and costly financial interventions than 'new wave' microfinance can provide, so this option effectively renders itself impossible right from the start.[65] But the unstated problem in the subsistence farming option is, as one might suspect, the fact that women are increasingly being expected to acquiesce to a future of unpaid labour. This result is hardly empowering. Indeed, as Manji suggests, '[the World Bank's] global land policy over the next decade will worsen rather than ameliorate women's social and economic position'.[66]

Another awkward issue for those seeing gender empowerment through microfinance is that in an increasing number of countries, above all in Bangladesh itself, commercialization pressures have resulted in the increasing abandonment of the solidarity circles concept in mainstream MFIs. The important thing for most 'new wave' MFIs nowadays is essentially to push out as much microcredit as possible.

It is best not to get bogged down in attempting to promote social mobilization and gender empowerment through solidarity circles. Yet recall that solidarity circles were originally portrayed by microfinance advocates to be *the* most important social innovation responsible for the empowerment of women, principally through the social capital accumulation route.[67] To those who have consistently argued in favour of such solidarity circles, then, their ongoing abandonment by many MFIs must surely be registered as a significant reversal in any gender empowerment scenario. Moreover, what is taking the place of solidarity circles in Bangladesh already looks pretty discouraging from a gender perspective. For example, as the *Wall Street Journal* reported in its survey of microfinance,[68]

> Harder-headed microlenders are stealing the spotlight [in Bangladesh] [...] One rising star is the Association for Social Advancement (ASA), [...] which boasts 1.5 million borrowers and just 0.7% of loans overdue, even by a week. Dispensing with borrower groups, ASA leans on borrowers' husbands and relatives if payments are missed, says the managing director, Shafiqual Haque Choudhury. To him, Grameen's [solidarity circles] approach is an ingenious idea that didn't stand the test of time.

Finally, we need to reiterate our earlier comment that microfinance advocates very often promote self-employment as the best way of escaping poverty, often without realizing or caring that entrepreneurial activity is not always what women in developing countries actually feel suited to or want to do. Many women naturally prefer more secure, child-friendly and better-paid work in a safe and clean environment, typically government work of some kind. These are valid wishes. But instead, and often on the basis of wrong-headed cultural stereotypes supporting the 'universality' of entrepreneurship, Rashmi Dyal-Chand points out that women in developing countries are increasingly being forcibly corralled into the most primitive forms of self-employment.[69]

Let me sum up these and other important worries using the words of Sally Williams, a former adviser to the central European delegations to the UN Beijing Conference on Women and to UNDP on microlending in central Asia. She had this to say:[70]

> I would like to point out that the vast majority of the success rates of the micro-credit programs such as Yunus's Grameen Bank is entirely

based on loan payback rates rather than whether the participating women have actually gotten out of poverty. In other words it's the success of the lender, not the recipient [...] Most of the wee loans at usury interest rates go to women for activities that require the involvement of whole families. Paying the high interest from earnings of a garden plot, a small kiosk, a phone service, or basket making generally requires a 16-hour day and help from family members. [...] I won't go into how belittled many women felt having to become a member of a group to get a loan rather than being respected as an individual because it places a tremendous burden on the women in the group to pay the interest for a member who becomes ill or has a problem in her family. We regulate predatory lending practices in some parts of the United States. These overseas lending programs are entirely unregulated and borrowers need protections.

Overall, the gender empowerment narrative cannot be taken very seriously. There is little historical evidence to support the contention that policy-makers set out to achieve, nor have they achieved, any major advance in this regard. The glossy PR handouts and jazzy websites of the main MFIs continue to tell many uplifting individual stories, but most independent research points to the fact that such examples are incredibly rare. In practice, microenterprise activity undertaken by women most often reflects the proliferation of hyper self-exploitative and patriarchal hegemony-strengthening outcomes – in a word, disempowerment. In fact, microfinance is essentially used instead to discipline and 'soften up' women, in order that they become more 'market-friendly'. Leading microfinance researcher Naila Kabeer effectively gives the game away here when arguing that 'women's access to the market [is] the primary route for their empowerment'.[71] In other words – and this point is absolutely crucial to understanding microfinance, not just in this gender context, but in general – *it is markets which are being empowered here, not women*.

Myths behind the 'new wave' microfinance model

In the 1990s, as I pointed out in Chapter 2, the 'new wave' micro-finance model began to replace the original Grameen Bank-inspired microfinance model as 'best practice'. As the 'new wave' model began its own rise to prominence, a specific subset of myths began to emerge to order to provide the required justification for the new arrangement.

Accumulating great wealth through microfinance does not mean that the poor lose out: it is a 'win-win' situation A pivotal feature of the 'new wave' microfinance model is the opportunity it presents to certain individuals to make their own personal fortune. This fortune is made not through *use* of a microloan, but through its *provision*. This personal enrichment process transpires in a number of ways. An individual might decide to establish her own MFI using international donor and/or government financial support to do so, promising poverty reduction benefits in return. An individual or group might also decide to gradually take over an MFI in which she/they work(s) and, again, where the initial capital was provided by the international donor community or from public funds. Still others attempt to become rich through buying into an MFI established with public or international donor funds, which is then aggressively restructured and turned into a highly profitable private business operation. Even future profit streams can be appropriated through an eventual IPO. All these techniques are part of the new method of wealth generation favoured by up-and-coming elites in the neoliberal era that emerged after 1980, termed by social anthropologist David Harvey 'accumulation by dispossession'.[72] Accumulating great wealth is easily achieved by quietly converting public and collective assets and income streams into private assets and income streams.

Advocates of 'new wave' microfinance contend, however, that this private enrichment process is actually a positive development for the poor in many ways. To get rich (to perhaps become a 'microfinance millionaire', as I call them in Chapter 5), one typically has to secure a greatly increased volume of microfinance for the poor. More volume is driven by more profit, which in turn also means more scope for higher pay and bonuses. Both parties thus appear to benefit. The individual admittedly becomes rich, but the poor also benefit from the increased availability of microfinance. Is this not, then, a classic 'win-win' market-driven outcome?

The problem with this 'win-win' scenario is that in historical practice it largely doesn't work like this. A close parsing of economic history tends to highlight, instead, how episodes of financial elite-building and personal enrichment are most often *detrimental* to the interests of the poor, especially to the rural poor. Personal enrichment typically involves what has been called a 'dualistic' methodology. Would-be financial elites seek to engage in a process of 'borrowing cheap to lend dear', the counterpart of which is the perpetuation and intensification of poverty and inequality in rural regions. Put very simply, within the context of expensive loans, rural producers are unable to produce their way out of poverty. The rural poor become caught in a local 'poverty trap', vainly striving to produce and earn more in order to escape their expensive loans, but never quite getting there.

For a good description of the adverse poverty impact involved in first constructing and then maintaining a local financial elite, we can usefully refer to the work of Carolyn Gates, who looks at the prototypical case of Lebanon.[73] The Lebanese financial elite was essentially created in the nineteenth century. Their starting point was being permitted to borrow at low interest rates in Beirut, and then lending out to the poor in the rural regions of Lebanon and Syria at usuriously high interest rates. Thanks to such high interest rates, however, all but a very small percentage of the rural poor found it impossible to produce, earn and reinvest enough to eventually make their way out of poverty. They remained poor. But meanwhile the financial elite was able to grow steadily richer and more powerful through their expanding range of lending activities. Of course, challenges to the power of the financial elite were forthcoming, first through popular movements and then through the offices of the state. But the financial elites were largely able to anticipate these challenges, and to head them off before they amounted to anything. Up until the 1930s, in fact, government efforts to respond to the passionate calls by the rural poor for affordable rural credit were consistently blocked by the powerful financial elite. The result is that even today Lebanon has still largely failed to escape a situation of generalized rural poverty. Similar examples abound right across the world.

Accordingly, as this 'dualistic' financial elite-building process plays out in developing and transition countries today via commercialized 'new wave' microfinance, there is no a priori reason, nor any concrete evidence accumulated to date, to conclude that a bright future awaits rural communities. It is therefore a myth to suppose that 'new wave' microfinance, and the processes leading to the sometimes spectacular enrichment of those standing behind it, must be performing a service that is of automatic and enormous benefit to the poor; the opposite is actually the case.

Demand for microfinance vastly outstrips the supply One of the most fundamental building blocks of the 'new wave' microfinance model is the assumption that the demand for microfinance far out-strips the ability of government and international donor-funded MFIs to provide it. Harvard academic and former president and CEO of ACCIÓN Michael Chu has called the presumed difference between demand and supply an 'absurd gap'.[74] Of course, since commercial-ized 'new wave' microfinance is held to be the only way that this 'absurd gap' is going to be filled, this rather conveniently rounds out the arguments in its favour. The commercialization of microfinance thus becomes an urgent necessity in order to extend the outreach of microfinance to as many underserved poor individuals as possible, thereby to help them escape poverty. In addition, let us not forget Muhammad Yunus's oft-stated claim that 'microfinance is a human right', which adds another humanitarian dimension to the urgent quest to ensure that microfinance is available to every last adult person.[75]

This very important claim to huge unmet demand is, however, a self-serving mirage. First, simply because an individual has not yet bought or accessed something, this does not mean that she is a potential client. There is a world of difference between *potential* demand and *effective* demand. Many microfinance advocates crudely assume that the potential demand involves every single self-employed poor person, jumping to conclude that this would all then translate into effective demand.[76] As even the microfinance industry itself is now grudgingly starting to admit,[77] there is no evidence to support such claims. In many of the microfinance 'saturated' countries, a high percentage of the self-employed choose of their own volition not to access microfinance. They do not do so because they can see no proper use for it, especially at ultra-high interest rates.

Second, a serious and growing problem for the microfinance in-dustry today is actually associated with the rapidly rising number of client 'drop-outs' and aggressive competition for clients between MFIs. That is, supply has shot way ahead of the demand. One obvious indication of this is that MFIs everywhere are increasingly caught up in a desperate struggle to find new clients to replace the growing number voluntarily choosing not to take on any new microloan. For example, Wright reports that in East Africa – a region not typically seen as especially well covered with MFIs – client drop-outs are nevertheless between 25 and 60 per cent per year.[78] According to the *MicroBanking Bulletin*,[79] in central and eastern Europe and in Middle East and North African countries the situation is the same; over 68 per cent of clients leave their MFIs on an annual basis. Research by the International Labour Organization (ILO) covering the operations of forty-five MFIs between 1999 and 2003 found 'an astonishing degree of client drop-out'.[80]

In Bangladesh, Pakistan and India there are ominous signs that the increasingly frantic drive to obtain new and retain existing clients is leading to a wave of 'hard-selling' practices. Many of the major MFIs have been privately alarmed about the growing oversupply worldwide, and some are now – finally – coming clean about their real fears.[81] Other MFIs have been developing and refining corporate strategies designed to work in markets where massive oversupply has been the norm for some time.[82] Importantly, nor are any of the microfinance stakeholders consulted in the authoritative 2008 *Banana Skins* report convinced of the 'absurd gap' argument.[83] The report shows that microfinance practitioners see their biggest concern today, as well as the concern that has most increased over the last ten years, as the rising level of competition for clients. Microfinance industry analysts, observers and investors all concurred. As the report summed matters up, 'The main problem is too much funding rather than too little.'[84] Indeed, because each MFI appears to be having more and more difficulty finding enough clients to maintain margins and survive, the report concludes that the stage is probably being set for some high-profile MFI casualties in the near future.

Third, it is also the case that a very significant proportion of effective demand for microfinance may be artificially stimulated. Clearly, as John Kenneth Galbraith famously argued in his path-breaking book *The Affluent Society*,[85] any argument made in favour of 'satisfying demand' must be instantly disavowed if that demand has had to be artificially created in the first place. Not unlike in the stunning case of the sub-prime mortgage and credit card markets in the USA,[86] in order to add additional clients MFIs are increasingly forced to massage and hide the true cost of the microloan they wish to sell, otherwise they simply cannot sell it. Existing MFI clients are also increasingly pressured to take out a new or a 'top-up' loan whether they really need such a loan or not. In fact, the poor are everywhere increasingly falling into an even deeper and permanent engagement with microdebt, with the need to cover regular, sizeable and growing interest payments now becoming a damagingly routine fixture in their everyday struggle to survive.[87] It 'helps' here that loan officers are increasingly financially incentivized along Wall Street lines, and so are generally more willing to do whatever it takes to bring in new clients and help existing clients into possibly unwanted debt, thereby to earn their bonuses.

Apart from a few underserved regions, it is the case almost everywhere in developing countries that the supply of microfinance has now overshot the genuine demand by some considerable way. It is therefore a myth to suggest that more effort is required to increase the supply of microfinance; the opposite is probably true, especially in those countries and regions wherein a major 'microcredit bubble' has clearly formed in recent years (see Chapter 5).

Commercialized MFIs will always respect their social mission

Advocates of 'new wave' microfinance firmly believe that it is possible to extensively commercialize an MFI and that it will still retain its original mission. Some key figures involved in the development of the 'new wave' microfinance model were aware of the potential dangers of 'mission drift', such as Maria Otero.[88] But it was thought that with sensible regulations, peer pressure and other measures, there would be no problem at all into the longer term.

Yet evidence that 'mission drift' has become a serious problem in the microfinance industry is now quite overwhelming. Numerous research outputs point to the growing separation between an MFI's original poverty reduction intentions and its later abandonment of such concerns. This feeling is backed up once more by the 2008 *Banana Skins* publication noted above, which reported that microfinance practitioners put 'mission drift' in second place among the most important problems facing the microfinance industry today. In its previous report in 1998, 'mission drift' was only marginally mentioned. In other words, as the commercialization of microfinance has got into its stride over the last ten years or so, its own practitioners agree that the average commercialized MFI has begun to veer significantly off course. In microfinance-oversupplied India, Arnab Mukherji, a researcher at the Indian Institute of Management in Bangalore, argues that 'We've seen a major mission drift in microfinance, from being a social agency first' to being 'primarily a lending agency that wants to maximize its profit'.[89] It is also puzzling, if 'mission drift' is assumed not to be a problem, why it is that the microfinance industry has increasingly felt impelled to establish its own institutions to police the industry in order that clients are not abused (see Chapter 5). Just as with the recent sub-prime mortgage and credit card fiascos in the USA, there is growing recognition within the microfinance industry that commercial pressures are increasingly forcing MFIs in developing countries to pressure and hoodwink their clients in order to obtain new business. This is, of course, a very serious case of 'mission drift'.

Given the rising number of interventions designed to stop the microfinance industry from veering away from its original mission to reduce poverty, it is very difficult to argue that commercialization has not affected the average MFI's social mission in a bad way. In fact, the 'new wave' commercialization model has added enormous impetus to the ongoing abandonment of the social mission aspect to microfinance.

High interest rates are not a problem for the poor since it is the availability of microcredit which matters most to them, not its price One of the original justifications for the establishment of the Grameen Bank was that it would displace the ultra-expensive credit typically provided by informal moneylenders. As Muhammad Yunus concluded, ultra-high interest rates prevent poor people from earning sufficient net income to begin to escape poverty. Instead, the poor are caught in a classic 'poverty trap'. Yunus found this situation to be an intolerable abuse of the poor. Nonetheless, with the arrival of the 'new wave' microfinance model in the late 1980s, this line of argument was dropped entirely. In its place came a new understanding that in order for an MFI to achieve full financial self-sustainability, the poor could,[90] and indeed should, be expected to pay whatever rate of interest would fulfil this overarching condition.

There is substantial evidence to suggest, however, that high interest rates remain a serious problem for the poor. First, one cannot get away from the basic fact that clients will inevitably end up worse off than otherwise would be the case under a subsidized interest-rate regime. High interest rates always eat into the typically minimal margins realized in a microenterprise, and this is painful for the poor. This is why, whenever asked, the poor overwhelmingly argue that they should not be subject to market-based interest rates, because they will simply *not* be able to generate a decent surplus. We cannot simply ignore their petitions on this issue, because there is so much evidence to back them up. In India, for example, the large National Sample Survey Organization reported that its latest 2005 mass survey showed that:[91]

[a] large proportion of microcredit clients are worse off after access-ing loans. Since higher interest rates on microcredit do not provide scope for savings and for investing in insurance, the dominant risk-covering factors for the poor, microcredit seldom propels the poor out of poverty. *Further, there are no businesses that can gener-ate profit after paying an interest of 24–36 per cent on capital.* (My italics)

Moreover, careful studies of the interest-rate elasticity of micro-credit show that the poor react very proactively to lower-priced microfinance. Using data from a randomized trial in South Africa, microfinance analysts Dean Karlan and Jonathan Zinman demon-strated that the poor's demand for microcredit is quite responsive to interest-rate changes.[92] In fact, there are many instances where the poor feel they have to 'shop around' for much cheaper microcredit as soon as they think they might be able to obtain it elsewhere. Consider also that one of the main proximate causes of panic and crisis in the microfinance industry is the entry of a state-owned MFI offering reduced interest rates on its microloans, which are readily taken up by the poor (see below). Often, too, groups of the poor continue the long historical tradition of attempting to set up their own financial institution able to offer much lower-cost credit. Mayoux reports that, in Uganda, women associated with FINCA rejected the high-interest-rate model once they had enough cash to go on their own.[93]

Third, we must deal with a major moral and ethical dilemma here. High interest rates are routinely justified by the microfinance industry not just as a way to attain financial self-sustainability, but to ensure that an MFI can generate significant profit as well. Profits are needed, so the argument goes, in order to expand the MFI (disburse more microloans, open new branches, etc.), thereby to increase the volume of microfinance available to other equally poor individuals. This justification effectively rests on a very shaky moral imperative, however: it is effectively asking one set of very poor individuals to generously agree to help out another set of very poor individuals. That is, the poor in one place and time are effectively being asked to turn away possible subsidies and pay high (market-based) interest rates not just to facilitate their *own* possible way out of poverty, *but that of other poor people too.* This is hardly the most equitable scenario. It should come as no surprise, then, to find that the poor generally resent such unorthodox forms of wealth redistribution, as we heard above when many poor individuals collectively reported to the World Bank that 'there is a limit to how much one hungry man can feed another'.

And, finally, an even more disconcerting fact is that if high interest rates are indeed 'no problem', then how do we explain the routine unwillingness on the part of MFIs everywhere, and also many instances of outright deception, when asked to clearly present their interest rates, fees and the total charges imposed on their poor clients?[94]

High repayment rates 'prove' that borrowers are succeeding with their expensive microloan As was emphasized in Chapter 2, the success of the Grameen Bank model was very much based on the simple fact that there was an almost complete separation of repayment from the ultimate success of any micro-project. Of course, it was largely not feasible to find out whether individual clients were making a success of their microenterprises or not, still less to help out in the event of any difficulties. Instead, high levels of repayment were secured thanks to various forms of social collateral (solidarity circles, personal guarantors, etc.). In fact, it was precisely because most income-generating projects actually *fail*, or at least fail to generate sufficient cash to repay the microloan, that the early MFIs were considered so astute in deciding to develop such social collateral-based lending methodologies. Recall too from the discussion above the fact that most microfinance is now very largely advanced for consumption purposes, and not for income-generating projects. Precisely because the microloan was not advanced in order to be used for any business project, high repayment rates therefore prove very little in terms of sustainable development and poverty reduction successes.

In fact, one of the most glaring features to arise in microfinance in recent years is the huge divide that separates microenterprise success and high repayment rates, and the associated fact that repayment in the event of an unsuccessful microenterprise venture further reduces the income and assets of the poor. To explain the disconnect between repayment and development, we must recognize the fact that the poor generally have fallback strategies that they deploy to repay a microloan when the original microenterprise fails.

First, clients borrow from family and friends to repay their original microloan. This is the easiest and least risky option in the event of getting into difficulty. But especially in cases where additional microloans have been taken out to try to save the business – as gamblers often continue to gamble in anticipation of 'the one big win' that makes up for all the previous losses – the relative ease in obtaining support across large family and friendship circles means that the hapless individual often ends up in very serious debt. This has been quite extensively documented in Bolivia, for example.[95]

Second, many existing clients choose to repay their original microloan by taking out another (often larger) microloan from another MFI. This turns out to be one of the principal ways that the poor in many developing countries have become awash in microdebt. As noted above, this has been a particularly worrying development in Bangladesh of late, with many analysts increasingly concerned at the dramatic rise in both loan recycling (using a new, larger microloan to repay the old, smaller one) and multiple borrowing across several MFIs.[96] According to Mathew, a similar problem has also arisen in India.[97]

Third, a range of family assets are simply sold off, from household utensils to roofing to equipment, vehicles and machinery. Worst of all is the fairly commonplace sale or seizure of family land, an asset that might otherwise be used to generate a rental income or produce enough food to ensure at least physical survival. This outcome inevitably risks plunging the family into much deeper and almost certainly *irretrievable* poverty. In Bangladesh, India and Pakistan, as in many other South-East Asian countries, land seizures from defaulting borrowers are very common and growing. In India, for example, it is estimated that about 14 per cent of farmers failing in their activities in any one year are forced to sell or mortgage their land in order to repay the original microloan used to advance their farming or off-farm microenterprise activities,[98] a sizeable increase on previous years.

Thanks to the above fallback strategies, high levels of repayment do not mean that the poor are successfully escaping poverty. In fact, they very often mean that, for reasons of shame, fear and future microloan availability, the poor are simply drawing down other financial, physical, social and reputational assets in order to repay their microloan, and thus getting poorer overall.

MFIs can be self-sustaining A variation on the 'high repayment rate equals poverty reduction' myth just noted is the idea that MFIs can all eventually become financially self-sustaining. Many of the most important advocates for microfinance, especially those on the right of the political spectrum, began to take notice of microfinance only when this aspect started to become common currency. High repayment rates were, after all, the aspect of Grameen Bank's early operations which alerted the international development community to its value. The poor can be helped into business with microfinance, and they will even pay for the costs of this financial support through high interest rates, as just noted.

Most in the microfinance industry, however, agree with the evidence showing that the bulk of MFIs are unlikely to reach financial self-sustainability. Of the 10,000 MFIs currently estimated to be operating in the world, only 3–5 per cent will become financially self-sustaining.[99] Manos and Yaron also point out that many of the MFIs substantially underestimate their dependence upon subsidy.[100] In other words, only the largest and most aggressively commercialized MFIs – that is, 'new wave' MFIs – are likely to be able to survive.

Conclusion

This chapter has shown that almost all of the fundamental building blocks that go into making up today's microfinance model, and which, in turn, constitute the public narrative, are largely nothing more than self-serving myths. The microfinance industry has proved supremely adept at 'creating its own reality'. The implications of this point are very significant indeed. If the microfinance industry is unwilling, or perhaps unable, to project a broadly truthful picture of what microfinance is all about, then we can only be led to assume that something is wrong. The worst-case scenario is that, as on Wall Street in the 1990s and early 2000s,[101] a deeply flawed public narrative has had to be deployed in order to provide cover for a growing range of unwholesome internal practices and inefficient external outcomes for the economy and society. We therefore need to look at the evidence on the ground to see whether such fears are legitimate or not with regard to microfinance. That is, we need to begin to answer the much more fundamental question: What role is the microfinance model *really* playing in terms of promoting sustainable economic and social development, and so also in poverty reduction? The next chapter begins to seek out an answer to this important question.

FOUR
Microfinance as poverty trap

'A Grameen-type credit programme opens up the door for limit-less self-employment, and it can effectively do it in a pocket of poverty amidst prosperity, or in a massive poverty situation.' Muhammad Yunus[1]

'Strikingly, 30 years into the microfinance movement we have little solid evidence that it improves the lives of clients in measurable ways.' David Roodman and Jonathan Morduch[2]

' ... tiny loans usually provided under microcredit schemes do not seem to lift large numbers of people out of poverty. Poor people need credit that enables them to go beyond meeting immediate consumption needs and build permanent assets.' World Bank[3]

'... it is becoming increasingly plausible to argue that the microfinance programmes installed by aid agencies and NGOs are not simply falling short of their hype (most observers agree on that) but are yet another faddish form of unhelpful help, an anti-development intervention that produces a short-run benefit but may misdirect and undermine sustainable development and poverty reduction in the longer run.' David Ellerman[4]

The previous chapter showed that a very large part of the rationale put forward in support of microfinance has been built upon a set of myths, some more egregious and self-serving than others. The purpose of this chapter is to move on from this deeply flawed narrative to consider whether microfinance nevertheless might still 'work' as a sustainable economic and social development policy.

Through support for income-generating activities the widespread belief took hold that microfinance could play a decisive role in poverty reduction. This was what apparently first drove Muhammad Yunus to experiment with microfinance in the late 1970s. Because it shared Muhammad Yunus's optimism and ideological commitment to indi-vidual self-help, the international development community right away began to support a massive expansion of microfinance. Microfinance very soon emerged as one of the most important poverty reduction weapons in the international development community's armoury of policy and programme support. In the early 1990s, Hernando De Soto began to build a lucrative career advising the international development agencies that the microenterprise sector was the perfect answer to joblessness and poverty in developing countries, and massive numbers of microenterprises would soon lift the poor out of their misery, starting in his native Latin America. Empirical work undertaken in Bangladesh in the late 1990s, much of it sponsored by the World Bank, seemed to undergird the belief that microfinance would have a positive impact on poverty and society. The widely presumed association linking microfinance to poverty reduction and local development remains just as strong today in the international development community. For example, Bernd Balkenhol, the current head of the ILO's Social Finance Programme, considers microfinance to be a crucial aspect of current development policy because it is 'the strategy for poverty reduction par excellence' (underlining in the original).[5]

In many respects, then, and putting the flawed public narrative to one side, we have here the critical issue at the heart of this book: does microfinance *really* lead on to poverty reduction through sustainable economic and social development?

What do microfinance impact assessments tell us?

An obvious first step in beginning to answer this question is to look at the large number of impact assessments that have been undertaken in the area of microfinance. The serious reservations I raised in Chapter 3 notwithstanding, impact assessments nevertheless do help us to at least begin to understand how microfinance might work in practice to influence development. Perhaps not surprisingly, the first and most comprehensive impact assessments were undertaken in Bangladesh, with the work of Mark Pitt and Shahidur Khandker most often cited. Drawing on material from a major Bangladesh Institute of Development Studies (BIDS) and World Bank data collection exercise undertaken in the mid-1990s, Pitt and Khandker initially pointed to strong poverty-reduction gains across a number of areas.[6] This result appeared to back up the faith the international donor community had had in Muhammad Yunus. Almost right away, however, other microfinance supporters disagreed with the conclusions reached by

Pitt and Khandker. The most important objection was lodged by Jonathan Morduch. Using the same data, Morduch could find no real positive impact, admitting only that such programmes seemed to reduce client vulnerability to an extent.[7] After these and other important challenges to the way the BIDS–World Bank data were processed, Khandker revisited the original data and methodology used. His revised conclusion was that microfinance programmes in Bangladesh still demonstrated a positive poverty reduction impact, but only a weakly positive one, mainly through clients being able to smooth their consumption and register marginal improvements in their assets and net worth.[8]

In other developing countries, many studies of microfinance impact have also been undertaken. USAID's AIMS project financed a number of important evaluations. As with the earliest studies in Bangladesh, most of these AIMS studies reported reasonably positive impacts from microfinance.[9] In the same vein, a major five-year impact assessment project, 'Imp-Act', found participating MFIs reporting a variety of direct and indirect positive impacts affecting both client groups and non-clients.[10] Khalily also summarized a number of impact assessments. His conclusion was that even when different methodologies are involved (econometric, descriptive and case study), microfinance programmes generally report a positive impact.[11] Finally, Nathanael Goldberg has provided a very useful summary of the results obtained from all of the major impact assessments undertaken to date.[12] His finding was that the majority of impact assessments purport to demonstrate some sort of positive impact. Only a small minority of these early studies suggested that there was no, or negative, impact produced by microfinance. Goldberg concluded his overview in a fairly upbeat fashion, claiming that 'This review of the literature provides a wide range of evidence that microfinance programs can increase incomes and lift families out of poverty.'[13]

Yet in spite of these seemingly fairly positive results, there are still those who remain quite unconvinced of the good news that impact assessments are supposed to be telling us. As noted in Chapter 2, a number of high-profile independent studies recently created something of a media stir by concluding that microfinance had little or no impact, and in some cases *negative* impact. Following on from several years of increasing criticism of microfinance on the margins of the microfinance industry and in academia, the mainstream media began to sense a change in the wind.[14] Even the World Bank began to publicly express its doubts as to whether microfinance is really an effective poverty intervention. The high-profile 2008 World Bank publication *Finance for All* concluded that 'More research is needed to assert whether there is a robust and *positive* relationship between the use of credit and household welfare, including moving out of poverty' (my italics).[15] For an institution that has been quite pivotal to the rise of the microfinance model, claiming that we don't know if the relationship between microfinance and poverty is even *positive*, never mind how robust it is, is a pretty radical admission. An even more explosive media headline was to come in 2009, thanks to David Roodman and Jonathan Morduch (again), who revisited the Pitt and Khandker data one more time.[16] A sophisticated replication exercise on the original data this time produced some quite astounding results; nothing less than the complete overturning of most of the key positive conclusions. Regarding the headline-grabbing results in the earlier Pitt and Khandker study, results that were hugely influential in ensuring the take-up of microfinance as a major poverty reduction policy, Roodman and Morduch obtained the *opposite* signs – that is, their results suggested negative impact. Among other things, this meant that Muhammad Yunus's endlessly recycled claim that '5% of Grameen borrowers escape poverty every year' was now deemed to have been quite inaccurate all along.[17]

Two important factors ignored by most evaluations As shown by the important work of Roodman and Morduch, and others, a growing number of independent analysts and institutions are becoming increasingly sceptical of the veracity of microfinance impact assessments. One of the main problems here is that almost all impact evaluators make the key assumption beforehand that 'microfinance works'. This then leads impact evaluators to attempt to design an impact assessment exercise confined to narrow issues that best help to confirm the original presumption. In particular, the focus tends to be upon *outreach* – how many individuals are actually served by microfinance – and *sustainability* – is an individual MFI able to keep itself going without the need for external support? These are both operational factors and they refer only to the *availability* of microfinance; they do not tell us anything whatsoever about the sustainable economic and social development impact of the microfinance model. It would be like assuming that the widespread availability of a particular drug confirms its applicability as a treatment for the illness it was designed to treat! The result is that almost all impact assessments are quite fundamentally and, I would argue, deliberately flawed.[18] In this section I will focus on two critically important impact issues that continue to be ignored within impact assessments. I refer here to local 'displacement effects' and the longer-term impact of client exit/failure. Let me briefly discuss both important issues in turn.

Displacement effects Displacement effects are a very common factor affecting microfinance and microenterprise programmes. Displacement effects (also known as 'spillover' effects) refer to the jobs and incomes lost in non-client microenterprises as a result of the entry or expansion of client microenterprises. Two mechanisms are generally involved here. First, the entry or expansion of client microenterprises may be achieved only by a reduction in the local market share previously enjoyed by incumbent non-client microenterprises (and note that in most developing countries incumbent microenterprises so displaced are likely to involve just as poor and marginalized individuals as client microenterprises). Lower sales in non-client microenterprises obviously translate into lower margins, profits and wages. In addition, some of the non-client microenterprises will find it impossible to survive in the now more crowded local market space, and so they exit the local market (see the next section below). A new coffee bar opened up with the help of a microloan might simply put out of business the coffee bar 50 metres down the road. Second, there are also likely to be some wider price effects. The additional local supply arising in new and expanded microenterprises very often causes a softening in the price of the product or service in question. This hurts incumbent non-client microenterprises, which have no other option but to face up to the lower local market price (that is, they are price-takers). All told, the incumbent non-client microenterprise will clearly be disadvantaged to some extent – or made poorer if you will – as a result of the programmed entry or expansion of the client microenterprise.

It is important to note that, in general, displacement effects are relatively much less problematic with regard to larger enterprise structures, such as SMEs. This is because SMEs typically locate a much higher percentage of their customer base from outside the immediate locality. So while displacement effects still arise – a new SME getting started in New Delhi will take some business away from an incumbent SME operating in Mumbai – the pain inflicted is generally diffused over a wider geographical area than just the local community. Moreover, much of economic theory holds such a displacement process in high regard, because it constantly displaces other less productive enterprises. This is an important industrial upgrading process captured by Joseph Schumpeter in his notion of 'creative destruction'.[19] So, even if an SME closes down owing to the establishment of more innovative competition elsewhere in the region or country, such forms of displacement might have a positive efficiency-enhancing effect at the national economy level. This positive impact, however, is generally not experienced in the microenterprise sector. A microenterprise displacing another microenterprise in the locality will likely mean nothing more 'transformational' than one trader or café or mobile phone time-seller taking business from, or forcing the closure of, their equally simple counterpart located in the same street or neighbourhood.

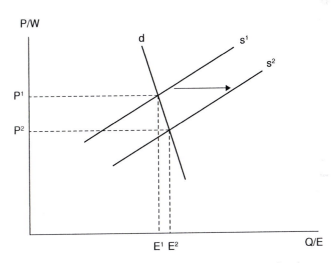

FIGURE 4.1 Simple response to an increase in supply of microenterprises

A simple supply-and-demand diagram helps to explain the basic local market dynamics here. Figure 4.1 shows the result of an increase in the local supply of goods and services thanks to the arrival of an MFI in the locality and its support for new and expanding micro-enterprises. Demand is typically relatively price inelastic. If the price of a haircut or a coffee or a counterfeit CD goes down, we tend not to increase our consumption that much. Supply is initially at s1, but with microfinance it shifts to s2. As a result of the increased supply, prices and self-employment wages fall from P1 to P2, though total employment and output may rise marginally from E1 to E2. The net overall impact, of course, depends on the strength of the general decline in prices and self-employment wages across the microenterprise sector, offset by any additional jobs and income created in the new microenterprises.

Because supposedly *additional* incomes and jobs in client microenterprises might actually be fully or partially offset by income and job losses arising in non-client-incumbent microenterprises, a microfinance programme might actually have no real positive impact in the local community whatsoever.[20] Crucially, most impact assessments simply do not capture such effects. This is because the assumption is made that the clients and the non-clients in any impact assessment are separate, just as in medical trials when patients are given particular drugs – the effect on one patient of taking drug A is entirely independent of the effect on another patient also taking drug A, and on the control group patient taking the placebo. So displacement effects are not that important. Impact assessments need not be specially designed to capture them. But if displacement effects *are* important – as I will show below that this is very much the case – then we cannot simply ignore them. Crucially, they suggest that there is a very powerful 'fallacy of composition' flaw inherent in the basic microfinance model. The microfinance industry is wrongly inferring that something is true of the *whole* – microfinance must create additional jobs and incomes in the community – based on the fact that it is true for *part* of the whole – microfinance can create additional jobs and incomes in one client microenterprise.[21]

Displacement effects in developing economies? In the developed economies, displacement effects have long been known to undermine, if not fatally compromise, microenterprise development policies and programmes. The classic example comes from the UK in the 1980s. As is well known, the Thatcher government came to power enamoured of the so-called 'enterprise culture'. Accordingly, rapidly growing unemployment in the early 1980s was addressed by a quasi-microfinance programme – the Enterprise Allowance Scheme (EAS) – a programme designed to increase the number of the self-employed and microenterprises coming from the unemployed and underemployed.[22] Importantly, too, the EAS had an overarching ideological purpose, which was to support the microenterprise sector as the future low-wage, non-unionized employment replacement for high-wage, unionized forms of employment. But no matter how dear the EAS was to the ideological project set in train by the Thatcher government, it could not survive the damagingly high displacement effects that soon became evident, which meant that almost no net employment opportunities were being generated in practice.[23] The UK government was reluctantly forced to discontinue the EAS after less than a decade of operation.

Do such damaging displacement effects also arise in developing countries? Consider the obvious case of Bangladesh. Recall that Muhammad Yunus initially expressed no concern for the simple displacement-type problems I have just outlined. As the quotation I cite at the head of the chapter indicates, Yunus founded the Grameen Bank on the basis of his confident belief that microfinance would work in any conceivable economic situation – poverty within a wealthy community, or poverty in a generalized poverty situation; it did not matter. Yunus was quite wrong on this, however. Perhaps nowhere more so than in his native Bangladesh have the very real absorption limits associated with microfinance-induced activity been so quickly exposed. As early as 1984, in fact, Ahmad and Hossain astutely reported that the seemingly positive initial results with microfinance in just one Bangladesh village were simply an illusion.[24] If scaled up into a major programme, they argued, it would very quickly be subject to diminishing returns because 'the competition among non-crop producers would increase and the members will need to count more and more on the markets of their own localities, which might lead to lower prices and reduction in their income'.[25]

For sustainable poverty reduction to take place, Ahmad and Hossain went on, it was necessary (among other things) for sustainable growth to occur in the local agricultural sector. Steadily growing agricultural productivity and incomes were first required, which would in turn lead to a rising level of local demand for the very simple locally produced and traded goods associated with microfinance. Yet the Grameen Bank was not helping here. Instead, it was mainly supporting either simple *non-farm* activities associated with goods and services that were already pretty much adequately supplied (for example, shops), or else it was supporting the most unproductive side of farming activities – that is, subsistence farms. Ahmad and Hossain therefore felt that a local upgrading and productivity-raising development trajectory would actually become a more *remote* possibility thanks to the arrival of Grameen Bank and microfinance. Overall, they were forced to conclude that 'The [Grameen Bank] approach of just providing credit and leaving the loanees on their own cannot therefore be a viable national antipoverty programme.'[26] Pointedly, Quasem later showed that most local income generated by new microfinance-induced traders was mainly a transfer of income from those already operating.[27] Osmani also confirmed that increasing microenterprise entry was helping to push down returns in incumbent microenterprises to below the (then) cost of borrowing.[28] Yunus's fundamental error in assuming that the typical local economy in Bangladesh could easily and productively absorb *any* number of new microenterprises had been pretty quickly exposed by his own compatriots.

Notwithstanding the fact that these early studies pointed out serious flaws in the Grameen Bank model, however, there was no stopping it. Today, a largely unproductive microfinance-driven scenario is pretty much what one *still* sees in Bangladesh. With a small formal sector (especially the public sector) and a very weak-to-non-existent social welfare net, most poor individuals in Bangladesh effectively have no other option but to join the growing throng of micro-entrepreneurs. There are now, of course, abundant opportunities to tap into microfinance should one wish to use it. One can at least hope to come out as one of the few lucky winners. But the result in most Bangladeshi cities is increasingly unfavourable. It is not easy making your way in a hyper-competitive microcosm of informal sector activity, a local environment marked out by high rates of microenterprise turnover and very low, and declining, financial rewards for most simple microenterprise activities. All of the most simple business areas have already been colonized by swarms of microenterprises, with any initial income gains made by the 'first movers' largely wiped out later on as the local competition rapidly balloons. An obvious example is the rickshaw sector. With more than 200,000 in operation in Dhaka alone, and with the returns averaging around a dollar a day for such backbreaking work,[29] this is no longer a sector wherein one can find an escape from poverty.

Very neatly illustrating the simple and fairly typical microfinance-driven adverse local dynamics involved today, we can specifically refer to one of Muhammad Yunus's own flagship anti-poverty programmes, GrameenPhone. Begun in 1997, GrameenPhone is a joint venture company formed by a non-profit member of the Grameen family,

Grameen Telecom, and the Norwegian telecom company Telenor. Telenor incurred almost no risk, while investing a very small sum indeed (only $40 million) in the establishment of the joint venture.[30] The poverty reduction angle was located in the so-called 'telephone ladies', teams of ladies who would access a Grameen Bank microloan (an average of $420[31]) in order to set themselves up in business with a mobile pay phone selling airtime on the GrameenPhone network. The project was a major financial success, breaking even in 2000 and thereafter making spectacular profits. It soon became known in financial circles as 'the diamond in Telenor's portfolio'.[32] At the same time, the project was also declared to be a major poverty reduction success. It was pretty soon employing an estimated 50,000 telephone ladies in villages across Bangladesh, all supposedly earning enough to begin to escape poverty.[33]

The project's high hopes of serious and sustainable poverty reduction, however, appeared to be dashed after just a few years. The initial phase saw generally one or two (well-publicized) telephone ladies operating in their village. In order to sell as much airtime as possible, however, GrameenPhone then pushed hard to increase the number of telephone ladies. With almost zero marginal cost, so long as the additional telephone ladies facilitated *some* net marginal increase in airtime use, and so revenue for GrameenPhone, this made perfectly sound business sense to GrameenPhone. Importantly, unlike in the developed economies where sales territory is the crucial variable in terms of the success of the salesperson, it appears not to have occurred to anyone in GrameenPhone to give each telephone lady their own exclusive territory. Thus, where just a couple of years earlier there had been perhaps a handful of telephone ladies in any one village, pretty soon most villages in Bangladesh had dozens of telephone ladies operating alongside each other in 'telephone streets'. From its initial plan to peak at 50,000 telephone ladies, by 2005 more than 280,000 telephone ladies were involved. Naturally, displacement effects began to bite. If initially (i.e. 1997) the yearly average income of a telephone lady was rather ambitiously planned to be somewhere in the range $750–1,200, by 2005 this had plummeted in practice to around $70.[34] The poverty reduction angle projected for GrameenPhone quite quickly began to evaporate. Most telephone ladies were soon forced into other, often unrelated, business areas in order to survive. 'The program is not dead,' reported Mazharul Hannan, chief of technical services at Grameen Telecom, 'but it is no longer a way out of poverty.'[35] In order to avert the damaging publicity of a growing wave of exits and strikes, GrameenPhone was forced to begin a desperate search to locate new business areas for the telephone ladies, such as providing Internet services through their mobile phones.[36]

While still a hugely profitable business model, particularly for Telenor, for the telephone ladies – supposedly a major focus of the entire GrameenPhone project – there is now little to be gained from engaging in such activities.[37] As one Grameen Bank loan officer said, 'Today, poor women who go into the phone business stay poor.'[38] It appears that once more we have to assume that the concept of the 'fallacy of composition' was not fully understood, or perhaps simply ignored.

In fact, displacement effects are registered everywhere Mexico also offers a further very good illustration of the serious problems arising as a result of displacement effects. As so often is the case in developing countries, with the formal sector shrinking in Mexico in the 1980s and 1990s, the default option left for the poor and unemployed was to move into some form of informal sector microenterprise. The rapid growth in the number of microenterprises in the poorest communities, however, allied to static or declining local demand, helped to ensure few net additional jobs, and generally always *falling* average incomes across the informal microenterprise sector.[39] Moreover, as Tilly and Kennedy note, it is increasingly not just in the poorest cities and rural communities that the informal microenterprise sector is growing completely out of hand, but also in the rapidly growing cities.[40]

Just one of the huge problems arising here is that the typical local economy in Mexico is reacting to the already bursting-at-the-seams informal sector through downward price adjustments. Prices for most of the very simple products and services produced in the microenterprise sector have been falling as 'poverty-push' new entry has been rising. In addition, lower turnover in individual microenterprises, as local market demand is shared out among a growing population of microenterprises, has been precipitating lower margins and incomes. This is why, following extensive liberalization in the economy from 1984 onwards and an associated wave of new microenterprise entry involving the newly redundant, we find that poverty levels in the self-employed microenterprise sector rapidly increased. Even as growth reappeared in the mid-1990s, poverty continued to rise in the informal microenterprise sector.[41] In many sectors and right across Mexico, many poor individuals are hugely angry at the declining margins and wages, as well as longer working hours, brought about by the unremitting inflow of 'poverty-push' microenterprises. Violent reaction has often followed, as was seen recently in the several-million-strong community of mobile street vendors.[42]

Equally adverse displacement effects have emerged in South Africa in recent years. With poverty levels barely changed and unemployment actually *rising* since the end of the apartheid system, like their Mexican counterparts South Africa's poorest have no other option but to try to survive as best they can in the informal microenterprise sector. With few other opportunities, most have been forced to fall back on simply buying locally in order to sell locally to others equally poor. Moreover, with many new 'poverty-push' entrants in these last few years, the margins and average incomes of incumbent individual traders have fallen considerably, especially in the major conurbations.[43] Many traders also use a small wooden barrow as the primary mode of distribution. This is a very unrewarding activity at best, and the hundreds of thousands of 'barrow boys' are some of the very poorest and most exploited individuals in the whole of South Africa. But things were made even worse in 2008. One of the official responses to the flow of refugees coming in from crisis-torn Mozambique and Zimbabwe was microfinance. A local MFI was provided with additional funds to offer the refugees the opportunity to start a little income-generating project of their own.[44] Quite predictably, however, many of the refugees simply copied what other poor South Africans were doing to survive, or what they were doing back in their home country, and so they established their own very simple street trading or barrow operation. Unfortunately, many of the struggling local operations run by poor South Africans were quickly displaced. The returns from such operations began to fall. Just as in Mexico, and also elsewhere in Africa,[45] the stage was set for violent confrontation, with many 'barrow boys' leading a ferocious assault on the refugee communities.[46] Failure on the part of the microfinance industry to understand the crucial economic and social dynamics that microfinance programmes precipitate can often be quite lethal – literally – for many of those involved.

Finally, the transition economies are also not short of such adverse economic and social dynamics, though – thankfully – violence has not yet become a feature. The Serbian economy has been struggling since 1990 to recover from transition to the market economy, multiple conflicts, political mismanagement, corruption and economic destruction. A number of UK government-funded surveys were undertaken in Serbia in the mid-1990s, in order to assess what development interventions were needed to address the severe and growing local poverty and unemployment.[47] Naturally, microfinance had been mooted by many international donor bodies as one of the solutions to rising poverty in Serbia.[48] Rather than endorse microfinance, however, the study argued against it. This was because it found that most local microenterprises, and many small enterprises too, were almost exclusively reliant upon local demand, which often made up to 90–95 per cent of their total sales. Further local increases in the number of microenterprises also targeting local demand would therefore achieve nothing more than displacing existing microenterprises struggling to survive. Because of simple displacement effects, there would likely be no net job creation or additional income generation within the community thanks to new microenterprises. Accordingly, the report recommended instead financially supporting mainly SMEs with the potential to tap into more distant, non-local markets. Whether or not this was its intention, by accurately highlighting the likely displacement effects of simple microenterprise development, the report added significant weight to the case against the deployment of microfinance in Serbia as a job generation and anti-poverty measure.

A growing number of high-profile intergovernment bodies are now finally beginning to accept the damaging impact of displacement. For example, the Inclusive Cities project, a global coalition of organizations supporting those in the informal sector, reported severe displacement impacts in most informal sector activities.[49] Following accelerated entry into many informal occupations, it was forced to point to increasing impoverishment and declining incomes. Displacement was particularly felt in the street vending sector, everywhere one of the mainstays for those with no other realistic employment option. The study found that, 'Street vendors [...] experienced a significant drop in local consumer demand. They reported the greatest increase in competition, as greater numbers of people who lost their jobs or had to supplement incomes turned to vending as a possible source of income.'

Perhaps the most incisive contribution in the context of displacement, however, is that of Mike Davis. In his important 2006 book *Planet of Slums*, Davis summed up both the limits to informal sector microenterprise growth and the debilitating impact of displacement.

He argues that it is a major policy folly to continue blindly encouraging expansion ad infinitum in the supply of microenterprises in developing countries, and especially in the growing slum communities around the globe. Recall, as Davis does, that the supply of informal microenterprises in Latin America more than doubled in the 1980s and 1990s, while poverty and suffering have risen almost in tandem. More microenterprises and the expansion of the informal sector in Latin America, he argues, are actually associated with precipitating deeper poverty and suffering, not less. Among other things, the optimistic late-1980s projections of Hernando De Soto have turned out to be quite wrong. Similarly in most of sub-Saharan Africa and South-East Asia. This adverse correlation has transpired, Davis argues, because '[the] space for new entrants is provided only by a diminution of per capita earning capacities and/or by the intensification of labour despite declining marginal returns'.[50] The microfinance-induced entry and expansion of microenterprises does not raise the total volume of local business, Davis stresses, so much as redistribute and subdivide the prevailing level of business between new and incumbent microenterprises.

But how can the microfinance industry simply ignore what appear to be very serious, if not fatal, 'spillover' impacts precipitated by microfinance? The answer is that everywhere in developing countries, the microfinance industry unquestioningly makes the assumption that a textbook version of Say's Law operates at the local level. Say's Law basically holds that the unending supply of the simple non-tradable goods and services that new or expanded microenterprises typically provide will, thanks to market and price adjustments, automatically call into existence sufficient local demand to absorb such goods and services. We saw above how adamant Muhammad Yunus was that the local economy in Bangladesh could productively absorb *any* number of microenterprises he managed to help into operation through the Grameen Bank. In Latin America in the early 1990s, Hernando De Soto felt just the same. Beginning with Yunus, however, and quickly followed by De Soto, the microfinance industry was quite wrongly led towards making the fatal assumption that the typical local economy in any developing country could elastically stretch to painlessly accommodate *any* increase in the microfinance-induced local output of non-tradable items; ergo there can be no displacement effects.[51] This misunderstanding of one of the most basic concepts in economics – the 'fallacy of composition' – therefore introduced a quite fundamental flaw into the microfinance model.

Client exit/failure A second important issue almost completely ignored by the vast majority of impact assessments is that of client exit or failure, and the associated problem of 'survivor bias'.[52] I define client failure here as the failure of the business activity originally financed by a microloan, in contradistinction to the mere exit of a client from a microfinance programme. In general, most micro-enterprise programmes encounter extremely high rates of failure. This is *especially* the case when, as in most developing countries, the individuals involved are effectively being forced into entrepreneurship by poverty (often termed 'poverty-push' entrepreneurship), rather than attracted into entrepreneurship by the possibility of some financial gain (often termed 'opportunity/profit-pull' entrepreneurship). Internationally respected SME researcher David Storey notes this when concluding that 'the single most important fact to be borne in mind when implementing measures for smaller firms is the high death rate of such businesses'.[53] Very much the same high death-rate situation in small businesses has been extensively documented in the USA by Davis, Haltiwanger and Schuh[54] and, more recently, by Scott Shane.[55]

The most important reason for studying client failure is that it has the obvious potential to propel many poor individuals into even deeper poverty than before they attempted their business project. The problems surrounding failure naturally start with the end of an income stream derived from a functioning microenterprise. Also lost will be any additional loans, savings, physical assets and local reputational capital also invested in the microenterprise. Some individuals, having failed in their original business activity, will opt to default on their microloan, seeing the loss of their local reputation and any collateral they might have advanced as the lesser of two evils. We also know from the juxtaposition of high repayment rates and rising failure rates, however, that the poor most often do *not* default on their microloan. The poor will, in fact, go to great lengths to repay any microloan, even though the original business activity for which the microloan was accessed no longer exists. What we tend to find overall, as I noted in Chapter 3, is a number of fallback strategies that arise to ensure that the microloan is repaid. This sounds very good indeed for the typical MFI, especially the 'new wave' MFI, which can achieve a high repayment rate irrespective of what happens to the microenterprise. But the problem for those interested in poverty reduction and development is that all of these fallback strategies have quite disturbing implications for the poverty status of individual poor clients.

With these important drawbacks to microenterprise development in mind, one would think that examination of client failure should be a fairly high priority in any impact assessment attempting to provide an accurate picture of the longer-term impact of microfinance. But it is not. This appears to be another serious problem with microfinance that microfinance advocates deliberately choose to keep quiet about for fear of undermining the general concept. Just as with displacement effects, one way to do this is to ensure that impact assessments are carefully calibrated to avoid any serious consideration of such failure issues. The result is that the microfinance industry is able to wilfully build up a further distorted picture of microfinance-driven outcomes. More charitably, it should be said, it is quite difficult to find those individuals who have failed with their microenterprise project, and quantify what happened to them. After failing, many individuals return to their traditional homes or move abroad in search of work. And failed clients – when they can be traced – naturally find it difficult to recount to researchers the humiliation and pain they and their family experienced when their microenterprise project failed. It is also socially awkward for researchers, too, who typically much prefer to interview and publicize the uplifting success stories.

At any rate, by largely focusing upon those individual microenterprises that manage to survive, while failing to register the impact of microfinance upon those that do not, most impact assessments fall into the trap of 'survivor bias'. This is the act of making wide-ranging assumptions based upon an examination of a few, possibly unrepresentative, survivors, while simultaneously ignoring the large number of exits or failures. This leads to some quite erroneous conclusions.

Consider, for example, the case of post-communist Poland in the 1990s. Poland at this time was plunged into its own 'shock therapy' unemployment problem. Just as in the UK in the early 1980s, Poland's neoliberal policy-makers and their Western advisers thought they had the answer to unemployment and poverty in the shape of the microenterprise sector. Indeed, nearly three million new microenterprises were registered in just a few years after the collapse of communism. Many analysts portrayed this microenterprise-driven phenomenon to be the key factor in the country's rapid post-communist economic revival.[56] Much of the supposed 'progress', however, was not quite what it seemed. First off, a very large number of the new registrations were simply existing informal sector microenterprises tolerated under communism, now converting over to a higher level of formality in order to operate under capitalism.[57] More important, however, was the almost equally high rate of *exit*. For example, in 1990 there were 140,000 new entrants, but offset by 120,000 exits. The total of registered self-employed individuals peaked at 31 per cent of the total working population as of early 1993. By 2000, however, this figure was significantly down (to 23 per cent),[58] and it continued to decline thereafter as new entry tailed off and exits continued to take their toll. All told, as in the similar microenterprise 'boom-bust' period in the UK in the 1980s, the net result after a decade or so was very much less *net* sustainable employment creation, poverty reduction and overall positive economic impact than had been excitedly predicted as the experiment was getting under way. With hindsight, one might actually say, the Polish microenterprise experiment was largely a failure.[59]

There is also much evidence to suggest that this 'exit' problem is also an acute one in developing countries. The first important remarks on the crux issue of microenterprise failure date back to the mid-1990s, to the work of David Hulme and Paul Mosley. Based on a major data collection exercise involving nearly all of the most high-profile MFIs around at that time, Hulme and Mosley reported on the 'considerable evidence [...] gathered during fieldwork that a minority of borrowers become worse off because of borrowing, that is credit from a case study institution increased their vulnerability'.[60] Hulme and Mosley also go on to provide additional evidence from a number of countries where failure is an important aspect of the MFIs' operation. Finding such high failure rates, Hulme and Mosley were led to conclude that 'there may well have been significant under-reporting of credit-induced crisis in most studies of finance for the poor'.[61] More recently, Peter Davis has warned about the negative impact of microenterprise failure in Bangladesh. From his field research in Bangladesh he reported that[62]

> Ten focus groups (9%) identified business losses or failed businesses as one of the three main causes of decline. Many poor households earn their livelihoods from small businesses and petty trading. These ventures usually work on very slim profit margins and are vulnerable to fluctuating prices, bad debts and cheating. Business losses often lead to very high levels of indebtedness.

Because they do not factor in the important aspect of microenter-prise failure, and instead provide only half – the good half – of the overall economic picture, almost all microfinance impact assessments are quite seriously flawed. Were Las Vegas casinos to use similar techniques to assess the poverty impact of gambling – focusing upon the small number of punters successfully graduating from slots to blackjack to the high-stakes roulette table, and ignoring the many more who go home after being relieved of their cash – we would be led into erroneously concluding that gambling represented a historic poverty reduction breakthrough! And although Alexander-Tedeschi and Karlan appeared to recognize the basic methodological error,[63] the widespread use of such flawed impact assessment methodologies nevertheless continued unabated. In short, client failure is potentially a problem of some considerable magnitude, yet it is one that remains mostly unregistered by the microfinance industry.

It has long been held of critical importance in public policy evaluation circles for the gains from a particular public policy to be balanced off against the losses.[64] In the context of microfinance programmes, I have argued above, this means an impact assessment simply must compare the overall impact (gains) made by clients and the survivors supported by microfinance, set against the overall impact (losses) incurred by the non-clients and the failures. If, for example, the income and employment gains registered by the (widely publicized) clients/survivors are actually swamped by the losses in-curred by the (largely ignored) non-clients/failures, then microfinance is very clearly destroying the economic and social fabric rather than repairing or strengthening it. This would be very useful informa-tion to have to hand. We could perhaps refine and redesign aspects of microfinance programmes. (For example, microfinance could be targeted mainly at those existing microenterprises seeking to invest in their business in order to cut costs; that is, without any require-ment for an expanded customer base to emerge. This would at least help minimize damaging displacement and exit impacts registered in the non-client community.) But even with such information, I would argue that we still remain unclear as to precisely what impact assessments are really demonstrating with regard to microfinance. We actually need some better way of assessing the longer-run impact that microfinance is having upon the typical local economy and its functioning.

Microfinance and key development triggers

Sustainable economic development is a complex process involving the interplay of institutions, governments and market processes. We do not know the exact policy recipe that best guarantees sustainable economic and social development – if, indeed, there is one. But in recent years we have begun to locate many of the most important and universal development 'trigger' issues. Here the so-called 'new development economics', a field of enquiry that emphasizes the importance of institutions and market imperfections,[65] has been particularly fruitful in supplying important insights and advances of relevance to local economic development policy and practice. One way of exploring the real impact of microfinance, then, is by reference to its effect upon the key development 'trigger' issues that we know underpin sustainable local economic and social development. Accordingly, in the rest of this chapter, I will foreground some of these core development 'trigger' issues, and I will try to explain how the microfinance model has impacted upon them to date in many of the supposedly 'best practice' country and regional examples of microfinance.

Microfinance and economies of scale One of the most important engines driving forward sustainable economic development is the ability of the enterprise sector to reap economies of scale. Experience from countries such as Italy after 1945, South Korea and Taiwan from the 1970s onwards, and most recently China since the early 1980s, shows how crucially important it is to invest in small enterprise units (including in agriculture) that can rapidly achieve minimum efficient scale of operations. A sufficient level of initial scale and investment is paramount to a microenterprise's survival and eventual growth, and thus also to it materially contributing to a local sustainable development dynamic and to poverty reduction. Scale economies ensure a low-cost operation and, eventually, the crucial ability to realize a reinvestible surplus. By definition, of course, microfinance produces microenterprises – that is, enterprises which are very small and so do not generally (at least initially) achieve minimum efficient scale. Nonetheless, it is vitally important to factor in the scale economies issue because otherwise suboptimal development trajectories are a real possibility, as I will show now.

Consider the example of India. Despite its rapid growth in recent years, India still has huge development and poverty-related problems. One of the most pressing of its development problems is the need to fill the so-called 'missing middle' that exists between, on the one hand, the small number of large internationally well-known computing and manufacturing companies and, on the other hand, the hundreds of millions of 'survivalist' informal microenterprises.[66] Put simply, India has so far failed to nurture an innovative and growth-oriented SME sector, one that would be capable not just of providing millions of desperately sought-after formal sector jobs in growth-oriented markets, but also of acting as an efficient subcontracting and supplier base for the large-firm sector. What accounts for this failure?

One reason stretching back at least two decades is that India's financial sector and rising entrepreneurial class has increasingly chosen to focus its attention upon the microenterprise sector. In the 1990s a raft of development-focused MFIs emerged to begin to intermediate a growing proportion of India's valuable financial resources (that is, its savings and remittances) back into the informal microenterprise sector. Adding to this supply of microfinance was a new generation of entrepreneur-owned MFIs, which began to emerge in large numbers from around 2000 onwards. These MFIs have little concern for sustainable local development, being far more interested in maximizing profits and shareholder value through making loans to whichever microenterprises can support their high interest rates and short repayment period. Their focus is therefore upon simple high-profit and low-risk household microloans.[67] Finally, caught up in the celebratory atmosphere surrounding microfinance and its supposed ability to 'help the poor', the Indian government has mandated India's biggest commercial banks to also expand their microfinance activities, especially through the networks of self-help groups (SHGs). Both state banks and privately owned banks are under such pressure.

As Aneel Karnarni convincingly argues, however, this financial sector trajectory represents a serious development setback for India. India's 'missing middle' is simply not being addressed. The hubbub created by the activity at the 'bottom of the pyramid' cannot disguise the fact that it is largely a weak force for the needed change in India compared to a dynamic and growing SME sector. He concludes that the growing focus on microfinance and microenterprises is quite dramatically *undermining* the productivity and overall efficiency of India's economy. 'The average firm size in India is less than one-tenth the size of comparable firms in other emerging economies,' Karnarni points out,[68] and so 'The emphasis on microcredit and the creation of microenterprises will only make this problem worse.'

But it is probably in relation to the agricultural sector where the lack of understanding of scale economies has proved to be the most destructive scale-related outcome of microfinance. The microfinance industry has long mooted that microfinance has an important role to play in agriculture. The common justification has been that it addresses the need to boost small-farm production destined for home consumption and the local market. Many of the Grameen Bank's first clients were, after all, accessing microcredits to undertake simple rice husking, milk cow rearing and chicken farming. In addition, microfinance has been slated to provide the basic financial resources and productive capacity needed to gradually construct sustainable local agricultural supply chains. In awarding the 2008 Conrad N. Hilton Humanitarian Prize to BRAC, which, alongside the Grameen Bank, is one of the most important MFIs in Bangladesh and in the world, the award committee neatly summed up much of what is widely assumed as possible thanks to microfinance:[69]

> microfinance, the indispensable multiplier. Money to pay for a cow. Fresh milk and something wondrous called 'income'. The cow became a dairy, then a milk distribution business. And the income went back to the village. The money became seeds, then crops. And the income went back to the village. And it became a school for non-formal education, a boat for a fisherman, a house, a university.

The emerging evidence seems to suggest, however, that this optimism is wildly misplaced. We need to recognize, first, that in both the developed and the developing countries, the most productively and socially efficient agricultural production structures are small family farms.[70] Small family farms are farms that essentially depend upon family and local labour, alongside a minimum/sufficient amount of capital investment, land and/or livestock to reach minimum efficient scale of operations. Alongside feeding the family itself, a sizeable percentage of total production is destined for the local market. As is increasingly coming to be understood, small family farms are more likely to maximize the potential to adopt important technologies and practices that create rural employment opportunities, raise agricultural productivity, relocalize the consumption of food, address food security issues, and all without damaging nature's goods and services.[71] As Norberg-Hodge, Merrifield and Gorelick emphasize,[72]

> Study after study carried out in many locations all over the world

show that small-scale, diversified agricultural systems have a higher total output per unit of land than large mono-cultures. The higher productivity of small farms is all the more remarkable in light of the fact that large landholders control most of the best land, while smallholders – particularly in the South – have been pushed to more marginal plots.

As just suggested, large-scale mono-crop agriculture is quite unproductive on many fronts. In fact, in many cases it largely depends upon government subsidies to continue. Some types of large-scale private agriculture in developing countries are highly financially profitable, however. But the problem here is that such plantation-type farms most often fail to offer any real sustainable economic and social return to the local community. For example, little meaningful or well-paid employment is produced thanks to extensive mechanization, while the financial returns are generally sucked up entirely by the wealthy landowner. The increasingly routine coexistence of successful plantation-style agricultural projects and endemic local/regional poverty shows the serious downside to this model.[73] Nor is large-scale socialized farming much of an answer here, as the poor agricultural performance of many former Soviet '*kolkoz*' and '*sovkoz*' demonstrate.

More importantly, a strategy of promoting agricultural activity that is centred on the tiniest of subsistence farms also cannot hope to substantively address the crucial economic, social and environmental issues currently facing developing countries today. While additional outputs from subsistence-type operations are, of course, useful to the individual/family, the fact remains that the very smallest farms have strict limitations in terms of being able to adequately feed the non-farm population. Thanks to the perpetual subdivision of land that takes place through inheritance, we can see the problem in many parts of Africa, Asia and Latin America today. The tiny plots of land that dominate in many parts of Africa, for example, are often unsuitable for even the very simplest of mechanization and cannot justify capital spending on such important inputs as irrigation, and it is unrealistic to expect significant economies of scale on both the purchasing side (seeds and fertilizer are very expensive per unit when bought in small quantities) and on any eventual sale of the surplus to market (taking just a few kilograms of produce to market is unrealistic – commercial buyers specify a minimum amount they are willing to purchase, etc.).

The economically, socially and ecologically optimum agricultural sector and rural financial policy today, then, is to focus support upon small family farming units that have reached minimum efficient scale. The crux problem here, however, is that microfinance is quite unsuitable for such small family farms. Nothing much can be done with small amounts of credit at high interest rates and over short repayment periods. Moreover, the higher risk involved in the more focused agricultural activities in a semi-professional family farm deters an MFI from seeking out such clients in the first place.

Those working in the tiniest of subsistence farms, however, often have much less resistance to working with microfinance. Often they simply don't appreciate the depth of the potential problems. Many simply have an urgent need for cash to keep going, and generally have nowhere else to go.[74] At the same time, the tiniest subsistence farms have actually been deliberately targeted by MFIs to become their agricultural client base. Put simply, so long as subsistence farmers can largely be made to repay their microloan through one of their likely income streams (or made to sell their land or other assets in the event of difficulties), it is not in the direct interest of the MFI to voluntarily stay away from such clients. In fact, given the ubiquity of subsistence farmers in many settings and the growing competition for clients everywhere, many MFIs eagerly look to this market segment for new clients. In short, the microfinance sector is everywhere in developing and transition countries managing to find an entry route into the subsistence farming sector.

What, then, is the overall result of the microfinance sector's move into subsistence farming? Unfortunately, in both developing and transition countries, it is not good at all. In fact, the growing tendency towards MFIs supporting subsistence farms at least partly accounts for why we find the dangerous primitivization and disruption of the agricultural sector worldwide. India is once more a good example of all that is wrong with a microfinance-driven approach to agricultural sector development. A country with a very large population of subsistence farms, India has around 650 million people living off the land. About 80 per cent of these small-scale farmers own less than two hectares. The proportion of marginal landholders increased from nearly 40 per cent in 1960/61 to 71 per cent in 2003, and they work only 22 per cent of the land.[75] Costs have increased on these subsistence farms, and the financial returns are inadequate.

One would be right to suppose that this marginalized sector

therefore requires external state support to upgrade technology and scale up, no less than European and US agriculture required support to scale up and break out of its subsistence origins.[76] But in India, thanks to the gradual marketization of the Indian economy and society in recent years, state support for such an important effort has declined precipitately. Investment in the rural sector is now around 65 per cent of what it was in 1985.[77] The previous system of special credit for farmers was phased out after 1991, and bank lending to agriculture has declined. In place of state priority lending came, among other things, rafts of commercialized 'new wave' MFIs and SHGs financed by loans from the commercial banks. Commercial bank credit to MFIs received a major boost in 2003 when ICICI Bank began to develop its so-called 'partnership model'. This was a way for ICICI to massively and quickly increase its lending via MFIs, which provide loan origination, monitoring and collecting services for a fee, but the loan stays on the books of ICICI.[78] The average loan size offered by India's MFIs was reported in 2008 to be no more than 3,500–5,000 rupees ($50–70) with a maturity of one year,[79] while the average loan size in India's large number of SHGs is not much higher, reported in 2008 to be around 6,000 rupees ($130).[80] In other words, both financial offers are pretty much unsuitable for anything other than the most primitive of agricultural activity on subsistence farming plots. In short, therefore, we find that while India's small farms began to find it difficult to access affordable credit from 1991 onwards, India's tiniest subsistence farms were soon being bowled over with offers of microcredit.

By all accounts, however, the profit-driven channelling of large quantities of microfinance to tiny subsistence farming units, most of which are not equipped to deal with it, has precipitated a disaster. It soon became apparent that the increased individual returns enjoyed by India's subsistence farms were simply too tiny and too insecure to justify engagement with commercial microfinance. The eventual result was the entrapment of several tens of millions of the very smallest subsistence farms in a vicious downward cycle of dependency and growing microdebt. In 2003, for example, it was estimated that fully *half* of the small farmers in India were in serious debt, the incidence of debt higher in the main agricultural states. Quite predictably, the highest figure – some 82 per cent of farmers – was found in microfinance-saturated Andhra Pradesh state.[81] Little additional agricultural output was actually secured thanks to this expansion of microfinance. In fact, most farms in serious debt ground to a halt. Among other things, this was thanks to the 160,000 farmer suicides registered in India since 1997, one of the most grotesque statistics associated with the growing entry of microfinance into the agricultural sector.[82] Many analysts blamed the government of India for allowing such an obvious microfinance 'oversupply' situation to arise. As *The Times of India* reported in relation to the rising number of suicides in rural communities, 'Having been in the business of creating self-help groups and promoting microcredit institutions, the government cannot absolve itself of responsibility.'[83] With so many tiny subsistence farms failing, while small family farms were increasingly unable to access capital on affordable terms and maturities, it was not at all surprising that rural incomes fell by 20 per cent in Andhra Pradesh in the decade after 1993.[84]

The massive increase in the amount of microfinance since 2000 has also been of little help to Mexico's peasant farmers (*campesinos*), who still constitute the mainstay of the country's agricultural sector. Since the passing of NAFTA (North American Free Trade Agreement) in 1994, most small Mexican farms have had a very difficult time remaining in operation. Immediately after NAFTA, subsidized US-produced corn (maize) began flowing freely into Mexico, a development that immediately began to negatively affect the millions of Mexico's small producers of corn. One possible way for the farmers to counter-attack was to invest in order to expand and diversify. But the harsh reality since NAFTA is that affordable finance for small farmers has become almost non-existent.[85]

Instead, rapidly growing access to 'new wave' microfinance from the 1990s onwards was quickly mooted as the answer. But because most small farmers found that it was impossible to repay the ultra-high interest rates demanded by Mexico's MFIs, microfinance was of no real use to them. They therefore remained without any real opportunity to access credit. On the other hand, the very tiniest of subsistence farms were now offered as much financial support as they could handle, yet (as in India) these were *precisely* the farms with almost no real productivity growth or sustainable development potential. From a sustainable-development point of view, the wrong clients were getting the support. The result was that agricultural productivity remained pitifully low in Mexico, and the agricultural sector stagnated. As the World Bank warned in 2004 in *A Study of Rural Poverty in Mexico*, 'An important factor explaining low productivity is lack of working capital, which may in turn be due to the *credit restrictions small farmers face that prevent them from using optimum quantities of inputs*' (my italics).[86] Family farms possessing some potential to commercialize and to make inroads into local supermarket supply chains found that they too could do nothing meaningful with microfinance, opening the door for other US agricultural exports to Mexico. Mexico has become a major net food importer (as recently as 1960 it was fully food self-sufficient). So, except for a very small minority able to export,[87] consolidating and expanding the most productive small farms in Mexico has become an almost impossible task. Thanks to the overarching shift towards microfinance starting in the mid-1990s, Mexico's agriculture sector has largely been helped to primitivize and stagnate, rather than flourish.

In Africa, too, the agricultural development impact of microfinance has been problematic. Microfinance industry advocates, such as the US-based Grameen Foundation's Alex Counts, still cling to the idea that the rapidly rising availability of microfinance will *eventually* produce some positive impact.[88] But because they misunderstand the requirements of sustainable agriculture, recommendations that microfinance be allowed even more of an opportunity to resolve the agricultural problem in Africa instead only add to the burden placed on Africa's poor farming communities. This is true especially with regard to its unpaid women, as emphasized by the work of Ambreena Manji I referred to in Chapter 3.

Consider one of the countries seeing a major improvement in agricultural productivity in 2007 – Malawi – where a government programme was introduced to provide subsidized fertilizer. Take-up of the fertilizer (and also better-quality seeds) was hitherto weak on account of the high prices of such items.[89] Such important inputs could have been quite easily purchased in Malawi prior to 2007 using a microloan, however, as many indeed recommended. But such important inputs were *not* purchased because of the high cost of microcredit. With very high interest rates, and in spite of the general food shortage conditions, the purchase of fertilizer using microcredit would have tipped the small farm into loss-making territory. So, rather than risk losing their remaining asset (their land) by defaulting on any microloan, the poor farmers just carried on tilling away as best they could.

In Kenya the availability of microfinance has massively increased in recent years, but the end result still remains very disappointing. Once again, the important small-farm sector has largely eschewed microfinance, because it was seen as far too expensive. Anyway, small farms are a risky proposition, and so avoided by MFIs in the first place. So the rising volume of microcredit in Kenya is being channelled elsewhere. Mostly it has gone into tiny subsistence farms and simple trade-based activities, both of which are unlikely to contribute to long-term growth and development. As Njoroge reports,[90] 'Credit constraints are frequently experienced by small holder farmers. In Kenya, the second-hand clothes trader is surer of accessing a loan than the rural farmer. Both businesses have different cash flows and microfinance business model favours one over the other.'

The situation seems to be repeating itself all across Africa. As Ehigiamusoe writes in *African Agriculture*,[91] 'Current trends in microfinance practice reveal the same neglect of agriculture. The proportion of the loan portfolios of microfinance institutions to farmers is insignificant. From Uganda through Côte d'Ivoire to Nigeria, microfinance institutions and banks pay little attention to agricultural financing.'

Interestingly, the World Bank neatly summarizes the reason why linking microfinance to agriculture is difficult:[92]

> Farm enterprises are rarely able to benefit as immediately and deeply from the most common techniques of sustainable microfinance as are small urban traders. This difficulty arises not only because of the short-term and progressive nature of the lending relationship but also because the relatively high break-even interest rates [...] that have to be charged for sustainable microfinance are often out of line with the rates of return that can be achieved in most of African farming today.

Overall, two crucial points stand out in Africa. First, most of the microfinance mobilized across the continent appears *not* to have been recycled back into the crucial agriculture sector, but into petty trading. Africa is becoming trapped as a continent of petty traders and nothing much else. Second, where microfinance *has* been made available for agricultural sector purposes in Africa, it has been largely channelled into the tiniest and least productive of subsistence farms, rather than into small family farms with growth potential. Good intentions and some rare good examples aside, the entry of microfinance into African agriculture has generally only contributed to its further primitivization and overall weakness.

Similar scale-related problems are common in the transition economies too. Consider, first, the results of a general project evaluation undertaken in Croatia by a major international consulting company.[93] The task was to assess the impact of the small amounts of capital disbursed to returnees and refugees as part of a 'start-up' package of support in an agricultural region heavily affected by conflict. The conclusion was that no sustainable development impact was realized. This conclusion was arrived at because it was found that none of the recipients could use the financial support provided to establish any sort of a sustainable agricultural enterprise. Instead, individual recipients were able to undertake only simple activities commensurate with the tiny sums of money allocated to them. This, the evaluation argued,[94] simply 'committed the village to remaining at a level of subsistence and denied the opportunity of building a farming community with complementarity between the farming activities'. The credits provided were 'too small, with too short repayment periods, and thus inadequate for longer term investment in farm businesses and buildings'.

This is a pretty damning picture, perfectly illustrating the general unsuitability of microfinance to agricultural activities. But do we find the same result when we look a little deeper into an individual agricultural sector in Croatia? The important dairy sector is the one obvious example to look at. With plenty of good-quality pastureland, an excellent climate, a plentiful water supply, and solid local demand for processed milk products, the sustainable recovery of the dairy sector was an obvious development and rural poverty reduction priority for the Croatian government in the aftermath of the Yugoslav civil war. It was also clear to both Croatia's and international agricultural specialists what had to be done to facilitate the process. For example, a major analysis of the dairy sector in 2005 by agricultural experts associated with the Agripolicy project concluded that,[95]

> ... as far as the economics and development of milk production are concerned, Croatia lags far behind the EU Member States. Most Croatian milk is produced on family farms and that production is expensive and insufficient to meet the needs of the dairy industry. There are a large number of small farms (2.8 cows per farm on average) with poor production capacities, 10,000 of the farms producing only 6,000 litres each per year.

As the Agripolicy expert group saw it,[96] the crucial task for the

Croatian government was to ensure that 'The farms which are not market oriented (presently almost half of all milk farms) [...] disappear while bigger farms with modern technology [...] develop.' Bearing in mind the need to coordinate policy across all agricultural sectors, the Croatian government was also implored to ensure that 'Agricultural policy initiatives should encourage only those programmes which will ensure the long term survival of this sector in a competitive market and/or those programmes which ensure some desirable social benefits.' The core recommendation provided by the Agripolicy team, as well as by many other specialized studies analysing the dairy industry, was above all for the country's scarce financial and technical resources to be used to rationalize the sector on the basis of scale. In other words, for an efficient dairy sector to emerge in Croatia, and for scarce financial and other resources to be used effectively, *the smallest dairy producers should be strongly encouraged to quickly exit the market.*

Since microfinance seems unlikely to be of any substantive use to a farm determined to upgrade operations and meet a minimum scale of operations, one might expect that MFIs in Croatia would be unwilling to engage with the dairy sector. Not so. As my own work with Dejan Sinković at the University of Juraj Dobrila Pula found,[97] the operations of one of the three MFIs operating in Croatia (DEMOS) were closely focused upon engaging with dairy operations. The focus, however, was upon supporting subsistence farms possessing one or two cows and requiring an additional cow in order to attempt to sell a little extra raw milk into the local 'green market', and/or to the small number of local processors. As predicted, however, most of these tiny dairy farming units were simply unable to survive at such low levels of output. Most ran into trouble not long after accessing their microloan, and it was only because they had been able to tap into Croatian government subsidy payments that they could repay their microloan. The microfinance-driven increase in the local supply of milk also contributed to reduced local raw milk prices, thus cancelling out much of the planned additional income boost to the MFI's clients. Non-clients in the dairy sector were none too happy either, of course, seeing their already minimal incomes from raw milk production falling as well. It also didn't help that the two main dairy processors opportunistically took advantage of the local oversupply. While initially agreeing to offer supply contracts to many of the MFI's clients, they nevertheless soon began to weed out those dairy units operating at less than minimum efficient scale (at the end of 2007 this meant 200 litres per day). Naturally, this mainly involved the MFI's hapless clients.

Importantly, however, repayment of the original microloan was still possible. First, this was thanks to access to Croatian government subsidies on 'three cow and above' farms, a factor that the MFI had known about beforehand (even offering some clients help to fill in the relevant forms!). Second, some clients later sold the cow(s) purchased with the microloan and repaid that way, thus ending their microfinance-supported income-generating project completely. Finally, some clients liquidated other family assets in order to repay the microloan.

In other words, we came to some pretty negative conclusions. The MFI was clearly keen to develop a microloan portfolio in the dairy sector. But this was not because of the development or poverty reduction potential, but mainly because it knew that repayment could eventually be secured by many factors other than the success of the individual dairy unit. All in all, while the MFI achieved its overarching goal – its own survival – the impact on the local community was quite negative. Most of the farmers who accessed microloans were worse off, the crucial dairy sector's overall growth and sustainability goals were manifestly compromised, while Croatian government subsidy payments aimed (among other things) at creating an efficient and sustainable dairy sector were effectively used to keep the MFI afloat.

Neighbouring Bosnia has also suffered exactly the same problems in the agricultural sector as Croatia, with the microfinance-driven proliferation of tiny inefficient producers quite effectively holding back the establishment of an efficient agricultural sector. Among other things, the necessary scale economies that could commercially justify the deployment of 'best practice' technologies still remain a rarity in the country.[98] Nearly half of the population are smallholders working their tiny plots of land, yet imports of fresh and processed foods into Bosnia remain significant.[99] Helping to explain matters is Christoplos,[100] who found that MFIs in Bosnia prefer to work with agricultural projects composed of a number of income-generating agricultural activities, rather than just the one. The reason for this was that no matter what happens to the particular agricultural project established with the microloan, it could be repaid from income arising from other activities on the family farm. The alternative for the MFI would be support for an agricultural project that was based on full-time potentially sustainable farming activities, but where there would be no alternative income source to repay the microloan in the event of the project getting into difficulty. Delinking the loan payment from loan use in this manner is actually very common. It is even recommended as 'good practice' for the MFI,[101] because the priority within the 'new wave' microfinance model is always and everywhere the financial survival of the MFI. This recommendation appears to hold, moreover, even if this means disadvantaging the local economy and the local agricultural sector. Even in the 'best case' scenario, MFIs will still largely end up supporting only agricultural projects even *more* likely than ever to be below minimum efficient scale, and so those projects that are even more likely to be unproductive and inefficient.

The end result of all this microfinance activity in the agricultural sector is inevitably support for a structure of part-time and below-minimum-efficient-scale agricultural units, which effectively preordains a country's failure to establish a sustainable, competitive and growth-oriented agricultural sector. Put bluntly, an MFI can clearly succeed with such tactics and become financially sustainable, but the local agricultural sector is destroyed in the process. The MFI then becomes a 'cathedral' of financial success in a desert of rural poverty that it has itself been instrumental in creating. As even long-time microfinance advocate Malcolm Harper concedes, the 'too expensive and too inflexible' terms and conditions involved in microfinance are simply unsuited to agriculture.[102] All the while, the most growth-oriented and productive family farms are effectively 'starved' of the financial help they urgently need. The collective organizations that have a track record of organizing subsistence farms in order to achieve 'collective efficiency',[103] through such as agricultural cooperatives, also go without funding. In the context of the two absolutely paramount considerations in developing countries today – sustainable rural jobs growth and local food security – microfinance is a risky, if not openly dangerous, intervention.

Summing up, by refusing to factor in the crucial issue of scale, the microfinance industry is responsible for channelling large amounts of scarce financial resources to many millions of individual microenterprises and subsistence agricultural operations that have almost no real growth or development potential. Effectively losing out are those farm and non-farm units with the potential to realize far higher productivity and social gains. All told, the focus on the tiniest of microenterprises and subsistence farms amounts to nothing less than building a 'house of cards'. There is therefore a huge downside and opportunity cost here to what Thomas Dichter has called 'the micro-credit paradox', a situation where 'the poorest people can do little productive with the credit, and the ones who can do the most with it are those who don't really need microcredit, but larger amounts with different (often longer) credit terms'.[104]

Microfinance and informalization The 'discovery' of the informal sector in the early 1970s provided huge impetus behind the micro-finance concept. The informal sector was thereafter validated as an important aspect of the local economy in developing countries, a sector that needed to be promoted as much as possible. By placing itself at the service of the informal sector, microfinance was quickly portrayed as a major development intervention too. Studies right across developing countries show that the overwhelming majority of an MFI's clients are informal sector microenterprises. If it were otherwise, and if working with the informal sector were for some reason disallowed, then microfinance would probably cease to exist in a matter of months. Intentionally or otherwise, microfinance is thus intimately associated with the legitimization and support for the informal sector everywhere across the globe. But is this microfinance-driven informalization trajectory actually beneficial?

Of late the role of the informal sector has increasingly been reassessed in terms of its contribution to sustainable development. Partly this change of heart has been precipitated by the rather obvious fact that the informal sector has massively expanded in the developing economies since the early 1980s, and in the transition economies after 1990, yet this development is manifestly *not* causally associated with sustainable economic and social development anywhere. Quite the opposite, in fact. The creeping informalization of the economy in both developing and transition countries is seen as responsible for a great many antisocial developments. It is unequivocally associated with the delegitimization of legal process, it has undermined respect for the tax system, it has sanctioned a casual approach towards health and safety and environmental regulations, and it has undermined the ability of democratically mandated governments to prohibit sharp business practices. All of these developments undermine social capital too, which, among other things, is also an important precondition for business investment. Increasingly, a business either has to travel the 'low road' practices of the rapidly expanding informal sector, or it is forced under. Worse, other more productive enterprises (i.e. SMEs) are also 'crowded out' by the informal sector. As management consultants McKinsey report,[105] 'By avoiding taxes and regulatory obligations, informal companies gain a substantial cost advantage that allows them to stay in business despite their small scale and low productivity. This prevents more productive, formal companies from gaining market share. The result is slower economic growth and job creation.'

Also, consider further why it is that business elites are often so supportive of microfinance and the microenterprises that they help create. This support might not arise because of any burning interest in poverty reduction, but because there are important economic benefits to the big-business sector. First, microenterprises indirectly support the movement to a much more 'flexibilized' local labour market, which will mean lower wage costs. With most developing economies experiencing a (sometimes vast) labour surplus, and with large numbers of informal microenterprises one of the typical 'poverty-push' responses to such conditions, the resulting heightened competition and desperation to survive generally lead to falling wages and deteriorating working conditions.[106] If the informal sector alternative becomes much less attractive as an employment option compared to the formal sector, it then becomes much easier for the formal sector business to enforce low(er) pay in its own operations. Second, microenterprise development directly supports the movement towards a much more compliant and much less costly raft of informal, non-unionized local supply chain partners, many of which are often also outside the tax system. By opportunistically dropping their formal SME suppliers and engaging instead with informal lower-cost microenterprise suppliers, large firms are able to drastically cut their own labour costs, tax bill and social responsibilities.[107] On both counts, therefore, greater informality at the bottom may thus help to further the commercial interests of large firms at the top. As should be clear, however, both these processes of informalization are also likely to raise the *overall* level of poverty, inequality and insecurity affecting the wider local community.

Informality is also seen as a very real threat to social peace right across the globe, especially in post-conflict zones, mega-city slums and areas prone to inter-ethnic strife. This is because, as Mike Davis puts it,[108]

Those engaged in informal sector competition under conditions of infinite labour supply usually stop short of a total war of all against all: conflict, instead, is usually transmuted into ethnoreligious or racial violence ... the informal sector, in the absence of enforced labour rights, is a semi-feudal realm of kickbacks, bribes, tribal loyalties, and ethnic exclusion ... the rise of the unprotected informal sector has too frequently gone hand in hand with exacerbated ethnoreligious differentiation and sectarian violence.

Put simply, the informal sector simply does not possess the sort of 'transformational power' widely claimed for it by Hernando De Soto and others. On the contrary, the unlimited expansion of the informal sector, and thus brutal and limitless competition within the local economy, is the most unlikely of precursors to increased investment. Even if one leaves aside the moral dimension, there are precious few examples where the increasing brutalization of poor individuals and the intensification of their day-to-day workload and suffering have successfully precipitated sustainable economic and social development outcomes. As Davis is forced to conclude,[109] 'DeSotan slogans simply grease the skids to a Hobbesian hell'. These severe downsides to informalization account for why most developing and transition countries today are now desperately trying to 'turn back the tide' and, through a variety of state and non-state interventions, rein in their oversized informal sectors.[110] Extending the informal sector with microfinance has thus come at a not inconsiderable price.

Microfinance and deindustrialization A major critique of neoliberal policies is associated with institutional economics and the careful study of historical development trajectories. Economists such as Ha-Joon Chang, Alice Amsden, Robert Wade and others have carefully charted the largely hidden history of Western capitalism and its rise to industrial dominance. These authors demonstrate how decisive industrial policies were to the ultimate success that today's developed countries achieved in the nineteenth and early part of the twentieth centuries, as well as to the rapid progress made by the East Asian economies since the 1970s.

One of the leading lights in this exciting new field of enquiry, Erik Reinert,[111] likens neoliberal policy to the Morgenthau Plan being lined up for post-war Germany in 1945. The Morgenthau Plan was designed by the wartime US government to deindustrialize post-war

Germany, with the aim of turning a previously mighty industrial power into a primitive and poor agricultural country that could never again challenge world peace. This was the price Germany was expected to pay for its role in initiating the Second World War. The idea was to obliterate all but the simplest and smallest enterprises with little industrial development potential, backed up by a prohibition on industrial research. The plan was quickly abandoned, however, when it became clear that an economically successful Germany was required to act as a buffer to the possible expansion of communist ideas emanating from the Soviet Union. Without this policy U-turn, Germany was facing a future with a seriously stunted industrial sector and, as intended, virtually no possibility of developing as an industrial nation, or of making a real dent in the horrific level of post-war poverty.

Instead, the victorious allies allowed the new post-war government to introduce a radically different economic policy aimed at kick-starting the country's industrial renaissance. With help coming from Marshall Plan funds, the new West German government introduced a range of financial packages to support 'bottom-up' industrial de-velopment and technology transfer in microenterprises and SMEs, special financial programmes for new technology-intensive enterprises, and the establishment of numerous subsidized longer-term business loan schemes through the regional state banks (*Landesbanken*). Very quickly, Germany's microenterprise and small industrial enterprise sector was reborn, and it soon began to thrive.[112] The medium-sized enterprise sector (*Mittelstand*) effectively became the core engine driv-ing rapid post-war growth. In fact, the West German state's concern to promote the *Mittelstand* came to be known as *Mittelstandpolitik* – the idea being that coordinated support for the *Mittelstand* could ensure competition in the industrial sector, while also providing a vital social and political pillar in post-war German society, particularly in rural communities.[113]

I raise the issue of the Morgenthau Plan here because, in a very real sense, we may quite easily describe microfinance as a modern-day version of the Morgenthau Plan. In general, we know that only very simple and unsophisticated microenterprises can service the terms and maturities demanded by most MFIs. Typically, these microenterprises are very simple trading, retail and service operations, with perhaps some very small production-based operations that can add value very quickly. Very few more sophisticated industrial microenterprises or

SMEs can effectively get started or expand with the assistance of microfinance. With microfinance today very much driven by the profit motive, there is an inbuilt bias in favour of short-term high-profit projects, and against longer-term projects likely to be of much more value to the local community, but which would struggle to repay high interest rates in their initial period of operations. Overall, to the extent that the local financial sector shifts in favour of microfinance – as we are indeed seeing right around the globe – the more an economy's scarce financial resources are directed towards ineffectual short-term projects, and away from business projects that offer far more to the economy and society into the medium to longer term. Microfinance as development policy very clearly facilitates the deindustrialization of the local economy.

In a roundabout way, the general development barrier I am referring to here has actually been consistently raised by many institutions, especially by the UN agency UNCTAD. In its 2003 annual report, for example, UNCTAD points to the serious lack of local industrial impetus and institutional support in developing countries. This weakness effectively consigns developing countries to a future marked out by almost 'no chance of nurturing the home-grown firms which are crucial to economic success'. What is needed instead, according to the lead author of the 2003 UNCTAD report, Yilmaz Akyuz, is 'the policy space: the ability to nourish, support and develop domestic industries, and the capability to compete in international markets and to supply the home market'.[114]

In transition countries the situation is slightly different, but no less problematic. With a long tradition of industrial development, the need is more to facilitate the cannibalizing of the old production and process technologies for adaptation and reuse in new microenterprise and SME projects. As David Ellerman has argued in relation to the post-communist economies,[115] such an industrial inheritance was of some considerable value. It represented a pool of 'genetic material' that could potentially be recombined in order to build upon the best of the past industrial investments, and not simply abandon them. A key requirement for this process to take place, Ellerman argues, is the presence of a supportive and long-term-focused financial regime; which is clearly not microfinance.

The argument I make in this important section is, therefore, that the increasing dominance of the microfinance model in developing countries is causally associated with their progressive deindustrialization and infantilization. Financial support to promote enterprises with productivity-raising potential, this being the ultimate precondition for sustainable economic and social development, is actually disappearing from the scene. The result is that the chances of any country creating the preconditions for its exit from poverty and underdevelopment are close to zero. As has been long recognized, notably in an influential article by William Baumol,[116] such a simple enterprise structure has very little chance of eventually precipitating growth and sustainable development. The temporary uplift often provided by microfinance (a little extra income, a boost to consumption spending, etc.) is therefore effectively being paid for into the longer term by the progressive deindustrialization and stagnation of the country concerned. This is a very high price to pay. A Morgenthau Plan-type policy is being implemented for real.

How not to go about development in Africa? Consider, as a first illustration of what I mean in practice, the hugely important case of the continuing economic failure of sub-Saharan Africa. This issue was recently the subject of a 2009 best-selling book, *Dead Aid*, by Zambian economist Dambisa Moyo.[117] Moyo's book is very relevant to the discussion here, though not because of her main thread – a denunciation of the international community for its provision of aid to African countries that go on to misuse it. Instead, her views are important here because of what she argues is one of the key solutions to the economic problems she highlights in Africa – microfinance. Microfinance, and therefore even more rafts of microenterprises, she argues, will hugely assist in supporting Africa's attempt to escape poverty and promote sustainable development. One has to say right away that Moyo's argument is seriously weakened by her own admission to not knowing much about the current issues and developments in microfinance.[118] Moreover, her central argument in favour of microfinance as a source of business investment is undermined because it uses very misleading data drawn from PR sources.[119] Such important caveats notwithstanding, does Moyo's thesis concerning the benefits of microfinance still hold?

As is well known, the African continent is replete with simple microenterprises. Many hundreds of millions of poor individuals effectively have no other option but to attempt to try to survive through very small-scale entrepreneurship. Support for this 'self-help' trajectory is provided by large numbers of international donor-funded

MFIs. Increasingly, too, Africa's own commercial banks are driven by simple market forces to 'downscale' out of SME lending (and other activities) and into the far more profitable world of microfinance. And even though as early as the late 1990s the very high drop-out rate being experienced by African MFIs was becoming a cause for concern,[120] and recently the huge over-indebtedness of many poor South Africans even forced the government to intervene,[121] Moyo nevertheless argues that Africa's microfinance sector urgently needs to be expanded even more.

This is a difficult argument to make, however. Framing all current and future financial support within Africa on the basis of the prevailing microfinance and microenterprise trajectory is, quite simply, not a strategy that will provide Africa with an exit out of its current malaise. As UNCTAD argues, and as Ha-Joon Chang more recently argued in his 2007 best-seller *Bad Samaritans*, the African continent urgently needs not more simple 'buy cheap, sell dear' microenterprises, but a robust light industrial foundation that will enable its entry into at least some mainstream production and manufacturing-based enterprises capable of productivity growth. Africa therefore also needs robust and far-sighted financial institutions that will help bring this about, which would not include the microfinance sector.

So far, very much as in the past,[122] the proliferation of microfinance in Africa is associated with *precluding* the chances of establishing the industrial foundations required for future growth and poverty reduction. The continent is fast becoming instead a vast reservoir of self-employed traders, and not much else. For instance, in Uganda, at least partly thanks to a sizeable increase in the availability of microfinance over the last ten years, small-scale trade now constitutes around 95 per cent of the urban economy.[123] Similar figures and scenarios prevail in most other African states. In Benin, when cross-border trade with neighbouring Nigeria was prohibited in 2004/05, the *entire* microfinance sector was thrown into crisis, since it turned out that the vast bulk of microcredit in the country was being channelled into the very simplest of cross-border shuttle trading operations.[124] In Kenya, Njoroge reports that 'Microfinance at its best pushes the rural active poor to urban areas and creates a nation of "traders and hawkers".'[125]

Nor is it just small-scale, industry-based, relatively technology-intensive, growth-oriented SMEs which will remain conspicuous by their absence. Even very small-scale subcontracting industries, perhaps serving larger FDI-driven enterprises operating in Africa, are unlikely to get started with microfinance behind them. In fact, Moyo actually raises exactly this issue herself, when lamenting the lagging share of employment in the SME sector in Africa, including in her native Zambia. Moyo makes the claim that the share of SMEs in Zambia is apparently just 40 per cent, which compares badly to the more than 80 per cent equivalent figure in Italy and Greece.[126] She does not, however, follow through with any discussion of one of the central reasons why this perceived lack of SMEs has actually arisen – the increasing profit-driven diversion of Africa's savings and international donor funds into the microenterprise sector, and so away from riskier and lower-margin work dealing with the sort of SMEs she otherwise desperately wants to see flourish.

There is also much evidence to suggest that even previously relatively industrialized African economies and regions – those that made important strides under the period of decolonization or with the help of raw materials exports – are also collapsing back into the very simplest of market-driven activities, greatly aided by the growing abundance of microfinance. Nigeria is an obvious example. Despite huge oil revenues since the 1980s, the country has nevertheless experienced a significant deindustrialization trend since then. Unlike other oil- and gas-rich African countries, such as Algeria and Libya (not to mention South Africa's apartheid-era policies that saw it forced to develop many SMEs capable of efficiently servicing an energy and military industry cut off from world markets), Nigeria adopted a neoliberal policy programme that discouraged proactively investing in SMEs capable of integrating into the oil industry supply chain. And from very early on,[127] nor has there been much investment directed towards developing a non-oil tradable sector capable of exporting. Nigeria's neoliberal policy programmes in the 1980s and 1990s emphasized instead only the need to cut government spending and to deregulate the financial sector in order to ensure, among other things, that financial support goes only to businesses capable of quickly repaying market-based interest rates.[128] Meanwhile, microfinance has boomed since around 2000, driven forward by rafts of new informal MFIs. Predictably, the informal sector has also boomed, with nearly 80 per cent of microfinance channelled into simple trade-based microenterprises alone.[129]

Nothing appears to have been learned, or done, in terms of improving Nigeria's chances of recycling its oil wealth and savings into 'bottom-up' industrialization and the gradual diversification of its economic base. Moreover, given government measures passed in 2005 to ensure that by 2020 microfinance becomes a very significant chunk of Nigeria's *formal* financial sector as well, an already adverse deindustrialization trajectory looks set to be considerably amplified.[130]

Unfortunately, then, there is very little evidence to suggest that an African continent built upon even more microfinance than at present will ever come to resemble any of the positive future scenarios outlined by Dambisa Moyo, and others in the microfinance industry. The reverse is much more likely to be true. Most microfinance projects in Africa are verging towards Morgenthau Plan-type interventions that are unlikely to improve the longer-term chances of Africa escaping poverty and underdevelopment. The minor poverty gains registered on some counts (consumption smoothing, subsistence farms producing additional food crops that can be consumed at home, and so on) cannot offset the longer-run debilitating impacts associated with the further degradation and infantilization of the local industrial and agricultural base. The likelihood is that more microfinance will end up accelerating the already strong deindustrialization trends in evidence virtually everywhere in Africa. Unless changes are made, the future for Africa is clear. As the executive director of the Johannesburg-based Textile Federation of South Africa, Brian Brink, warns, 'De-industrialization is a real threat. We have to decide whether we go down that slippery path. What happens then? We all become a bunch of traders.'[131]

Microfinance doesn't help elsewhere either Nor can we say that Africa is the exception here. Thanks to the growing abundance of microfinance, most other developing and transition countries are encountering the same primitivizing and deindustrializing impetus that is clearly under way on the African continent. The situation in Latin America is little different.

There is no question that Mexico's economic structure is increasingly becoming dominated by the tiniest of informal microenterprises. More accurately, substantial growth in the number of tiny micro-enterprises, most spectacularly in the case of street hawking, has come at the expense of a significant weakening of Mexico's previously relatively well-developed, innovative and technology-intensive SME sector. As economist Santiago Levy points out,[132] this is a major worry with regard to Mexico's long-term future. One of Mexico's principal problems today is low growth, and, Levy points out, it arises at least partly because of 'Over-employment and over-investment in small informal firms that under-exploit advantages of size, invest little in technology adoption and worker training.' Put simply, as many analysts in Mexico are arguing today, the Mexican economy is undergoing an irreversible process of 'changarrization' (a reference to the term *'changarro'*, an informal microenterprise or 'mom and pop store').

A key problem here is that market-driven pressures are making the Mexican financial sector much less interested in supporting the sort of enterprises that Mexico *really* needs. For example, using data from the National Survey of Microenterprises undertaken in 1994 and 1998, Woodruff reported that in the second half of the 1990s the Mexican banking system registered a drop in loans to microenterprises (though many microenterprises were still able to access a microloan from other informal sources).[133] Importantly, he found that the shortage of formal bank credit in the 1990s resulted in the average microenterprise becoming relatively *less* technology intensive and even *smaller* than before (usually losing any employees it may have had, for example). Moving into the new millennium, it then became clear that microfinance was becoming an increasingly abundant offer in the Mexican financial sector thanks to the large numbers of newly established MFIs. Predictably, this new supply was overwhelmingly channelled into the very smallest of *changarros*, and increasingly into simple consumer lending too. Moreover, as Mexico's existing commercial banks desperately tried to recover from the banking collapse of the mid-1990s, they increasingly sought to rebuild their financial strength through high-profit microfinance. Pointedly, much of the capital Mexico's commercial banks needed for microfinance applications in Mexico was found by reducing their exposure to the lower-profit and more risky SME sector: bank lending to formal sector SMEs fell in Mexico in the new millennium, going from 60 per cent of total lending to just over 48 per cent in six years.[134] As economist Santiago Levy explains once more, the problem today is that 'There are more resources to subsidize informal employment than formal employment', so that 'Mexico is probably saving less and investing in less efficient projects.'[135]

Over the last two decades, therefore, the financial sector in Mexico has quite dramatically shifted into working with the sort of microenterprises that lie at the heart of Mexico's 'changarrization' (deindustrialization) malaise, on the one hand, while progressively abandoning the much more productive and employment-generating SME sector, on the other. Mexico's future as an industrial economy is therefore coming under increasing threat from this largely profit-driven reorientation of its financial sector in favour of microfinance. Even the business-elite-friendly Mexico Employers Association laments these changes and the current 'changarrization' trend, arguing that the country is gradually reversing most of the important industrialization and oil-industry-financed development gains made in the previous couple of decades.[136]

In South-East Asia, too, Morgenthau Plan-style dynamics have also been at work in the most microfinance-saturated countries. The obvious example is Cambodia. A country whose financial sector is now pretty much dominated by MFIs and microfinance, Cambodia has signally failed to 'take off' in the manner of either neighbouring Vietnam or Thailand.[137] A good illustration of why this situation has arisen involves ACLEDA, the largest MFI in Cambodia, its second-largest bank and also (as in a growing number of countries and regions) its most profitable bank. Clark reports that ACLEDA, founded by UNDP in 1993 as an NGO project, has become an icon within the microfinance industry.[138] This is because, in fewer than twenty years of operation, ACLEDA is now responsible for a very significant and still-growing proportion of the total savings mobilization in Cambodia, as well as a similar amount of total microlending activity. It is also, as just noted, an extremely profitable institution. Following its conversion into a private for-profit commercial bank in 2000, its financial performance continued to impress. International investors began to take note, and soon a line began to form of those most interested to get a piece of the action for their rich shareholders.[139]

Consider also, however, that more or less all of the local savings that ACLEDA successfully mobilizes for on-lending (i.e. 91 per cent as of 2004) are then recycled back into the very simplest of microenterprises – that is, mainly street hawkers, cross-border shuttle traders, simple kiosks, fast-food stands and petty services. In 2005, for example, more than 70 per cent of the loans advanced by ACLEDA went into the trade sector alone, with only 3 per cent of its disbursed loans going to help upgrade and develop the hugely important agricultural processing sector.[140] Meanwhile, influenced by the commercial success of ACLEDA, the more traditional local commercial banks have also moved into providing only highly profitable microcredit, and they now shy away from traditional business project lending to an incredible degree.[141] Overall, with a high and growing proportion of local savings recycled into highly profitable microfinance programmes, as opposed to being channelled into more productive and growth-oriented SMEs or other efficiency-enhancing projects, ACLEDA is playing an important role in *undermining* the country's desperate attempts to escape extreme industrial and agricultural backwardness.[142] ACLEDA is yet another microfinance sector 'cathedral in the desert'.

Finally, in eastern Europe's transition economies, the deindustrialization and primitivization of the average local economy thanks to microenterprise development has effectively set back the region's development chances by decades. With hindsight, as I noted earlier, we now realize that Poland's 'micro-entrepreneurship miracle', alongside a block on proactively supporting SMEs,[143] achieved very little of lasting economic significance. One particularly adverse outcome was that virtually the only production-based microenterprises and SMEs that managed to start and/or remain in business during this heady period (in fact, they initially proliferated) were low-value-added 'loan system'-type business operations, especially in textiles. In addition, Poland's lead in many promising small-scale technologies, its highly skilled population and its immediate past history of exciting domestic innovation activity were all largely abandoned as the source of new sustainable enterprises.[144] Thanks to the establishment of a number of MFIs in the early 1990s, notably Fundusz Mikro, the already debilitating deindustrialization trajectory was accelerated.[145] Surveying the long-term damage done to the Polish economy as a result of its high-profile foray into market-driven microenterprise development, Hardy and Rainnie could only conclude that 'the emergence of a flea market [...] is no basis on which to build successful local economic development'.[146]

Also within eastern Europe, the Balkans is another region where we find an abundance of Morgenthau Plan-type trajectories in operation thanks to microfinance. In the aftermath of the Yugoslav civil war, Bosnia's impressive industrial enterprise sector and associated technological/institutional infrastructure were still a significant and very valuable inheritance. Most large technology-intensive enterprises, however, immediately had to begin to downsize and to reduce employment. One way they attempted to do this was by encouraging technical staff to depart after having established for themselves a new microenterprise or 'spin-off' in a relatively technology-intensive area.

Many of the highly skilled technical staff in Bosnia's largest and most innovative companies were indeed keen to depart under such conditions, such as in the Sarajevo-based EnergoInvest. Accordingly, business plans were prepared, ideas were tested and national and international market contacts re-established. Almost none of these proposals came to pass, however. The principal reason was that the financial support was simply not there.

Because the international donor community had ensured that Bosnia would become the Balkan 'test-bed' for microfinance, and part of this strategy included the need to ensure that other competing financial institutions were blocked,[147] potential entrepreneurs had access to microfinance and virtually nothing else to help establish their new business. It was either microfinance or 'no finance'. For most prospective entrepreneurs, those with sophisticated products or processes, with distant break-even points and with complicated technologies involving 'learning-while-doing', it was a case of 'no finance'. As a result, most of the large technology-intensive enterprises in Bosnia downsized after 1995 with almost no associated boost to the structure (quantity and quality) of the local microenterprise sector and the local SME sector.[148] A major industrial inheritance, skills base and R&D tradition – an asset that most developing countries would *desperately* like to be in possession of – was thus largely abandoned without even a whimper. As UNDP lamented in 2002,[149] the result is that Bosnia has now been 'condemned to reliance on a grey, trade-based, unsustainable economy rather than a production-based one'.

Microfinance and 'connectivity' One of the most important areas of policy research in the 1980s was into the connections that link enterprises together vertically and horizontally. Researchers found that individual microenterprises and SMEs were able to successfully overcome the disadvantage of small scale by coalescing together with other enterprises into 'industrial districts'. They were able to reap so-called 'collective economies of scale'.

One of the seminal texts on this issue is Michael Piore and Charles Sabel's 1984 book *The Second Industrial Divide*,[150] which predicted the survival and re-emergence of small firms, because they were increasingly able and willing to link together horizontally and vertically in efficiency-raising networks and clusters. The large-firm system – termed 'Fordism' – had reached its limit. Fordism was increasingly being joined in many of the regions, if not entirely displaced, by rafts of dynamic small firms cooperating with each other in the 'industrial districts'.[151]

The end result of these insights was a new paradigm of local economic development policy, one that saw great value in directly supporting the interconnections between enterprises far more than (just) the simple internal production arrangements or capitalization of any one individual enterprise.[152] Emerging at around the same time was a parallel concern with the need to promote subcontracting arrangements and so-called 'commodity chains' as the most important way of upgrading small enterprises. These were highly efficient forms of inter-enterprise cooperation mainly involving vertical hierarchies of mixed-size enterprises, and where longer-term collaboration and risk-sharing were more important than simple short-run cost minimization.[153]

Importantly, the efficiency-raising potential of many of these forms of inter-enterprise collaboration very often extended to microenterprises. In northern Italy, for example, microenterprises were pulled into regional and international supply chains by the famous '*impannatori*' (intermediaries). High post-war levels of social capital and solidarity in the 'Red Regions' helped to ensure that traditional forms of exploitation and insecurity were minimized.[154] Similarly, in postwar Japan, as Nishiguchi recounts,[155] dynamic microenterprises were encouraged to become an important part of the industrial supply chain. Provided by their larger partner enterprises with the very latest technologies, secure contracts, prompt and decent financial payment and other forms of support in order to motivate them, they were soon able to excel in their performance (delivery times, quality, cost, etc.). Networks of local government institutions worked alongside these microenterprises too, helping with training, further capitalization and new technologies. Indeed, reflecting on the successes of both the Italian and Japanese microenterprise sectors since 1945, Linda Weiss was forced to conclude that 'the core of modern micro-capitalism is not competitive individualism but collective endeavour'.[156] Some development programmes today also recognize the crucial need to connect microenterprises, such as through marketing cooperatives and buyer consortia.

In contemporary microfinance policy, however, such beneficial grassroots 'connectivity' dynamics are quite fanciful. MFIs today 'succeed' only in the narrow sense of producing rafts of new (albeit often temporary) informal sector microenterprises. The overwhelming majority of these new entrants, however, have no need, wish or ability to meaningfully cooperate in order to begin to forge the required productivity-enhancing horizontal ('proto-industrial districts') and vertical (subcontracting) connections. Especially within the 'new wave' microfinance paradigm, the additional investment and support required to identify and support suitably 'connectable' microenterprises are seen as an unnecessary financial burden. What matters to an MFI is simply whether or not a client microenterprise can repay its microloan.

This is not to say that some forms of connectivity are not promoted through microfinance. In agriculture, for instance, the concept of 'contract farming' has been quite widely promoted by offering a microcredit to potential small-farm participants. The 'contract farming' system is, however, principally of benefit to the final buyer or processor, and is not particularly meant to be of benefit to small farmers. Microfinance is cunningly used here to avoid the need for the final buyers or processors to make any additional investment in the small-farm suppliers. The small farms thus also get stuck with much of the risk involved in the event of failure. Controlling the farmers in this way also helps to reduce costs into the longer term; for example, by regularly switching and abandoning some farmer-suppliers as a form of disciplining measure. Many family farms seek a way to get around these low-return contract farming operations, in order to develop sustainable farming operations of more benefit to themselves. Agricultural cooperatives are the obvious mechanism. But with only microfinance on offer, this option is typically made impossible.

Overall, then, we can say that the basic 'raw material' required for local efficiency-raising 'connectivity' is a very unlikely outcome of contemporary microfinance programmes. Microfinance mainly operates like a football academy that exists solely in order to turn out players with possibly excellent individual skills, but all of whom have no understanding of the importance of the teamwork required to win the match.

Microfinance and import dependency One of the main sectors microfinance has traditionally supported right across the developing and transition countries has been cross-border shuttle trading, along with the associated web of small-scale retail operations (shops, kiosks, street hawking) that then sell on imported items. Such simple trade-based activities are often initially very profitable in the aftermath of conflict, natural disaster, economic collapse and so on. They are therefore natural MFI clients because they can cover the high interest rates and short repayment periods demanded. This is what is known as a 'pull' factor. There are also 'push' factors at play here, however, principally the ease of entry into such activities for those with no skills, experience or cash. For example, cross-border trading has exploded in importance in many countries, driven largely by unemployment and abject poverty rather than by the chance to make decent financial returns.

It is widely accepted that the instant expansion of such simple trading activities results in some valuable additional income being generated by those directly involved, and perhaps also some jobs are quickly created. This is why in the aftermath of natural disaster or conflict, the rapid rise in such activities is often tolerated and may generate positive benefits for the local community. Until local production can restart, for example, it is of some considerable benefit that such microenterprises are able to access needed products from unaffected neighbouring countries or regions. Some of the cash raised is eventually reinvested in production-based activities, which will create local jobs and income too.

Overall, however, the longer-term impact of such developments is seriously debilitating and largely offsets the meagre initial benefits I have just recounted. For a start, microfinance has very clearly played an important role in promoting irreversible import dependency. One of the most damaging features of the neoliberal programmes that developing countries were forced into during the 1970s and 1980s was the collapse in local manufacturing and agricultural production brought about by instant trade liberalization. An ensuing flood of (often subsidized) imports was facilitated largely by the massive proliferation of small shuttle trading and importing ventures, many of which were attracted away from production-based activities and into the newly profitable area of importing. The conclusion reached by an important study undertaken by SAPRIN in conjunction with the World Bank[157] was that the largely uncontrolled surge of imports needlessly contributes to 'the failure of many local manufacturing firms, particularly innovative small and medium sized ones that generate a great deal of employment'. Microfinance support for such 'quick and easy to enter' shuttle trading and importing activities thus leads to import dependence. Local production possibilities get wiped out too.

Microfinance thus underpins an import-dependency dynamic that is pretty much irreversible. A stark illustration of what I mean comes from the agriculture sector in post-communist Poland. After 1989 a large shuttle trader population quickly emerged into formality and began importing into Poland agricultural items from neighbouring countries, including Germany to the west and Russia, Ukraine and the Baltic states to the east. These nimble, mainly urban-based, microenterprises often made small fortunes for their owners. They also proved quite damaging, however, to Poland's economy overall. For example, their activities greatly helped to turn a $557 million surplus on agricultural products with the EU in 1989 into a $333 million deficit by 1993. This instant splurge of imported food items, many of which were very cheap because they incorporated subsidies derived from EU farm support programmes, led to farm incomes in Poland falling very dramatically (by around 50 per cent). By 1995 around 60 per cent of Polish farms were technically bankrupt and rural poverty began a dramatic rise to new heights.[158]

There is also a wider 'crowding out' problem to factor in here. Because simple cross-border trade is a quick payback activity, and often quite profitable (at least in the early stages), MFIs and other financial institutions naturally want their 'fair share' of the gains from such activities. The result is that the real local cost of capital typically rises to match the opportunity cost (i.e. the margins made on cross-border trading). Interest rates are hiked up, of course, but so too are hidden charges, 'one-off' fees, membership subscriptions, and so on. But because small-scale manufacturing operations are likely to be much less profitable in the short run, this phenomenon of temporary higher local cost of capital precludes any realistic possibility of obtaining and servicing a business loan. To appreciate the downside, one needs only to look at some of the border locations in the Balkans, where temporarily high local capital costs arising as a result of this 'crowding out' cross-border trading phenomenon permanently destroyed both long-standing production operations and new ventures.[159]

Thus seen, many of the supposed gains derived from the well-publicized small-scale cross-border trading ventures and tiny stores associated with microfinance are actually offset by the structural disadvantages and distortions thereafter frozen into the local economy. Import dependence is the main outcome, which is a long-term financial drain on any economy. Moreover, high profits and rents earned on large import operations typically become embedded, and so constitute a strong deterrent to the eventual (re-)establishment of local production operations.

Microfinance and social capital A common claim made in the microfinance literature relates to the potential for microfinance to help build and extend social capital in poor communities. Many analysts have routinely portrayed the Grameen Bank's famous solidarity circles as evidence of it successfully building and extending social capital and solidarity within the local community. Constant interpersonal interaction engendered through participation in solidarity circles, among other things, is said to construct the sort of bonding and bridging social capital described by Robert Putnam as the crucial 'glue' that holds local societies together.[160]

From another angle, however, the supposed links between microfinance and social capital are largely nothing more than an illusion. While even critics of microfinance accept that the Grameen Bank did indeed very successfully tap into pre-existing stocks of local social capital and local solidarity in order to ensure high repayment rates, as Rankin argues this fact does not validate the related claim that microfinance is also *constructing* social capital and local solidarity.[161] We need to recall, first of all, that by recasting individual survival as a function of individual entrepreneurial success (i.e. in a micro-enterprise), the bonds of solidarity, shared experience and trust that exist within poor communities are undermined. This is a truism. And as Colin Leys has argued,[162] history shows time and again that recasting community development and poverty reduction activities as commercial operations – the central operating principle of the 'new wave' microfinance model, remember – is likely to seriously reduce levels of local solidarity, interpersonal communication, volunteerism, trust-based interaction and goodwill. Accordingly, it would seem logical to expect that microfinance would be on a hiding to nothing in terms of being able to create productive forms of social capital.

On closer inspection, this is indeed the case. In fact, it is increasingly being recognized that social capital and local solidarity are more often *destroyed* by microfinance than encouraged.[163] Aminur Rahman was one of the first to get to grips with the reality here. Hiding behind high repayment rates at the Grameen Bank was a world of strong social pressure upon female members, and the routine ostracizing of defaulting borrowers.[164] In demonstrating that the 'shaming' of female loan delinquents is a routine practice in Bangladesh, Lamia Karim also shows that it greatly contributes to the crushing of any sense of local gender solidarity and community.[165] We should also recall that, thanks to commercialization pressures, the original innovation universally said to engender social capital within microfinance – solidarity circles – is now being abandoned in an increasing number of MFIs.

In Latin America, the individualism and competitiveness inherent in the microfinance model often clash with traditional values, especially those of the indigenous populations. Rather than creating so-called 'bridging social capital' – the sort of social capital that brings heterogeneous communities closer together – microfinance very often *widens* already wide cleavages. This is especially true with regard to the operation of 'new wave' microfinance, given that many senior employees in MFIs and their supporting organizations overwhelmingly tend to place a high value on their inclusion within the mainstream banking system and international banking circles, rather than on their closeness to poor clients. In Bolivia, for instance, the main MFIs work extensively in the communities of the Aymara and Quechua. But the MFIs also make sure that they remain both geographically and culturally as far apart from this client base as possible. Most documentation is in Spanish, or even English, for example, rather than in the two native languages of the country spoken by the Aymara and Quechua peoples. A further problem is caused by the preferred business location. As Holman very perceptively remarks,[166]

> the central offices or headquarters of major MFIs [in Bolivia], with few exceptions, are located in the wealthiest banking areas of downtown metropolises. The edifices are often fabulous colonial mansions or luxurious skyscrapers, paid for largely with the interests of the poor. By choosing these status symbols as headquarters, MFIs are proclaiming their legitimacy to the regular banking industry, but they are also creating an elitist divide between their ostentatious wealth and their clients' poverty. Aymara and Quechua people often feel like the downtown banking areas of the cities are culturally foreign and by locating MFIs' headquarters there, the industry is reinforcing a cultural separation from the majority of its clients.

MFIs in many parts of Africa have often been seen as taking advantage of those in poverty and have built up very little social capital. In increasingly microfinance-saturated Uganda, for example, commercialized MFIs have built up a very bad reputation in the local community. Local analysts Kaffu and Mutesasira report that[167] 'At the moment most MFIs are perceived to be "opportunistic and uncaring". Successful MFIs will have to position themselves to be seen as business partners interested in understanding customer needs and responding to them. MFIs will need to work hard towards shedding the image of being "vultures" preying on the clients' financial illiteracy.'

More widely, Hulme and Mosley reporting on their research into the impacts of several high-profile MFIs,[168] including Grameen Bank, found little evidence of class-based solidarity between borrowers, raising the obvious possibility as they saw it that 'the most successful borrowers [...] pursue individual and household strategies for advancement based on adopting the practices of the dominant social groups (such as purchasing land through distress sales, paying low wages, operating exploitative tied transactions), rather than practising solidarity with less-successful group members'.

Consider also the fact that everywhere the spectacular microfinance-driven rise of the informal sector has unequivocally resulted in the destruction of social capital (see above). As Davis vividly argues,[169] in today's increasingly unregulated business space an enterprise is forced to survive by adopting the 'low road' practices of the rapidly expanding informal sector. If it does not, it goes under. Solidarity is inevitably destroyed as the distorted business ethics and morals that emerge under such Hobbesian conditions gradually percolate into other enterprise structures (i.e. SMEs), institutions (i.e. government) and across all levels of society. All of this problematizes the microfinance industry's intimate association with the informal sector.

Conclusion

This chapter started by looking at the microfinance industry's own impact assessments. I noted that, for many obvious reasons, most impact assessments are seriously incomplete. I pointed out that two factors are ignored which are really quite fundamental to the likely net sustainable impact of microfinance in the community – displacement and client exit. The rest of the chapter was dedicated to a closer examination of the microfinance model in practice. By foregrounding the main 'triggers' that we know underpin sustainable local economic development, and assessing what impact microfinance has typically made within the context of each category, I was able to begin to explain why it is that the microfinance model largely frustrates development. I concluded not only that the presumed economic development and poverty reduction 'power' of the microfinance model is far less than the international development community has been led to believe to date, but that microfinance has been, and is, a major contributory factor in the destruction of the main positive economic and social development trajectories. In fact, I argue that microfinance constitutes a very powerful 'poverty trap'. In the next chapter, I will go on to explain why it is that the turn to 'new wave' microfinance in the 1990s has manifestly accelerated this already deleterious trajectory.

FIVE

Commercialization: the death of microfinance

'The organizations that develop in this institutional framework will become more efficient – but more efficient at making the society even more unproductive and the basic institutional structure even less conducive to productive activity.' Douglass C. North[1]

'Are [neoliberals] "true believers", driven by ideology and faith that free markets will cure underdevelopment, as is most often asserted, or do the ideas and theories frequently serve as an elaborate rationale to allow people to act on unfettered greed while still invoking an altruistic motive?' Naomi Klein[2]

This chapter will explore how the move to the commercialized 'new wave' microfinance in the 1990s has created huge problems for the microfinance model as development policy. I start by first looking back at one important example of financial sector commercialization in the UK financial sector. This example shows how and why it is a process that often goes spectacularly wrong for the poor, yet always seems to go quite well for the wealthy and powerful, a juxtaposition that is rarely coincidental. I then move to discuss the commercialization of microfinance that has taken place since the early 1990s. I find that the same dichotomy exists: enormous benefits for those promoting the commercialization of microfinance, but not for the poor and the poor communities at the receiving end. I end by discussing in a little more detail one of the most spectacular episodes of commercialization, that of Compartamos in Mexico. Perhaps more than any other recent example, this episode highlights the huge gulf between the original high-minded goals of microfinance and the current reality. Since Compartamos is positively viewed by many, and even described by some as the 'future of microfinance', it is important to see what lies ahead as we continue down the commercialization road.

Background to commercialization

Commercialization is intended to create more efficient and motivated organizations. In the case of a private company, the recommendation in theory is very clear. As Milton Friedman famously said, 'the sole and only purpose of a private business is to maximise profits'. The commercialization philosophy was central to the rush towards privatization pioneered in the UK in the 1980s, quickly spreading to virtually all countries thereafter. The assumption in this case was that the most efficient form of enterprise was possible only under full private ownership. All forms of non-private and/or collective ownership were defined as suboptimal.[3]

Much of the thinking behind commercialization and privatization is, however, mistaken. As Chang and Grabel show,[4] there is actually little empirical evidence to back up the widely made claims for the overwhelming superior performance at all times of privately owned companies. Publicly owned companies are often very efficient. In fact, under certain conditions, notably in post-1945 western Europe and in East Asia from the 1960s onwards, public companies were able to drive development forward far better than private companies and financial institutions impelled by purely private and short-term objectives. Note, too, that privatized companies very often do not register the productivity gains widely predicted for them as a result of the simple change from public to private ownership, notably in the UK's famous privatization experience.[5]

In the case of development-focused organizations, one might assume that things would be a little different. In the main, such organizations are deliberately established as non-profit organizations pursuing a developmental mandate, rather than profit. Neoliberals continue to assume, however, that such organizations should also be privatized or commercialized, so that they will also become 'more efficient' through (among other things) more incentivized management. Importantly, development organizations previously in receipt of regular public funding would be able to forgo it, perhaps by selling their services, thus helping to cut public spending. Even where privatization was not legally or politically possible, such as in healthcare or other services, if such organizations could nevertheless still be forced to act 'as if' they were private profit-driven bodies, then they would still register large efficiency gains.

In the majority of cases where public or non-profit organizations have been forced into a process of commercialization, however, the results have been almost universally negative, if not quite disastrous. In many cases, the organization was stripped of its original rationale and transformed into a vehicle whose operative goal was simply to generate profit, among other things in order to generate high salaries, bonuses and dividends for those having assumed control of it. Let me illustrate in a little more detail one important commercialization episode that encapsulates all that can go wrong with such a concept. Because it involves the commercialization of a financial organization quite similar in mandate and operations to an MFI, it is particularly useful in helping frame the discussion of commercialization to come.

Commercialization of the UK's building societies It would be difficult to find a better example where commercialization has delivered little for the vast majority but bestowed huge benefits upon 'insiders' and other close associates than the demutualization of the UK's long-established building societies (saver-owned financial institutions). The building societies originated in the late 1700s and the drive by the poor and their supporters to establish a source of low-cost housing finance. Owned by the savers, and with various checks and balances in place to ensure that they remained dedicated to their founding mission, success quickly followed. By the early 1900s, the UK's building societies had become the dominant force in housing finance, and a very important player in the mobilization of savings, insurance and other services of value to the poor and working classes.

The UK government's ideology in the 1980s, however, held that the building societies would operate more efficiently if they were taken out of mutual ownership and restructured into private commercial banks. This would inject more profit-driven practices and business savvy into what were until then very conservative lending and saving institutions. With significant support from senior managers eyeing much larger salaries if demutualization went ahead, and egged on by a new class of so-called 'carpetbagger' members eyeing up the profits windfall to be made from a quick sale of the shares to be distributed to existing saver-members, one by one the large building societies were demutualized and commercialized. Initially, at least, their new-found commercial freedoms saw them prosper in financial and reputational terms. Looking back now, however, the whole episode of commercialization was an economic and social disaster. It was not just a major setback for the UK economy, but a major blow for the poor communities wherein such organizations had arisen many years ago.

As intended, demutualization and the creation of a shareholder-owned private bank came with the unfettered freedom, as well as the obligation, to pursue maximum profit. This would generate further competition in the sector and so more efficiency and a better service to clients. Higher dividends would then ensue too. The former members having received their allocation of free shares would, of course, be very much better off. So far, so good.

The stage was actually being set, however, for a multitude of commercialization-driven sins. As widely predicted, demutualization gave the new private banks the freedom for senior managers to hike up their own salaries and bonuses, which they predictably did right away. The banks then began to move into high-profit but much riskier projects and speculative activities. This move initially hiked up profits, and so ensured high dividend payments for the new owners. It also conveniently provided 'cover' for even higher salaries and bonuses for senior managers. Meanwhile, in spite of supposedly more competition in the sector, but with hungry shareholders to feed and senior managers' inflated salaries and bonuses to meet too, the prices on many products and services gradually began to go up in real terms. This was in contravention of the market-based justification for demutualization paraded before the members and the general public in the time leading up to the act itself. Former members thus had to balance the immediate gain represented by the free shares received on demutualization against the longer-run higher cost of mortgages and other services. Of course, for new customers there was just a downside (higher prices), especially first-time homebuyers finding the cost of a mortgage higher than before.

The tragedy of commercialization finally peaked with the collapse and takeover of virtually all of the main building societies that had been established from the late eighteenth century onwards. These institutions had accumulated many years of solid service to the community, and particularly to poor members seeking to purchase their own home. Their downfall was related to risky investments designed to hike up profits at any cost. In a matter of years, a number of long-established institutions providing real benefit to the poor were destroyed. The global financial crisis that began in 2008 then finally put paid to the few remaining demutualized building societies, not one of which managed to survive as an independent entity. For example, long the world's largest building society, the northern-England-based Halifax Building Society succumbed to the financial crisis in a most dramatic way. After its demutualization the decision was taken to enter into a number of takeovers and a merger that took it into areas of business it had little prior knowledge of. It jumped into many risky and speculative projects, especially speculation on commercial property, which all ended up making massive losses as the global economy began to deteriorate. Now known as HBOS, it eventually had to be rescued from its own managers by the British government, and it was handed over for virtually nothing to one of its main banking rivals. Contrast this embarrassing fate with that of the building societies that in the 1990s chose to remain as mutual saver-owned institutions, such as the Nationwide Building Society. Relying on traditional safe practices of retail deposits, minimal use of wholesale funds and almost no contact with exotic instruments like derivatives, all of the old building societies managed to survive the global financial crisis largely intact.

Consider now a little more of the shocking detail surrounding the most high-profile commercialization disaster, that of the Northern Rock Building Society in the north of England. Probably the best account of this tragicomic episode has been provided by Larry Elliot and Dan Atkinson, in their brilliant 2008 book *The Gods that Failed* (which I will mainly draw upon now). Northern Rock was the Newcastle-based building society that in 1997 demutualized and converted into a 'flashy, stop-at-nothing' bank.[6] Under the guidance of its young dynamic managing director, it grew rapidly into one of the major lenders in the housing market. Spectacular growth of 20 per cent per year was achieved, however, only by taking at least two huge risks. First, in the absence of sufficient savings from clients, Northern Rock began to use large amounts (eventually as much as 80 per cent) of short-term money-market funding to expand its property mortgage portfolio. Second, Northern Rock became infamous for its willingness to work with the riskiest clients, on the basis that, with apparently permanently rising property prices and accompanying economic prosperity, such clients could eventually float off their initial debt and repay successfully. But even in the case of default, rising house prices should still see the bank getting its money back through the quick sale of repossessed property.

As long predicted, the property market finally took a downward turn in 2006/07, however, and defaults started edging up. When the global economy began to head in a seriously downward direction at the end of 2007, all short-term funds were immediately cut off. With no alternative arrangements in place, Northern Rock plunged into the crisis its detractors had long said was inevitable. Savers quickly became aware that Northern Rock was unable to obtain further funding on the money markets. This started the first full-blown run on a British bank since 1866. Northern Rock was immediately taken into public ownership. A £24 billion loan from the government, plus further guarantees, was provided to stabilize the newly nationalized bank. With UK government support, new management and a complete change of operating philosophy, Northern Rock was able to survive. All told, as Elliot and Atkinson conclude, demutualization and the aggressive commercialization set in motion as a result have been hugely damaging to the UK economy. Northern Rock was emblematic of the debt-laden, short-termist and ultimately supremely destructive financial system that had resulted in the UK thanks to the massive 1980s drive for greater commercialization.

An important lesson from Northern Rock needs to be emphasized in the specific context of our discussion of commercialized microfinance. The commercialization process quite quickly destroyed the institution's long-standing goal of providing quality low-cost services to members. The senior management team replaced this historic 'mission' with a new central goal and a new subsidiary goal: first, maximize short-run profit, thereby to, second, maximize (or at least justify) the extremely generous and rising financial rewards accruing to those same senior managers. In addition, a transparently false public narrative was constructed to shield the shareholders and wider public from what was actually going on. Many who should have known better bought into the idea that Northern Rock was genuinely aiming to serve the public, even as it engaged in an increasingly bizarre series of financial acrobatics to maximize short-term profit, and as senior managers hiked up their financial rewards to spectacular heights. Many financial analysts went along with the deception, for no other reason than it correlated with their own ideologically driven view that the financial sector (always) needed to be liberalized. In short, those seeking personal enrichment strongly favour commercialization as the required 'cover' to achieve this goal. But the process of commercialization opens the door to powerful impulses leading to 'mission drift', institutional chaos and even an institution's eventual demise.

The gathering storm

Let us now return to the specific issue of microfinance commercialization. As noted, the commercialization drive taking place in the late 1980s began to produce a growing number of financially self-sustaining MFIs around the globe. The ambition and intent were that such examples would and should be rapidly multiplied across the globe. Progress has been slow, however, and there are still relatively few fully self-financing MFIs in operation around the world (see Chapter 3). Nonetheless, commercialization and financial self-sustainability remain the ultimate goals of the microfinance industry and the wider international development community. It is clear that 'new wave' MFIs are already beginning to dominate the microfinance industry. Accordingly, we need to examine what the future holds for the poor once this global scenario transpires. So what are the results in those localities, regions and countries that have been touched the most by commercialized 'new wave' microfinance?

Bolivia's excellent adventure Long one of Latin America's poorest countries, Bolivia is also the Latin American country where the 'new wave' commercialization model has made the most rapid inroads. The microfinance sector in Bolivia has been described as 'one of the jewels in the crown of microenterprise finance',[7] as well as the world's most important example of the commercialization of microfinance. By the late 1990s Bolivia enjoyed an extensive raft of strongly commercialized MFIs. Bolivia is also home to one of the pioneering examples of a commercialized MFI – BancoSol. If it is at all possible for any one country to demonstrate the far-reaching poverty-reducing and development benefits of commercialized microfinance, then it should be Bolivia. In practice, however, other than simply delivering 'more microfinance', the commercialization-driven expansion of microfinance in Bolivia has produced pretty much the opposite of what was originally promised by the microfinance industry.

First, it is almost impossible to find any meaningful correlation between the quite dramatic expansion of microfinance in Bolivia since the late 1980s and positive changes in the level of poverty and development. As Vik notes,[8] the emphasis in Bolivia is almost exclusively upon the performance of the individual MFI, and the performance indicators used often conceal (perhaps deliberately) the lack of impact on poverty. Some researchers, notably microfinance specialist Paul Mosley,[9] *do* claim to have found evidence that poverty reduction gains through microfinance took place from the late 1990s onwards. But it was also admitted that much of the evidence for this understanding was unreliable. For one thing, researchers were unable, or perhaps unwilling, to factor in the issue of 'drop-outs' and failed clients, the numbers of which began to rise quite dramatically in the late 1990s.[10] If these unfortunate individuals are eventually dumped into deeper poverty, as I argued in Chapter 4 is typically the case, and as much evidence from Bolivia confirms,[11] then the supposed 'gains' registered from microfinance need to be significantly adjusted downwards. At any rate, the fact is that it is widely agreed that until the advent of the Morales government in 2006, there had been more than two decades of almost *no* progress in reducing the level of income-based poverty in Bolivia. Real GDP per capita was actually lower in 2006 than in the late 1970s, and a massive 64 per cent of the population were living below the poverty line in 2006.[12]

So, if there exists in Bolivia a robust correlation between sustainable poverty reduction and a local financial system effectively dominated since the early 1990s by the provision of commercialized microfinance, it remains an extremely well-hidden one. In fact, as the new Morales government very much seems to think is the case, there is indeed a correlation between microfinance and poverty; but they are of the belief that it is one where microfinance *exacerbates* poverty, not resolves it (see next point).

Second, as previously discussed, it matters greatly not just that finance is available to enterprises, but also to *which* enterprises. When not simply disbursing consumption loans, the overwhelming predilection of Bolivia's MFIs to date has been to work only with the very simplest informal microenterprises, and to eschew contact with more sustainable enterprise projects. The longer-term result of this commercialization-driven preference is that it has gravely undermined the modest light industry and agricultural production and processing base that Bolivia had painfully built up from the 1950s through to the 1970s.[13] Dazzled by high repayment rates and the large profits enjoyed by Bolivia's MFIs, the international development community and the microfinance industry remained oblivious to the fact that Bolivia's light industrial and agricultural structures were very effectively being starved of capital on appropriate terms and maturities, and so were gradually disintegrating. These valuable foundations were steadily replaced by a microfinance-induced bazaar economy, alongside the continuation of primitive subsistence agriculture for the majority of

Bolivians working the land. In short, commercialized microfinance appears to have *undermined* the long-term fight against poverty and underdevelopment in Bolivia.[14]

Third, thanks to the very rapid profit-driven expansion in the supply of microfinance in the late 1990s, Bolivia was plunged into an economic crisis. Initially, as in all speculative episodes, the profit-driven overselling of microfinance created an atmosphere of progress and euphoria. For sure, the poor generally had more money to spend on consumption goods thanks to microfinance, and perhaps also a little could go into income-generating projects, or saved in order to make the first couple of repayments. Even though it was well known that many poor individuals were accessing multiple loans from different MFIs,[15] many simply seeking to repay their existing microloan(s), the implications of this trend were largely ignored. 'New wave' microfinance advocates were particularly pleased with the progress apparently being made thanks to Bolivia's almost total adoption of their recommendations. Inevitably, however, the turn-around came. Large numbers of poor borrowers began to find they could no longer repay their higher debt levels, and default rates began to rise rapidly.

By 2000 the entire financial sector in Bolivia had plunged into crisis. Domestic investment began to decline alarmingly. MFIs concentrating on high-profit consumer microloans were particularly hard hit. Bolivia's microfinance sector, and the wider financial sector, began to reel. Between 1999 and 2000 two of the largest MFIs, BancoSol and Prodem, lost 25 and 45 per cent of their clients respectively. With almost no progress to show in terms of sustainably reducing poverty in what was Latin America's showcase for microfinance, the Bolivian economy and society then began to buckle under the pressure of the immediate withdrawal of the supply of microloans. Even the most determined supporters of commercialization were left struggling to present an explanation as to why the 'new wave' commercialization model had imploded in such a destructive manner.[16]

Since the microfinance collapse of the late 1990s and early 2000s, things have recovered somewhat. One major result linked to the overall failure of microfinance, however – both its earlier inability to address poverty and promote sustainable development, and then its eventual crisis – was that it finally brought to a head the growing popular disenchantment with neoliberal policies. This eventually resulted in a vote for radical change in the 2005 election, elevating to power the leftist Evo Morales. To those involved in the microfinance sector in Bolivia, as well as for neoliberals in the country and everywhere else, this was seen as a major blow.[17] While not completely abandoning commercialized microfinance – at least not yet – the Morales government has nevertheless very definitely edged it aside as it tries to address high poverty in Bolivia. A new Bolivian constitution passed in early 2009 implicitly repudiates many of the traditional methodologies and programmatic outcomes of microfinance, such as simple petty trade-based microenterprises, and stresses instead the urgent need to rebase Bolivia's future upon restarting local production and the promotion of sustainable agricultural activities.

Two new programmes are seen as important in moving away from the negative outcomes of microfinance experienced in the two decades before the Morales government. First, steps were quickly taken to create a state development bank for SMEs – the Banco de Desarrollo Productivo (BDP). Among other things, the BDP is designed to begin to pilot the typical local economy in Bolivia away from its reliance upon simple trade-based activities and unproductive subsistence farming, and towards a much greater focus on supporting meaningfully scaled-up industrial and agricultural production-based activities. One of the major concerns in Bolivia, as noted above, was the large and growing percentage of Bolivia's savings (including large remittance income flows) being recycled into very simple microenterprise activities, mainly petty trade-based activities.[18] Those behind the establishment of the BDP saw no way to deal with poverty in Bolivia if there was no attempt to directly address this debilitating trend.[19] Microfinance in Bolivia effectively constituted a 'poverty trap', monopolizing valuable funds that could otherwise have been offered to the most growth-oriented enterprises. The BDP aims to break Bolivia out of this microfinance-driven 'poverty trap', by supporting instead the establishment of an enterprise sector based on at least some modest levels of technology, innovation, non-local market penetration, higher-value-added operations, scale economies, and so on. One might describe the BDP as fully compatible with successful East Asian development banking models, as well as the successful Brazilian development banking model, and so a first step in the right direction.

Alongside the BDP, a second important programme introduced by the new Morales government involved the increasingly popular conditional cash transfer (CCT), entitling the very poor to a small cash sum on condition that they take their children for health check-ups or ensure that they go to school regularly, for example (see Chapter 7). CCTs are slated to help the very poorest maintain a minimum level of consumption. CCTs will also address the huge issue of inequality in Bolivia, since they represent an elemental form of wealth redistribution. Finally, and equally importantly, it is also hoped that CCTs can replace the poor's debilitating dependence upon ultra-expensive consumption loans provided by some of the newest and most aggressive MFIs.

Overall, Bolivia's more-than-twenty-year experiment with commercialized microfinance has thrown up almost no independently verifiable evidence to show that it has achieved anything positive. On the contrary, with poverty levels rising and industrial and agricultural disintegration accelerating during microfinance's rise to ubiquity, and then a commercialization-induced 'oversupply' crisis the almost inevitable consequence, the massive increase in the supply of microfinance appears to have done far more damage than it has done good. The result is that the microfinance industry has been forced on to the back foot. Arguing that much of the most recent damage was caused by an influx of new MFIs serving the consumer loans sector, including one very large MFI (Acceso FFP) that was a subsidiary of a large private financial company based in Chile, key advocates in the microfinance industry essentially had to condemn the increased competition and lower interest rates that resulted.[20] Yet these are two of the principal *benefits* most often claimed for the 'new wave' microfinance model, now being portrayed as the villains of the piece. This highlights the desperate effort by 'new wave' microfinance advocates to try to pin the blame for an oversupply-related crisis on anything but the real culprit itself – commercialization. (It also doesn't help their case to find that the private microfinance sector in Bolivia is once more coming under serious pressure thanks to the commercialization-driven oversupply phenomenon – see below.) In the same vein, the microfinance industry cannot credibly explain why it is that almost total microfinance saturation in Bolivia over the last twenty years or so has produced no palpable impact on poverty. This fact also starkly contrasts with the rapid reduction in poverty brought about by a number of successful programme interventions undertaken by the new Morales government from 2006 onwards,[21] including its establishment of a sizeable number of growth-oriented SMEs and cooperatives.

Who wants to be a 'microfinance millionaire'? One rather obvious outcome of the commercialization trajectory in microfinance has been the rise of a group of 'microfinance millionaires'. Though his subsequent fame and public speaking and consulting services have made him a wealthy and influential individual, Muhammad Yunus is also noted for having extracted little personal financial reward directly from the Grameen Bank he founded. Other high-profile individuals in the microfinance movement are much less grounded in altruism, however. Many private individuals in at the founding of what was to become a major MFI have subsequently and very opportunistically moved to convert their original position as an employee into stratospheric personal wealth. More importantly, the lure of actually becoming a member of this exalted club has itself become a major 'feedback' driver behind the increasing commercialization of microfinance.

The first objection to this trend is a general one. Profiting so egregiously from the suffering of poor individuals is morally and ethically wrong. In the aftermath of such catastrophic misbehaviour on Wall Street in recent years, many would surely now agree. Of course, some hold that big business and savvy entrepreneurs can make healthy profits in poor communities while greatly benefiting the poor. This is a perennially powerful 'win-win' idea that has not gone away – which would be fine, if it were true. Unfortunately, the idea was given renewed legitimacy by C. K. Prahalad, the author of the 2004 best-selling book *The Fortune at the Bottom of the Pyramid: Eradicating Poverty Through Profits*.[22] Because Prahalad's book supposedly provided renewed moral and economic justification for the activities of many entrepreneurs and multinational corporations (MNCs) in developing countries, it became extremely popular in politics, business and international development policy circles. Even a cursory inspection, however, shows that most of Prahalad's signature ideas fall down.[23] And as I point out in the next section, Prahalad's idea that 'inclusive' supply chains will greatly benefit the poor is also usually quite mistaken. In fact, what seems to be happening is that, in the name of advancing their cause, the poor are yet again being taken advantage of. As noted Indian agricultural economist Devinder Sharma indignantly describes it,[24]

> There can be no better business opportunity than starting a
> micro-finance institution with assured returns and 100 per cent loan

recovery. You can even think of trading on the stock exchange after a couple of years. And still more importantly, you can hold your head high and claim that you are helping the poor to come out of the poverty trap. You don't have to feel ashamed and morally guilty. The elite in the society have knowingly (or unknowingly) given you a license to loot.

Moreover, and my second point here, in truth the 'microfinance millionaires' are actually very bad for sustainable local economic development. From a moral standpoint, of course, it is for the individual to decide whether or not they are 'repulsed by the idea of MFIs making profits from low-income people'.[25] But if the end result of 'making profits from low-income people' is that such low-income people are actually made much worse off, then it becomes an economic development and equality issue, and it ceases to be (simply) a moral or ethical issue. The problem is that the lure of such huge financial rewards *inevitably* distorts and misdirects the institutional response to poverty, especially rural poverty. This becomes clear if we refer once more to the classic 'dualistic' financial structures found in many developing countries, structures that are almost wholly antagonistic to development and poverty reduction. Financial sector 'dualism' did not arise to help the poor – it actually undermined their attempts to escape poverty – but primarily to construct a new financial elite through exploiting the poor. 'New wave' microfinance and the inevitable outgrowth of 'microfinance millionaires' are simply 'dualistic' financial structures under a different name.

In addition, third, we also need to remember that entrepreneurship in the microfinance sector is quite different from conventional productive entrepreneurship. Entrepreneurship associated with the 'microfinance millionaire' approach is typically founded on the risk incurred and funds provided not by the entrepreneur hoping to make his or her fortune, but by someone else – that is, by the international donor community, the local government and various others. It is wrong that, if the MFI succeeds in passing through the very risky start-up stage thanks to crucial support from public and other external bodies, the future 'microfinance millionaires' can then take over and radically restructure the venture in order to benefit personally from thereon in. But if the MFI fails as it goes through this risky initial phase, those same individuals simply lose their job and walk away otherwise unharmed, leaving the public bodies (and the general population, through taxation) to absorb any losses. In other words, we are not talking about conventional productive entrepreneurship here, but an unethical and one-sided Wall Street-style 'accumulation by dispossession' process. The future 'microfinance millionaires' can appropriate all future profits in an MFI, but if there are any losses then, no problem, they are simply socialized.

Microfinance-led 'inclusive' supply chains: who is really meant to benefit? A new model that has emerged in international development circles in recent years sees the poor as an opportunity, rather than a responsibility or burden. One of the main ways that this new model ostensibly seeks to help the poor is through their inclusion in subcontracting arrangements involving national companies and, preferably, MNCs.[26] C. K. Prahalad's 'bottom of the pyramid' idea, just noted above, has been very influential in promoting the idea of 'inclusive' supply chains. Some of the international development agencies have also been active in this field, notably UNDP.[27] Consider also that one of the main costs that businesses typically incur when attempting to expand into a new market is the setting up of a functioning supply chain. Especially in developing countries, the opportunity for profit may be possible only if the supply chain is established on the lowest possible cost basis. One way that businesses in developing countries have attempted to reduce the financial outlay and risk involved in constructing a supply chain is to pass on the costs and risks to other weaker parties in the supply chain (that is, the poor). Technically speaking, this is nothing more than efficient supply chain management.[28]

A growing trend here is to use microfinance in order to construct an 'inclusive' distribution chain. Large national companies and MNCs working in developing countries are now being encouraged to use microfinance as a way of inserting individual microenterprises into their distribution chains. This is done in order to greatly reduce the costs and risks to the large company or MNC. The technique is generally as follows.

The large company starts by identifying a group of poor individuals in the country in question who might wish to become part of their distribution chain. Members of this group of poor individuals are then helped to contact a local MFI and to obtain a microloan, which they can use to advance-purchase some item to be sold or simple machine to be used. The large company often provides some other inputs to the new distribution chain members, such as training, storage, billing services, and so on. Importantly, the fiction is created that such microenterprises are independent businesses, rather than – which is actually the case – an integral component in a top-down-driven distribution chain with almost no ability to do any other business outside of the supply chain. In fact, some distribution chain agreements specifically forbid the microenterprise undertaking business with any other party. This fiction of independence is generally needed for two reasons. First, to ensure access to a microloan, which might be refused if it became clear that the microenterprise was actually an integral part of a formal/legal distribution chain, and not an independent microenterprise at all. Second, there are important tax advantages independent microenterprises can take advantage of that formal/legal distribution chain participants cannot, principally opportunities for tax avoidance. Overall, the attraction of such a distribution chain arrangement is clear: the large company can establish and operate a distribution chain at a greatly reduced cost and risk, while the poor are offered the opportunity to become 'independent' microenterprises right from the start. A 'win-win' situation surely?

Well, this is the theory anyway. But it seems that in most cases serious long-term problems arise which swamp most of the short-term benefits. One very central problem that arises is that in order to maximize sales and profits, the large company typically seeks to quickly establish as large a number of microenterprise partners as possible. While this maximizes sales of the final good being distributed, it also rapidly diminishes the local market share held by each individual microenterprise. This in turn quickly forces the microenterprise into a situation of bare survival. Of course, what we are describing here is yet another example of the 'fallacy of composition' problem raised earlier. In developed countries, as I noted in Chapter 4, the issue of sales territory is a crucial issue subject to very precise legal undertakings regarding its size, advertising commitment, rules for those transgressing into someone else's sales territory, and so on. But in developing countries it seems that large companies are extremely reluctant to agree to such conditions. The result is that, through no fault of their own, the poor involved in the distribution chain mostly end up in great difficulty later on.

Recall once more the example raised in Chapter 4 of the Grameen-Phone 'social business'. Suspicions arose early on that the business model was actually fundamentally flawed, and that the intentions behind it were not what the general public and international development community were being sold. As we saw, although the very first wave of telephone ladies did fairly well from their microenterprises, all those coming later did not do well at all, because by then – as could have been expected – the local market had reached its upper limit. Rather than generate new customers, the telephone ladies became engaged in a desperate struggle to grab customers from each other, with the result that the poverty-reducing benefits disappeared for most involved. Suspicions were raised further when a dispute broke out between Telenor and Grameen Telecom. Partly because the entire project was so hugely profitable, Telenor decided to renege on an initial deal it had apparently agreed to with Muhammad Yunus back in the late 1990s, which was to pass on free of charge its 62 per cent holding in GrameenPhone over to the non-profit Grameen Telecom. The idea was that the Grameen telephone ladies would then benefit as shareholders in a business that they had clearly had a major hand in setting up and running. This was easier said than done. Part of the problem was that the initial deal with Telenor was made when it (Telenor) was under full public ownership. In the meantime, the group was part privatized and its new private profit-seeking majority shareholders were now very reluctant to give away the 'diamond' in its portfolio. A deal was finally reached in late 2009, prior to the announcement that an IPO of GrameenPhone was planned for October 2009, allowing Telenor to capitalize on its ownership stake when it chooses to do so. These delays and machinations help to illuminate the real and conflicting motivations that too often lie behind projects ostensibly meant to serve a social purpose but which, coincidentally we are inevitably told, generate a huge amount of value to the MNCs and large companies taking part.[29]

Similar distribution chain problems to GrameenPhone's already seem to be emerging in the latest social business case involving Grameen Bank, this time with the French company Danone. In 2006 Grameen Bank and Danone formed Grameen Danone Foods Ltd (GDFL), formally one of the first multinational social businesses. Established with a fifty-fifty ownership structure, GDFL was designed to manufacture and distribute a yogurt product (*Shakti doi*), which Danone claims has a number of health benefits as well as nutritional content. Danone put $500,000 of its own money into GDFL, with the rest coming from the Grameen Bank. According to Ghalib and Hossain,[30] the original deal is that Danone expects only its initial capital to be returned after three years, and any profit made in future is to be reinvested back into GDFL, less a 1 per cent dividend to its shareholders. As with most initiatives concerning Grameen, the project was an instant media sensation.[31]

As in the case of GrameenPhone, however, a little later on it became clear that the saleswomen were going to benefit far less than they had initially been led to believe. What had happened? First, around 1,600 saleswomen were initially located to sell the yogurt locally, with each saleswoman averaging sales of around sixty to seventy pots per day. Partly thanks to a rise in milk prices, however, but partly also thanks to further growth in the number of saleswomen and, initially, a weak product (not sweet enough), average sales and earnings per seller soon began to decline. Many of the saleswomen gave up the business because servicing the original microloan became much harder on such low turnover, which in turn created some repayment problems. The initial period of well-publicized excitement and intense PR activity soon began to give way to growing anger and disillusion among many saleswomen in the distribution chain.[32]

Another problem was that low demand in rural areas precipitated a decision to produce a much larger pot of yogurt to be sold at a higher price, and mainly to much richer individuals resident in the capital city, Dhaka. There is now a possibility that the urban community will become the main market, with a gradually declining percentage of product routed back to the rural communities to be sold at lower prices. Moreover, we must remember that such cross-subsidization is a useful pro-poor concept, but experience from many parts shows that it all too often gets phased out at some future stage as commercialization pressures come to the fore.

We also need to highlight the extent to which Danone has been able to build up, very cheaply and almost risk-free, a major distribution and 'visibility' platform for its future dairy product lines planned for Bangladesh. As an entry strategy, the tie-up with Grameen has been very useful indeed. But, we must ask, is it right that Grameen should basically establish an MNC in a poor country that otherwise has plenty of dairy organizations capable of servicing local demand? In addition, Bangladesh itself and neighbouring countries are not inexperienced in building large-scale organizational structures, such as farmer-owned dairy cooperatives, that can work very well for the poor as a poverty reduction tool. India's experience with milk cooperatives supported through 'Operation Flood' is the most obvious example of the enormous potential to reduce poverty and promote sustainable development through collective action, thanks to pro-active government support helping small dairy farmers to form their own cooperatives and to thereafter expand.[33] Might it not be the case, then, that Grameen is being used as the 'Trojan horse' to allow Danone to enter a market that would not otherwise take kindly to its products? And might not the existence of the high-profile 'social business' option displace organizational alternatives, such as coopera-tives, that would be far better, as in India, in terms of promoting sustainable poverty reduction?

Fourth, it is of real concern to many that the health benefits claimed for *Shakti doi* yogurt remain to be definitively proven by anyone outside of GDFL. This worry arises because, in Europe, Danone is struggling to defend itself against widespread claims that it has been cynically inventing health benefits for one of its main product lines (a probiotic milk drink), a strategy apparently adopted as part of an aggressive effort to build market share at all costs.[34] What might Danone's borderline-legal actions in Europe suggest in terms of the company's motives in establishing its social business with Grameen Bank in Bangladesh?

On the face of it, the GDFL experiment in Bangladesh seems like another example of a somewhat cynical business strategy increasingly being adopted by MNCs in developing countries, one that sanctions the use of microfinance to build a distribution chain that is by far of most benefit to the MNC. The MNC takes almost no risk and invests a tiny amount of capital. The risk and investment required to build the distribution chain are largely taken on by the poor participants invited into the project, using a microloan. Because the project is very neatly marketed as 'of benefit to the poor', a number of other important benefits arise for the MNC. The business attracts good publicity in the country, high-level contacts with government are forged, and the MNC is given significant freedom to conduct busi-ness transactions just as it wishes. Most importantly, the MNC gains entry into a country and can begin to build up its market presence and visibility alongside the immediate project. Meanwhile, the poor directly involved appear to gain very little in comparison with the MNC, and probably would have been better off had they been helped to embark upon establishing a cooperative instead. The wider local and national community eventually suffers too, losing an important element of local demand thanks to the eventual profit, dividend and management fee repatriation to the rich Western countries.

Rather than functioning as a genuine poverty reduction opportunity for the poor, Muhammad Yunus's 'social business' concept is a Janus-faced innovation. Certainly, it is a brilliant new opportunity for MNCs everywhere. The sustainable poverty reduction side, however, is often largely nothing more than good PR. Even if malice aforethought is not proved, it still remains the case that much of the optimism generated with regard to highly commercialized microfinance-driven distribution chains and 'social businesses' would appear to be very seriously misplaced.

The growing need to enforce fairness and transparency in microfinance One of the abiding myths of microfinance holds that a commercialized MFI will remain true to its founding mission to serve the poor. Microfinance is about poverty reduction, and, so the argument runs, however this objective is reached, it still remains the objective of an MFI no matter what happens to its organizational structure. Some even go so far as to claim that selflessly serving the poor is 'in the DNA of microfinance'.[35]

The growing commercialization of microfinance, however, has led to this overly optimistic scenario coming under serious review. In fact, there is a growing realization that converting MFIs into straightforward profit-seeking businesses inevitably means that there is always a loss, *often a complete loss*, of the original social mission. Above all, in the absence of strong regulations and controls, and with so much prior encouragement to deploy Wall Street-style methodologies and tactics, it seems that too many profit-seeking commercialized MFIs are all too often willing to hoodwink and abuse their poor clients.

As we will see below, the case of Compartamos has stimulated a flurry of initiatives designed to rein in the worst practices of MFIs. But even before this high-profile example hit the headlines, many individuals within the microfinance industry had taken steps to try to ensure that microfinance would not become an abuse of the poor, and that MFIs would not simply transmute into a 'feel-good' version of the sort of 'doorstep lending' organizations found in the developed countries. One such body formed to try to prevent abuse of the poor clients is the 'Alliance for Fair Microfinance'. Established in 2007 by a group of high-profile microfinance practitioners, including Malcolm Harper, one of the leading lights in the microfinance field for many years, the Alliance aims to promote client interests in an industry that is rapidly becoming the preserve of hard-nosed professional managers and investors. The Alliance quickly garnered an impressive roster of practitioner-members alongside its high-profile founder-members. It states:[36] 'In microfinance today, growing numbers of practitioners are relying on practices that would be considered illegal or unethical in mature financial markets – untrue information, unlawful repossession, and usurious interest rates in particular. Lack of adequate customer protection in emerging markets thus easily opens the door to exploitation of poor people.'

There is also 'MicroFinance Transparency', a body formed as a direct response to the Compartamos affair. Founded by Muhammad Yunus and Chuck Waterfield, a long-standing microfinance adviser, MicroFinance Transparency describes itself as a global initiative seeking fair and transparent pricing in microfinance. The justification for Yunus's involvement was, in his own words that, 'Microfinance emerged as a struggle against loan sharks, so we don't want to see new loan sharks created in the name of microcredit.'[37] Waterfield has called the new body 'an industry-based truth-in-lending effort'. Very quickly the organization has put together a long list of supporters, and financial support was quick to arrive from many international development bodies in order to spread their message. By their own estimates nearly 60 per cent of the world's microfinance clients are now covered by their campaign.[38]

Another upshot of the Compartamos affair was the establishment by a self-selected group of senior microfinance advocates of a code of conduct for the microfinance industry. The so-called 'Pocantico Declaration', named after the conference centre in New York in which it was drafted, is essentially an attempt to save the microfinance industry's reputation in the face of a growing realization that the commercialization of microfinance has effectively subverted its original purpose. An initiative of Deutsche Bank, the Boulder Institute and CGAP, the Pocantico Declaration is designed to re-establish the poverty reduction credibility of the microfinance industry within the international development community (Compartamos's massively successful IPO more than established its credibility in the hard-nosed world of the international financial community).

Seen from the outside, it is telling that even long-time microfinance advocates feel they had better move fast to rein in the burgeoning unethical activities of the 'new wave' commercialized MFI sector. This is an obvious sign that things are not working out as the microfinance industry promised they would. Moreover, while probably mainly well meaning in intent, it remains to be seen what these campaigns, organizations and uplifting statements can actually achieve. One possibility is that such campaigns might even end up being manipulated and circumscribed by those they are designed to regulate. For example, ACCIÓN, probably the most important non-state body promoting the commercialized 'new wave' microfinance model, announced in April 2008 a new 'Campaign for Client Protection'. It maintains that this campaign is about establishing what amounts to a microfinance Hippocratic oath. It is not beyond the bounds of possibility, however, that such an initiative might actually be something else; a somewhat cynical attempt to shape, or put a limit on, the unfolding consumer protection measures directed at commercialized microfinance (e.g. interest rate caps). Such a spoiling tactic is not without precedent.[39]

All told, the deliberate injection of Wall Street's values and methodologies into microfinance in the 1980s, not least by those (such as ACCIÓN) now taking steps to supposedly curtail otherwise entirely predictable Wall Street-style developments, has created a financial juggernaut that has now taken on a life of its own. Given this multibillion-dollar Wall Street-style industry, with huge wealth to be made by those who can gravitate into key management and/or ownership positions in an MFI, as well as in the constellation of support services dependent upon commercialized MFIs (research, advisory, evaluation, etc.), changing course now will surely be determinedly resisted.

And yet another microfinance crisis emerges in Andhra Pradesh In recent years India has made enormous progress in expanding the supply of microfinance. From the 1990s onwards, one state stood out as having achieved almost total saturation with microfinance – the state of Andhra Pradesh. As Ghate recounts,[40] Andhra Pradesh became known in the 1990s as the 'Mecca' of microfinance in India. It was the HQ for the four largest MFIs and the location for more than half of the self-help groups (SHGs) linked to banks and channelling bank finance down as microloans to SHG members. With the blessing of the authorities, and very much as per the commercialization model, large numbers of private business people also began to jump into the field of microfinance. Finally, also caught up in the general excitement surrounding microfinance was Andhra Pradesh's state-owned SHG – Velugu – which was also encouraged to rapidly expand. The result, according to Ghate once more,[41] was that '92 per cent of poor households in AP had already been covered [by Velugu] by March

2005 [and it was aimed] to cover the rest by the end of 2005'. Many in the microfinance industry, and in the Andhra Pradesh and Indian governments, were keenly anticipating the huge poverty reduction and development benefits that would flow from this superabundance of microfinance.

Instead of generalized progress, however, in early 2006 the microfinance sector was plunged into crisis. The state government of Andhra Pradesh raided and temporarily closed down the offices functioning in one district (Krishna), setting off a shock wave right across India. The raid was an immediate response to a rapidly growing number of complaints about usurious interest rates and highly commercialized MFIs 'hard-selling' microloans to poor individuals with almost no realistic way of repaying (at least not at the interest rates that they had originally, and perhaps unwisely, agreed to). A further aggravating background factor was the rapidly accelerating number of suicides, which most studies relate to rising farmer debt. In just three months in 2004 (May–July), for example, more than four hundred farmers committed suicide in Andhra Pradesh, and the numbers were rising fast.

The Andhra Pradesh microfinance crisis caused many analysts to question the previously thought immutable notion that 'more microfinance equals more development', and also to warn about the huge build-up of micro-debt elsewhere in India.[42] It was bad enough that microfinance had apparently done little to counter the increase in rural poverty and agricultural sector distress experienced in Andhra Pradesh in the run-up to the crisis in 2006. But it was obviously discomforting for many in the microfinance industry to find, yet again, that the microfinance sector was creating serious economic and social distress in precisely a region where it had achieved almost total 'saturation'. This was not an optimistic portent, particularly for those other Indian states striving for even more microfinance. Indeed, some other Indian states were already experiencing the negative impacts of having achieved their own oversupply of microfinance.[43]

Although there were several proximate causes for the events in Andhra Pradesh, the primary underlying force behind the crisis was the rapidly growing commercialization of microfinance. A number of adverse developments were involved. One was the toleration of a very large number of multiple memberships, which most MFIs agreed to in order to build market share. Multiple memberships in the three largest MFIs had reached 82 per cent by 2006.[44] Such adverse market signals notwithstanding, many new private MFIs continued to enter the market in search of their own fortune. And the banking system, particularly the largest bank – ICICI Bank – also continued to expand its highly profitable microfinance portfolio through SHGs. Local informal sector lenders also began to see a rise in clients quite openly seeking a new loan to repay other MFI loans, which, once more, they openly accepted in order to continue building market share (and for individual loan officers to obtain their bonuses). In this context, Shylendra has also reported on the rapid growth of 'client poaching'.[45] All told, MFIs in Andhra Pradesh were widely seen as 'behaving like businesses' – that is, building market share at almost any price, while also setting interest rates that were deemed by many to be far too high for the poor clients (especially rural clients) that they were actually supposed to be helping.

As I explained in Chapter 4, the agricultural sector in India, but particularly in Andhra Pradesh, was particularly hard hit by its engagement with commercialized microfinance. With mounting evidence of a crisis in agriculture, the state authorities had to commission a major report to look into the problems – the 'Report of the Commission on Farmers' Welfare, Government of Andhra Pradesh', released in late 2004. It noted that 'Agriculture in Andhra Pradesh is in an advanced stage of crisis'[46] and that 'The heavy burden of debt is perhaps the most acute proximate cause of agrarian distress. The decline of the share of institutional credit and the lack of access to timely and adequate formal credit in the state have been a big blow to farmers, particularly small and marginal farmers.'[47] A major problem was that far too many of the *least* productive subsistence farms were able to access a microloan, when it was clear that they could really do almost nothing with it. Any marginal increase in productivity was simply not enough to cover the high interest rate charges on the microloan that gave rise to it.

The overall result of these factors was that the subsistence farmer population in Andhra Pradesh got into a 'microdebt trap' in a big way. As noted in Chapter 4, in 2003 it was found that 82 per cent of farm households in Andhra Pradesh were indebted – the highest proportion in India – compared to around 49 per cent at the all-India level. Aggarwal also showed that a much higher proportion of the loans accessed in Andhra Pradesh were for current expenditure as opposed to capital expenditure, suggesting that not much longer-term investment in the agricultural sector was being financed in this way.[48] Worse, as the farmers began to slide farther into debt, they were trapped even more into growing high-risk cash crops, rather than crops that might be sold but could at least be used as food for the family if not. This was because the most indebted farmers desperately needed the cash payments to clear their expensive and, crucially, *growing* debts. The combination of a more market-driven agricultural sector associated with India's opening up to the global economy in the 1990s, alongside commercialized microfinance as the main substitute for previously affordable state credit, was thus a deadly one for many of the state's subsistence farmers.

The Andhra Pradesh crisis has led to a number of changes to its microfinance model, some possibly just temporary. There was, first, a slowdown in the expansion of microfinance in Andhra Pradesh. The banks cut their supply of credit to the SHGs, for example. Local MFIs also began to cut back on their operations. Second, there was a general lowering of interest rates. The two largest MFIs – Spandana and SHARE – announced they were cutting their interest rates from the 31 per cent and 28 per cent levels that prevailed in the period 2002–06, down to 28 per cent and 24 per cent in the post-crisis period.[49] The many costs and fees added on to a microloan, often imposed without the farmer's knowledge, were apparently also brought under a little more control. Third, many subsistence farms were henceforth avoided as potential clients, given that they rarely had the capacity to generate sufficient income to repay any microloan.

The most important policy lessons arising from the Andhra Pradesh experience, however, are the crux issues of availability and impact. Why was it that dramatically easy availability of microfinance did *not* produce the anticipated local economic development and poverty reduction impact in Andhra Pradesh? As with the example of Bolivia and Bangladesh, once again we find no causation leading from more microfinance to accelerated poverty impact: in fact, once again we find the reverse. The end result of achieving almost total 'saturation' of microfinance in Andhra Pradesh was not generalized economic and social development progress, as the microfinance industry had convinced the international development community would be the case, but a setback to economic and social development instead.

The dramatic switch into high-profit consumer microloans The market mechanism is often said to be superior to all other forms of allocation mechanism, because a market-driven financial system is assumed to be able to always and everywhere channel finance to where it is of most value to society. Conversely, when the market mechanism is suppressed or distorted in some way, the end results are very often poor. A market-driven financial system, however, very often produces a seriously negative impact that contravenes this market rule. Nowhere is this more evident than in the dramatic switch into high-profit/low-risk consumer microloans.

It is now increasingly accepted that somewhere between 50 and 90 per cent of microloans are actually accessed for simple consumption purposes, rather than to support income-generating activities. This move into consumer lending has been a quite dramatic trend in the last few years. A number of developments are responsible. Many of the new microfinance banks, including conversions from NGO-type MFIs, have become very heavily involved with low-risk/high-profit consumer loans in order to ensure their financial self-sustainability. For the same reasons, many private commercial banks in developing and transition countries, especially foreign-owned banking groups, have chosen to 'downscale' into consumer loans. Worse, there is some evidence that the weakest banks are those most interested in high-profit consumer microloans,[50] seeing such business as perhaps the only way to their eventual salvation but thereby introducing more risk into the local financial system. Consider Table 5.1, which summarizes some of the most dramatic instances of change around the globe in recent years.

Put simply, what we are seeing here, thanks to the commercialization of microfinance, is the profit-driven diversion of a nation's valuable savings flows into simple 'no-development' uses, and concomitantly out of all *other* uses that we know are likely to be of much high development value to society – principally SME lending. Some microfinance advocates who accept that a fundamental change has taken place here nevertheless respond with a casual 'so what?' They point out that poor people appreciate an inclusive financial system, so at least *some* benefit is derived here. This point might just make some sense if we were to assume an unlimited amount of funds, so that we could cover all possible demands. But if we now return to the real world, we are confronted by scarcity, choices and opportunity costs. We need to emphasize the fact that simple consumer loans impart almost *no* perceptible development impact compared to enterprise loans. Important empirical evidence was forthcoming on this score in 2008, thanks to a major study undertaken by economists

TABLE 5.1 The rise of consumer microloans in selected countries

Country	Comment
Bosnia	In Bosnia the average real growth of credit to households between 2001 and 2006 was about 50%, compared to the real growth rate for credit to enterprises of only 13.5%.[51]
Croatia	Consumer microloans rose from almost zero in 2000, but by 2006 were almost 35% of GDP. Many of these consumer microloans were taken out in euros and Swiss francs, adding a serious element of risk relating to currency movements.[52]
Estonia	Consumer loans have massively increased in the country since 2000, with the volume of consumer loans rising by 125% in just one year (mid-2005 to mid-2006).[53]
Hungary	In Hungary more than a third of all bank lending by 2008 was in the form of consumer microloans, rising from almost nothing in 2000.[54]
India	Only between one fifth and one third of microcredit disbursed in India is used for an income-generating activity.[55] Microloans as of 2006 constituted 15% of all commercial bank lending in India, a large rise from just five years before. These new funds have come from a relative decline in other portfolio assets, including SME loans.[56]
Mexico	The arrival of foreign banks in Mexico saw mortgage and household consumption lending explode, going from 15% in 1999 to around 45% of total lending by 2007. Bank lending to formal enterprises (SMEs) fell in Mexico in the new millennium, going from 60% of total lending to just over 48% in just over six years.[57]
Serbia	From almost zero in 2002 commercial banks' portfolios of consumer microloans expanded nearly tenfold, eventually amounting to almost 22% of total bank assets and around 12% of GDP as of late 2007. During this same period, the share of consumer loans in total private sector credit more than quadrupled to 41%. Meanwhile, funds for SMEs (except for trade credit) are very difficult to locate, and almost non-existent for start-ups.[58]
South Africa	From 2002 household debt (consumer microloans) quadrupled in volume in just five years. As many as 300,000 South African households are now classified as 'over-indebted' after having accessed a consumer microloan with no income to repay.
Ukraine	Consumer loans as a category have dramatically increased in recent years. Rising from almost nothing as recently as 2005, by 2008 household loans accounted for nearly 50% of total outstanding loans of the banking sector. Around 50% of these retail loans were made in foreign currencies.[59]

attached to the World Bank.[60] Covering forty-five countries in some considerable depth, the study showed a significant impact on GDP per capita growth only from enterprise-level credit, with almost no impact registered by household microloans.

In fact, it cannot be overemphasized: consumer loans, while no doubt of some use to the poor in terms of consumption smoothing, are nevertheless simply *not* a major driver of sustainable economic development and poverty reduction. This suggests, at a minimum, that the benefits of both options need to be compared before we declare which is preferable. The crux of the problem we inevitably find here is clear, however: the vast amounts of cash increasingly being directed into consumer microloans (savings, aid funds, investments, etc.) effectively mean that the important enterprise sector is being 'crowded out'. This effectively ensures that the wider economy is undermined into the longer term. A short-term palliative for the poor individual as consumer thus comes at a very high price for the poor individual as employer/employee.

In Bangladesh, for example, one can now see that the overarching emphasis upon microfinance as a source of consumer loans (as well as 'no-growth' microenterprise loans) has produced a major deleterious effect in this 'crowding out' context. The supply of microfinance in Bangladesh is reaching new heights. Just two MFIs alone (Grameen and BRAC) account for nearly $7 billion of microloans disbursed, much of which is supported by local savings.[61] Meanwhile, however, SMEs operating in Bangladesh are finding it extremely difficult to access capital to support their ongoing operations, while 'start-up' capital is an almost unknown concept. In fact, in terms of the availability of affordable capital for SMEs today, Bangladesh now stands out as one of the *worst* performers compared with virtually all other low-income countries. Research by the UK government's DfID aid arm summarized the situation in Bangladesh, as of 2008, as one where[62] 'The financial system – including banks, capital markets and the micro-finance sector – is inadequate to support long term investment financing for growth. Smaller firms, responsible for the lion's share of employment, have severely limited access to financial resources. *Rural areas, with the highest potential for lifting low income groups out of poverty, are cut off from most financing mechanisms*' (my italics).

Think about this – in the most microfinance-saturated country in the world there appears to be almost *no* capacity whatsoever to meaningfully support SMEs, especially in rural areas where poverty is heavily concentrated (and note that 'Grameen Bank' in the local language means 'Rural Bank'). This is no coincidence. In fact, the hugely powerful microfinance industry in Bangladesh has served to divert attention and huge quantities of financial resources *away* from one of the most important productivity-raising destinations – SME development – and it now very efficiently and profitably channels these financial resources into 'no-growth' microenterprises and, increasingly, into consumer microloans. The opportunity costs arising from this 'crowding out' phenomenon, I would argue, and DfID researchers seem to agree, are simply huge: microfinance is destroying the potential for SME sector development and growth in Bangladesh, *and so therefore the longer-run possibility that Bangladesh will ever escape underdevelopment and generalized poverty.* This is probably not the end result the international development community envisaged when first supporting Muhammad Yunus and the Grameen Bank all those years ago, but it is what has transpired nevertheless.

To their credit, a growing number of MFIs have finally begun to sense that enormous dangers lie ahead if they continue to shift financial resources *into* high-profit consumer loans and *away* from virtually everything else. Interestingly, a number of major MFIs have decided to make a stand on this important issue, and some have even begun to move out of this field of lending. A few of the more creative MFIs even use the fact that they avoid consumer loans as a unique selling point in their marketing effort! For example, Pro-Credit Bank Serbia, part of the global Pro-Credit group of MFIs, publicly announces as part of its mission statement that[63] 'Unlike other banks, our bank does not promote consumer loans. Instead we focus on responsible banking, by building a savings culture and long-term partnerships with our customers.'

This statement – and particularly the use of that word 'responsible' – is a very dramatic admission, by one of the most prestigious MFIs in the entire microfinance sector, that there are serious problems and opportunity costs associated with the shift into consumer loans. Many of the most prominent MFIs, however, including Grameen Bank, have resorted instead to simply trying to play down the fact that they now mainly function as consumer lending operations.

Realistically, we now need to portray microfinance and MFIs on a par with the developed countries' fraternity of aggressively profit-seeking US-style 'payday lenders'. These are profit-driven financial institutions that exist not to promote poverty reduction or development, but simply to siphon off a further layer of wealth and income from the very poor.[64]

'Microcredit bubbles' The worst-case scenario for microfinance is that of stoking up a 'microcredit bubble' similar to the US sub-prime 'bubble' that caused so much havoc to the US financial system. 'Microcredit bubbles' appear to have already been foretasted in the case of Bolivia and Andhra Pradesh state in India. Financial analyst Graham Turner also points to a household consumption loan bubble of enormous proportions existing in many of the world's poorest countries, one that when it bursts fully will inevitably create huge damage.[65] Even Muhammad Yunus was warning the London-based *Financial Times* as early as mid-2008 that[66] 'The world's biggest banks risk creating a subprime-style crisis for millions of the planet's poorest people if they continue to plough money into the booming microfinance sector.' With rural incomes declining in spite of the ubiquity of microfinance, many researchers are finding that the poor are simply substituting microfinance for lost income. Accelerating contact with microfinance has de facto become the main coping strategy for very large swathes of Bangladesh, creating the potential for a serious reversal when the bubble bursts.[67] The *Wall Street Journal* also ran a series of articles in mid-2009 expressing its concern over the possibility of microcredit bubbles emerging, particularly in India.[68]

Countries newer to microfinance have fared particularly badly of late. In my own research and consultancy work in Bosnia, I have long argued that microfinance has been a seriously adverse development intervention in that country,[69] not least since microenterprise failure rates very quickly rose to endemic proportions (of those microenterprises established between 2002 and 2003, World Bank researchers estimated that just under 48 per cent of them exited within *one* year of their establishment[70]). Even what few marginal gains there have been thanks to microfinance are now rapidly disappearing, thanks to the emergence in 2009 of what microfinance supporters describe as Bosnia's 'microfinance meltdown'.[71] This dangerous new development for the country is marked out by defaults now rising very fast (above 10 per cent in October 2009), commonly up to five or more microloans held per client, increasingly frantic competition for the few remaining individuals wishing to enter the world of microfinance, and most MFIs now moving into loss-making territory. Most recently it was also revealed that possibly as many as 100,000 personal guarantors are now being sought out in Bosnia to repay the microloans they (perhaps casually) agreed to personally guarantee for friends and relatives.[72] Overall, it would seem that the massive commercialization-driven expansion of microfinance in Bosnia has been a serious development policy error, one that other post-conflict countries clearly need to learn from in order to try not to repeat it.

But, then, going against the wishes of the international development community and attempting to halt the expansion of microfinance is not easy. Even countries having already experienced a 'microcredit bubble' and its subsequent bursting appear to be able to do little to prevent it reoccurring. For example, in Bolivia there are now serious worries over the huge microloan over-indebtedness that has returned in the last few years, mainly affecting the privately owned commercial microfinance sector.[73] The possibility of *another* microfinance 'bubble' crisis in Bolivia is now apparently being seen as a very real one.

Overall, an increasing number of international MFIs are finally beginning to register what others less enamoured of the microfinance model have been saying for some time: that a dangerous 'sub-prime-like' microfinance bubble has been created in many developing and transition countries, and urgent action is now required to avoid a major global meltdown. In general, two scenarios now beckon. First, there is a sub-prime-style bursting of the microfinance bubble. This outcome would be extremely bad news for the developing countries. It would set back their poverty reduction ambitions quite considerably, if indeed it did not usher in a period of extreme economic and political turbulence. But even if, second, the current 'microcredit bubble' is deflated gradually, thanks to the fallback methods I reported above – income diversion, using remittances, raising cash from asset sales, guarantors repaying microloans, and so on – the end result is still likely to be pretty bad for most developing countries. Already buffeted by an economic crisis originating in the developed economies, they now find that personal consumption, wealth, income and investment spending are all gradually declining as microloans are retired rather than rolled over or extended. We can envisage that (artificially inflated) employment levels will return to the pre-bubble trend, average incomes of the poor will similarly decline, inequality will rise (especially if forced assets sales are involved) and other negative economic and social impacts will inevitably be felt. This would indeed be an inglorious end to their entire commercialized 'new wave' microfinance episode.

The perfect storm – the 'Compartamos affair'

For many, the self-destructive nature of the Wall Street-style 'new wave' commercialization drive has been best captured by the case of Compartamos, one of Mexico's largest financial institutions. Though Compartamos has been operating since 1990, its 2007 IPO brought into full view a range of practices and outcomes that had previously been largely ignored. The result of the revelations at Compartamos was a major schism within the microfinance industry. On the one side stand the 'new wave' commercialization proponents. Their claim is that Compartamos shows the way forward in terms of how best to quickly and sustainably raise the availability of microfinance. Notable among these proponents were ACCIÓN, which was both an investor in and an adviser to Compartamos, and CGAP, which provided mainly technical advice. On the other side of the argument are those appalled at what was exposed by the IPO. Particularly troubling was the ultimate end result of Compartamos's preference for interest rates upwards of 100 per cent, a policy which seemed designed to facilitate mainly the personal enrichment of a small number of individuals in and around Compartamos. The cold calculations involved in securing quite dramatic levels of personal enrichment, and the obvious counterpart losses incurred by the very poorest and most vulnerable in Mexican society as they struggle to repay ultra-high interest rates on tiny microloans, appear to contradict virtually everything the microfinance model – and Compartamos – was originally meant to stand for. In the wake of the IPO, a much deeper reflection on Compartamos's activities, strategies and poverty impact began, as well as deeper reflection on the legitimacy of the entire 'new wave' microfinance model.

Compartamos was established in 1990 by a Catholic social action group called Gente Nueva, beginning its life as an NGO (Asociación Programa Compartamos). The original inspiration was apparently a visit to Mexico by Mother Teresa. Helping Compartamos to get started was a $4 million package of grants and soft loans provided by a number of international development agencies, plus some additional funds from several wealthy private Mexican supporters hoping to benefit the poor in their country. Compartamos began to grow quickly, serving poor rural communities in Mexico. Between 1998 and 2000, equity amounting to $6 million was provided in order to facilitate faster growth and to incentivize the directors and senior managers (who also became shareholders). Those providing the funds included the directors, senior managers and their family and friends, as well as a number of external advisory bodies, such as ACCIÓN and the World Bank's International Finance Corporation (IFC) arm. ACCIÓN took an initial 18 per cent shareholding that was paid for by the US government.[74] The World Bank's IFC arm took a 10 per cent shareholding. CGAP provided a grant of $2 million to Compartamos in 1996, but it did not become a shareholder.

Right from the start Compartamos's client base was overwhelmingly women (98 per cent of clients). Thanks to a policy of maintaining very high interest rates, over 100 per cent for long periods of time,[75] Compartamos was able to achieve full financial self-sustainability by 1997, and very high profits thereafter. Flush with its success, in 2000 Compartamos transferred its operations into a regulated for-profit finance company, known in Mexico as a 'sofol' (*Sociedad Financiera de Objeto Limitado*). Nearly 40 per cent of the shares of the new *sofol* were retained in Compartamos AC, a social-mission NGO controlled by the original core employees of Compartamos, now directors and senior managers of the *sofol*. Into the new millennium, Compartamos's growth accelerated. Part of the reason was its very aggressive move into urban areas with high concentrations of potential clients (though not necessarily the poorest). It also helped that Compartamos was able to tap into external capital. For example, it issued around $70 million of bonds on the Mexican Securities Exchange. On top of this, Compartamos also raised a further $65 million of loans from a variety of Mexican banks and commercial institutions. In 2006, Compartamos received its full banking licence. Part of the justification for this move was so that it could begin to generate deposits. Profitability in the new millennium became extraordinarily high, exceeding that of all of its Mexican counterparts by some considerable way (for example, $57 million in 2006). All told, return on equity between 2000 and 2006 averaged a massive 52 per cent.

In the summer of 2007, Compartamos underwent its long-planned IPO. Thirty per cent of the existing shares were sold to institutional investors, overwhelmingly located abroad. The three main institutional shareholders at the time of the IPO were: Compartamos NGO (39.2 per cent), ACCIÓN (18.1 per cent) and IFC (10.6 per cent), with directors and managers (23.7 per cent) and other private Mexican investors (8.5 per cent) making up the remainder of shareholders. These existing investors received $450 million for the 30 per cent of the shares released at the IPO, of which $150 million went into the pockets of private shareholders (directors, senior managers, friends and family), who also retain around $300 million of shares in Compartamos (as of the value at the time of the IPO). Several of the directors and senior managers saw their shares in Compartamos valued at several tens of millions of dollars each. ACCIÓN's nearly $1 million investment was valued at as much as $300 million. Overall, at the time of the IPO, Compartamos was valued at nearly $1.4 billion. The return on the original $6 million investment was calculated at this time to be around 100 per cent per year, compounded for eight years.[76]

The reaction If initially the full ramifications of the Compartamos IPO were lost on its main supporters, high-profile individuals like Muhammad Yunus were in no doubt whatsoever what the IPO signified. Yunus immediately jumped in to condemn Compartamos in the most forthright language possible.[77]

> I am shocked by the news about the Compartamos IPO. Microcredit should be about helping the poor to get out of poverty by protecting them from the moneylenders, not creating new ones [...] When socially responsible investors and the general public learn what is going on at Compartamos, there will very likely be a backlash against microfinance. The field may find it difficult to recover if corrections are not made.

Sam Daley-Harris of the Microcredit Summit Campaign chimed in that microfinance was 'in great danger of being [about] how well the investors and the microfinance institutions are doing and not about ending poverty'.[78] Chuck Waterfield, one of the first to draw people's attention to the huge importance of the Compartamos IPO to the microfinance model and its future trajectory, summed up his feelings thus:[79] 'Not only are they [Compartamos] making obscene profits off poor people, they are in danger of tarnishing the rest of the industry [...] Compartamos is the first but they won't be the last.'

Initially, the greater part of the microfinance industry took the offensive. Arguing that those against the IPO seemed not to like profits, they fully supported the right of the canny shareholders to secure huge profits: this was capitalism, after all. Belatedly realizing, however, that the IPO had created a perfect storm of criticism across the international development community, and wider still, and that it was clearly damaging everything they had painstakingly built over the previous thirty years or so, the microfinance industry switched to damage limitation mode. Key officials in CGAP began to tone down their earlier support for Compartamos. Explicitly referring to Compartamos, Elizabeth Littlefield, then a director of the World Bank and chief executive officer of CGAP, now said that[80] 'Without commercial foundations microfinance cannot become the profitable business it needs to be to survive. But without firm ethical principles and a commitment to benefit poor people's lives first and foremost, it will no longer be microfinance.' Referring to the ultra-high interest-rate policy, CGAP also had this to say in a note released just after the IPO:[81]

> looking at the facts available to us, it is hard to avoid serious questions about whether Compartamos' interest rate policy and funding decisions gave appropriate weight to its clients' interests when they conflicted with the financial and other interests of the shareholders. It is not yet clear how much Compartamos' decisions on those issues differed from what one would expect from a purely and forthrightly profit-maximizing company and its investors.

Some advisers to Compartamos claimed as the storm broke that CGAP had all along argued against Compartamos's ultra-high interest-rate policy, but that they (CGAP) were simply unable to get their own way on this key issue. Given that CGAP was extremely close to Compartamos right from its inception, many have wondered, then, why nothing was done to even highlight that they had reservations about the policy of ultra-high interest rates. There is simply no record of any action taken, or public or private admonition, to suggest that the high-interest-rate policy (or any other policy) was not acceptable to CGAP. Moreover, Compartamos CEO Carlos Danel is on record as saying well before the IPO that CGAP largely went along with their policies, stating '[CGAP] didn't try to drive us in another direction [...] They helped us do what we wanted to do, but better.'[82] In truth, CGAP really began to register its disquiet only *after* the IPO, when it became clear that the whole episode was turning into a PR disaster for itself and for the wider microfinance industry.

As one of the principal investors and advisers to Compartamos – and, remember, the institution that former ACCIÓN president and CEO Maria Otero says *invented* the commercialization model – ACCIÓN also came under strong criticism. It also had particular difficulty trying to explain its unflinching support for Compartamos's ultra-high interest-rate policy. Put on the defensive, ACCIÓN could only tough it out, try to contain the debate to the issues it felt strongest about, and generally put forward its own version of events.[83] But its long-standing support for Compartamos's Wall Street-style tactics was to prove difficult to live down, especially when in late 2007 Wall Street itself began to collapse in a frenzy of greed and naked self-interest many would argue was not unlike the behaviour ACCIÓN had freely sanctioned in Compartamos. One form of damage limitation, as noted above, was the founding by ACCIÓN of its 'Campaign for Client Protection'. Otherwise, ACCIÓN did nothing to disavow the commercialization model: how could it, when the commercialization model had been quite fundamental to its strategy and operations over the last three decades, and to the 'new world' of microfinance it had been instrumental in creating.

Finally, what of co-CEOs Carlos Labarthe and Carlos Danel, the two main protagonists in Compartamos itself, and now fantastically rich individuals thanks to the IPO? There was no word for quite some time. But when finally pressed for a reaction to the large amount of negative publicity, including their effective excommunication by Muhammad Yunus from the global group of the microfinance 'great and good', they eventually took to issuing a 'Letter to Our Peers'. In this letter they restated their rationale for promoting high interest rates and the eventual IPO – to expand Compartamos as quickly as possible, thereby to also expand the volume of microfinance available to as many poor Mexicans as possible. Labarthe and Danel also stressed that they were absolutely *not* driven to attempting to shape policies, developments and events within Compartamos in order for themselves and other senior staff to benefit personally. At all times and in whatever they did, they insisted, they had the very best interests of their poor Mexican women clients at heart.

Key problematic issues raised by the Compartamos episode

For those primarily interested in sustainable development and poverty reduction, the following interrelated issues are the most contentious ones to have arisen in connection with Compartamos, the ones signalling that 'new wave' microfinance appears to have reached a disturbingly negative climax.

Who cares if ultra-high interest rates damage poor clients? Perhaps the most controversial issue surrounding Compartamos prior to its IPO was its policy of high interest rates, at times rising above 100 per cent annually; many quite justifiably saw this aspect as harming the poor clients that it was established to help. Whichever way you look at it, Compartamos's clients were repaying as interest a very large proportion of the tiny income they earned in their microenterprises. For those accessing a microloan for consumption spending, the interest-rate burden on the individual and family would amount to a considerable imposition. The justification for high interest rates put forward by Compartamos, as just noted, has always been that high interest rates led on to high profits, which in turn underpinned the rapid expansion of Compartamos. With more microfinance made available to Mexico's poorest, so the Compartamos argument went, more of the poor were able to escape their poverty. For example, CGAP expressed its own toleration of the high interest policy in Compartamos by arguing that 'any profits were going to be used to reach future customers rather than escaping into anyone else's pockets'.[84] This view sounds quite positive, but it is actually a deeply flawed and self-serving line of argument.

First, almost no concern was registered, nor evidence collected, as to the *actual* impact of ultra-high interest rates on Compartamos's poor women clients and the wider local community. There is only the presumption that it is benefiting these poor women and the local community. But, to my knowledge, no real hard evidence that it is having the presumed effect on poverty has ever surfaced.[85]

Second, an important equity and moral issue comes into play here. The very poorest women in Mexico are effectively struggling to repay their ultra-expensive microloans in order to make sure other equally poor women in future, and elsewhere in Mexico, *and even outside of Mexico*,[86] can also have access to microfinance. The huge ethical and equity implications raised by this expectation have, to my knowledge, not been meaningfully addressed by anyone in Compartamos, or by their main advisers, but they are quite staggering.

Third, it is accepted, even by supporters of Compartamos, that the IPO and introduction of private investors will inevitably increase the pressure to maintain ultra-high interest rates, not reduce them. As we noted earlier in Chapter 3, CGAP itself pointedly concluded that[87] 'In light of what the new investors have paid for their shares, they will certainly have little sympathy for interest rate policies that do not stretch profits to the maximum.' There is surprisingly little comment on the important fact that one of the most widely stated benefits of commercialization – lower interest rates – is not actually expected to transpire. In fact, commercialization is now seen as militating *against* this positive development.

Fourth, given that 82 per cent of the shares released at the IPO were bought up by foreign institutional investors, many representing the wealthiest citizens in the developed world, and with only 12 per cent sold to Mexican investors, there is a strong argument that the resulting long-term capital outflows can only damage the poor in Mexico. The very poorest communities in Mexico are effectively losing local demand and wealth, which is being siphoned off to rich communities outside of Mexico.

Fifth, Compartamos has down the years appeared to consistently refuse to seek access to much cheaper sources of finance – savings mobilization in particular – that would have allowed for interest rates to have been greatly reduced. This, too, is an operational aspect that is open to much criticism. One possible explanation put forward for this preference is that with other types of financing it is much easier to channel the main benefits of high profitability towards shareholders.

Employee capture Another problematic issue for many, even for those supportive of the 'new wave' microfinance concept, is the lack of transparency in Compartamos's entire structure and operations. While Compartamos has always claimed to be concerned to 'keep the transparency [with which] we began our operations [as] an NGO',[88] the reality would suggest otherwise. Just to understand the structure and operations of Compartamos requires the services of a forensic accountant. David Richardson of WOCCU (World Council of Credit Unions) is one such accountant, and his study of Compartamos is extremely revealing. Recall that one crucial issue was why the development-focused shareholders in Compartamos – ACCIÓN and IFC – felt unable to push Compartamos, as they say they wanted to, to establish much lower interest rates. As major shareholders, they seemingly had sufficient power to do this. The answer to this puzzle, however, seems to lie in who *really* controls Compartamos. The main shareholder is the Compartamos NGO with 39.2 per cent of total shares, which in turn is controlled by the directors and senior managers in Compartamos the commercial bank. Consider, then, the implications in Richardson's own words:[89]

> But what of Compartamos AC, the non-profit NGO who controlled 39.20% of the votes? After reviewing the ownership structure of this

NGO, I found that three of the four founding members just happened to be stockholders of Financiera Compartamos, the Finance Company (SOFOL). Furthermore, one of those three members was a Full Board Member and the other two were alternate Board Members. In other words, Compartamos, AC, the non-profit NGO who is the largest stockholder of the Financiera Compartamos (SOFOL), happens to be controlled by three Financiera Compartamos Board Members who are all private investors with a vested interest equal to 6.79% of the company!

It might, or might not, be coincidence that such structures very clearly appear to be working for the benefit of senior employees, rather more than for the poor clients or the community.

Programmed financial enrichment of the senior personnel One of the supporting arguments deployed by Compartamos was that working with the very poor is not easy, so that they had to offset the additional costs on servicing tiny microloans by charging ultra-high interest rates. Following up on this claim led the aforementioned David Richardson to once more try to find what financial data were publicly available. For a major financial institution supported with public funding, there was not much. But persistence paid off, and Richardson found that Compartamos's cost structure was indeed extremely high, suggesting considerable inefficiency. But, interestingly, this inefficiency was not because of higher branch costs or some other factor that Compartamos management could perhaps deal with, but mainly because costs were high in one particular area: *the financial rewards paid out to management itself*. In fact, from around 2000 onwards, the directors and senior managers rewarded themselves with almost Wall Street-style salaries and bonus payments. Because they show the dramatic extent of financial inefficiency in Compartamos, Richardon's findings here are worth quoting in full.[90]

> How can the Compartamos expense ratio be 4 TIMES greater than [the credit union] CPM when it has fewer employees and fewer branch offices??? In my previous post, I made the following observation: 'WOCCU has conducted some studies of savings deposit costs in credit unions, and we have found that 49% of all costs are linked to salaries, particularly the salaries of the executive management team. Perhaps, in addition to huge profits at Compartamos, there may be huge salaries as well?' Unfortunately, salary information is

not available, so it is only speculation at this point. I believe it is high time, however, that there is more transparency regarding executive compensation in Microfinance. Even though there has been a code of silence from the [Compartamos] IPO beneficiaries, I am pleased to tell you that I hit paydirt the other day as I scoured the 279 page Spanish IPO prospectus. On page 177, it says that during the calendar year 2006, 25.35 million pesos ($2.3 million dollars) were paid to the Board of Directors and executive staff for bonuses, salaries, and 'special compensations'. If you take the 10 Directors and 2 Executives and divide 12 into $2.3 million, you have $194,163 dollars per person! 5 of these people were also stockholders in Compartamos, so this yearly compensation was in addition to the lucrative value of their stock. Needless to say, in a credit union, the Directors and managers can never be stockholders who profit personally, and many Directors are volunteers with a very modest stipend for their time and expenses. This compensation is way off the chart for any credit union leader.

Not content with this, as Richardson notes, the directors and senior managers also began to generously reward themselves via dividend payments. Owing to Mexican law dividends were not paid out from 2001 to 2003,[91] but after that things got a lot more interesting. Modest dividends were paid out in 2004 and 2005.[92] By 2006 the cash dividend was a handsome 164 million pesos (approximately $15 million), or about one quarter of total earnings (632 million pesos). The dividend posted in May 2008 was a record, around $20 million or about 51 cents per share. But this was then topped in 2009, when the dividend paid out was a new record of 67 cents per share (around $20 million in total, but this was because the peso was devalued by 23 per cent).[93] In other words, directors and senior managers were doing very well here too. In just a few years all of the Compartamos shareholders received enough cash dividends in order to pay back their initial investment of 60 million pesos ($6 million). Moreover, the total of earnings left after the cash dividend was paid out was capitalized to retained earnings, which will ultimately benefit the shareholders when their remaining shares are sold.

Paying out handsome salaries, bonus payments and dividends to directors and senior managers was, and is, quite legal. The fact remains, however, that many see this Wall Street-style strategy as out of keeping for an institution established with public and international donor funds, and with a specific mandate to focus on doing everything possible to help the poor. It goes without saying that no one from Compartamos has consulted directly with their very poor women clients to ascertain whether such Wall Street salaries and bonuses are what they really want to see too.

De facto privatization of public and donor investment Recall also that Compartamos was established with significant financial and technical help from the international development community, which also fully accepted the risks involved if the institution folded in its early years. This assistance was gratefully accepted by the original employees of Compartamos. But this social investment was then de facto privatized by the directors and senior managers of Compartamos. An initial investment by the international donor community meant to build an institution that would operate on behalf of the local community of the poor in Mexico was instead used to begin a process that would lead to the private enrichment by a small group of its original employees.

Not only is this process of wealth accumulation ('accumulation by dispossession') unethical to my mind, it also gives rise to a significant future moral hazard issue. Equally savvy individuals everywhere now realize more than ever before that the international donor community can quite easily be drawn into financially supporting their own individual dreams of wealth and power, just so long as these individuals couch their request for support in sufficiently catchy terms of 'wanting to help the poor'. Once the first chance arises, however, the original mandate can then be kicked aside, and the institution can become private property and subject to private enrichment goals.[94] Already in India, Bangladesh and Mexico we see the negative results: large numbers of savvy business people canvassing donors and governments for funds in order to establish an MFI designed to enrich the owner far more than anyone else. Compartamos is now a brilliant role model for those also seeking to benefit from the 'accumulation by dispossession' process.

'Changarrization' simply ignored Finally, we get to the part where we simply must ask what Compartamos actually *has* achieved in terms of its original poverty reduction and 'bottom-up' development mandate. Did it, does it and will it in future contribute to sustainable poverty reduction in Mexico? As I pointed out in Chapter 4, there is very little evidence that microfinance is achieving anything in development terms in Mexico. It is mainly serving to inflate the already vast numbers of '*changarros*'. And, as I have pointed out, analysts are becoming increasingly concerned that this 'changarrization' trajectory represents an existential threat to the entire functioning of the Mexican economy. So this cannot be good. Local savings, commercial funds and donor funds that could conceivably go into far more sustainable and pro-development business projects in Mexico are simply not doing so. Put simply, entrepreneurs in possession of a somewhat sophisticated and formal sector business project find little support. Interestingly, there is nothing on record (that I could find) which tells us whether or not Compartamos agrees or disagrees with the growing assessment that Mexico's development prospects are being sabotaged in this manner.

Essentially, recycling local savings and commercial funding into the very simplest of informal '*changarros*', or else into consumption lending, is a hugely profitable business activity for Compartamos. It is a business activity that has continued regardless of the mounting concern in Mexico and elsewhere that such forms of lending do not support sustainable growth and development, but actually undermine it. Support for the 'changarrization' of the local economy is therefore a trajectory wilfully, rather than accidentally, driven forward by Compartamos (as by other similarly aggressive profit-driven MFIs in Mexico, it should be added). In an obvious echo of Wall Street's concern for the eventual consequences for the US economy of its risky and speculative activities – that is, virtually none whatsoever – Compartamos has also demonstrated an apparent lack of concern for the fact that it is likewise contributing to undermining the structural foundations of the Mexican economy. Thus, over the longer term, it can be argued that Compartamos is actually *damaging* Mexico's chances of enjoying sustainable economic and social development, and so also poverty reduction.

Conclusion

The 'new wave' approach to microfinance rests its main a priori case on the claim that commercialization will facilitate the largest possible availability of microfinance at the lowest possible cost to governments and the international donor community. Quite apart from the fact that in this book I challenge the widespread contention that 'more microfinance equates to more poverty reduction and development', there are also serious problems associated with the specific claims made for commercialization. In the growing number of cases where the microfinance industry has achieved its central goal – microfinance is made available to anyone who might want it – even microfinance advocates have been forced to concede that the results have been very far from satisfactory. In fact, where microfinance saturation has been achieved and celebration should be in order, the broad experience is actually pretty disastrous – institutional crisis, 'microcredit bubbles' and local economic collapse. Moreover, examination of the Compartamos case graphically shows in detail how commercialized MFIs are associated with a whole host of antisocial and anti-poor developments, especially their easy 'capture' by senior staff. Perhaps we should not be surprised that Wall Street-style commercialized microfinance is producing mainly Wall Street-style outcomes. At any rate, we have reached the devastating finale for the 'new wave' microfinance model as a development and poverty reduction policy. The light at the end of the 'commercialized microfinance-as-poverty-reduction' tunnel is actually an oncoming train.

SIX
The politics of microfinance

'I believe that "government," as we know it today, should pull out of most things except for law enforcement and justice, national defence and foreign policy, and let the private sector, a "Grameenized private sector," a social-consciousness-driven private sector, take over their other functions.' Muhammad Yunus[1]

'It was Friedman who in 1962, with the publication of "Capitalism and Freedom," first proposed the abolition of Social Security, not because it was going bankrupt, but because he considered it immoral.' Interview with Milton Friedman[2]

The preceding chapters have called into serious question the widespread claims that microfinance can play a major role in promoting sustainable economic and social development, and so also poverty reduction. Microfinance is, in fact, a 'poverty trap'. This being the case, the obvious point to raise right away is why on earth would the international development community have wanted to help establish microfinance, and continue to support it over the next thirty or so years? The purpose of Chapter 6 is to briefly address this apparent conundrum.

To get to the heart of this issue, we first need to refer to a number of important insights from the institutional economics field. One very central insight is that the process of institutional development, and the evolution of associated organizational models, is largely contingent upon a complex interplay of economics, politics, ideology, self-interest, ethics and the exercise of power. Importantly, we must right away reject the idea that there is a Darwinian process that ensures the most efficient institutions or organizational models will emerge and be sustained over time. On the contrary, as accepted by writers as diverse as Marx writing in the nineteenth century and, more recently, the conservative institutional theorist Douglass North,[3] we know that 'bad' institutions and organizational models are often allowed to survive, and may even be *encouraged*, because doing so is in the interests of the economically and politically powerful. Microfinance institutions have been universally promoted on the basis that, as institutions established with an obviously positive purpose – addressing poverty – this simple fact alone must mean that they are, *by definition*, a 'good thing'. But history, as well as many of the arguments made in this book, demonstrates conclusively that this need not necessarily be the case.

Going farther, Steven Heydemann very usefully reminds us of the equally important historical fact that institutions and organizational models are most often encouraged to change, or are blocked from changing 'as a result of intentional actions by economic and political elites to preserve institutional arrangements that provide them with significant distributional advantages'.[4] In other words, institutions may well have a laudable stated public purpose, but their *real* reason for existing, changing or not changing can most often be put down to the 'distributional advantages' that accrue to key individuals and groups associated with these institutions. This important point within the institutional economics paradigm is demonstrated almost perfectly in the world of microfinance, as Chapter 5 showed, by the progress of the 'new wave' microfinance model since its establishment in the 1990s. Initially based upon an ideological (neoliberal) conviction that commercialization simply had to be 'best practice', the grubby Wall Street-style reality that quickly emerged instead pretty much confirms the broad thrust of Heydemann's argument.

The upshot of all this is that to really explain institutional development, and so also microfinance institutions, we first have to expose the hidden narrative.[5] In this chapter I want to do two things to this end. In the first section I briefly explore the motivation and views espoused by the microfinance sector's supremely iconic pioneer – Muhammad Yunus. Thanks to microfinance, Yunus has come to be seen as one of modern history's most important and effective campaigners against poverty. Even leaving aside for a moment the important issue of whether or not microfinance actually 'worked', do his views, actions and reactions down the years really justify this mantle? In the second section, I go on to point out that the microfinance model is actually almost perfectly consonant with the goals and imperatives of neoliberalism. This seems very strange. After all, neoliberalism is certainly not a political philosophy that favours the poor. As even its own supporters unashamedly accept, neoliberalism took shape in the 1950s on the basis of firm conviction that, thanks to political democracy, the poor were becoming *over*-empowered and indulged. The horrendous outcome, as neoliberals saw it, was the full panoply of Keynesian-inspired forms of government intervention, progressive taxation, excessive regulation, social welfare rights and bloated public services. Neoliberals therefore sought to restore power to a 'lean and mean' business class, using the fullest extension of market forces and private business freedoms, alongside a hugely 'downsized' state, as the way to do it. So where does microfinance fit into this schema?

Bringing capitalism to the poor to make capitalism safe for the rich

At least until very recently,[6] it would be difficult to describe Muhammad Yunus as anything other than a very deeply committed supporter of free market capitalism. As Chapter 2 highlighted, Yunus's belief in microfinance is based on the fact that it helps the poor to fully embrace the standard (neoclassical) capitalist wealth-creation mechanism – individual entrepreneurship. The very poorest can become micro-entrepreneurs within the local capitalist economy, and so they will finally get their small 'piece of the action'. Crucially, the community will begin to escape poverty to the extent that it becomes possible for many, if not *all*, of its poor inhabitants to engage with income-generating activities. The poor do not need the state to intervene on their behalf, or to exercise their collective capabilities to achieve change through social movements, trade unions, and so on. The poor certainly do not need wealth redistribution! All they need, in fact, is individual entrepreneurship, self-help and a microcredit. Put another way, Yunus fully supports the capitalist status quo, but argues for a little bit more effort to include more of the poor within its reaches in order to give it further legitimization in their eyes.

Going farther, we can see that Yunus is actually wedded to the idea of maximizing the *opportunity* for the poor individual to escape poverty. A poor individual just requires a microcredit, and she can engage in an income-generating activity, and so *hope* to escape from poverty. Yunus would appear to have little time for the idea of securing *by right* a generalized poverty reduction outcome (sometimes called the 'basic needs approach'). No matter that this is an aspiration that many of his contemporaries have passionately argued for – for a long time Amartya Sen[7] – it is not a vision that Yunus appears to have shared. Instead, his understanding of poverty and local society famously leads him to pronounce microcredit itself to be a 'human right'. According to this logic, Yunus does not appear to see it as a 'human right' to have access to a basic income, to decent employment, to basic healthcare, or even to simply the basic supply of food which makes human survival possible. These latter benefits should be forthcoming only on the basis of individual microenterprise success underpinned by microfinance. This approach very firmly places Yunus at the philosophical heart of Western neoliberal capitalism, epitomized in the popular writings of such arch-neoliberals as Milton Friedman[8] and George Gilder.[9]

It is also indicative of Yunus's distinctly rosy – some would say naive[10] – view of business and capitalism to find that he has increasingly sought to partner up Grameen Bank with MNCs. It is well-known that many anti-poverty activists, NGOs and others with an interest in poverty reduction find his desire for intimacy with international big business puzzling.[11] As Chowdhury points out,[12] Yunus has routinely worked with, and has accepted many prizes and awards sponsored by, MNCs almost universally seen as some of the worst offenders when it comes to the poor, to the environment and to sustainable development.

Most recently, Yunus has begun to portray these links with MNCs as directly advantageous to the cause of poverty reduction through what he calls 'social businesses' – businesses that are 'cause-driven' rather than 'profit-driven'. MNCs link up with a local business to form a 'social business' with poverty reduction a key objective of this new organization. Presenting these ideas in his 2007 book *Creating a World without Poverty*, Yunus boldly claims to have made another historic breakthrough in the promotion of poverty reduction (the first being microfinance). One of the main ways in which 'social businesses' can help to reduce poverty, Yunus argues, is by working alongside microenterprises as distribution chain participants, or 'micro-franchises'. Grameen Bank can provide the necessary microloans for poor individuals to insert themselves into the distribution chain of a 'social business', with the idea being that both parties to the transaction – but especially the poor – will do well. As previous chapters show, however, these uplifting ideas for 'social businesses' and 'inclusive' distribution chains do not seem to pan out over the longer term. Pointedly, so far at least, 'social businesses' in practice appear to be far more about quietly benefiting the long-range strategic plans of the powerful MNCs involved, while offering a few minor benefits to the poor if they quietly go along with the whole experiment (charade?). Crucially, the poor are all too conveniently denied a range of 'bottom-up' organizational structures, notably cooperative enterprises, which have far more potential to directly facilitate poverty reduction and social inclusion.

Most damaging of all, however, is the fact that Yunus has not been shy of providing evidence himself that brings into question his genuine commitment to the poor. As the quotation cited at the head of this chapter illustrates, Yunus has many times registered his support for one of the most extreme 'anti-poor' demands insisted upon by neoliberal policy-makers and business elites everywhere. This is that state institutions should be replaced by privately owned market-driven institutions designed to respond, not to genuine human need, but to effective demand (that is, demand backed up by purchasing power). Yunus is effectively asking the poor to forget about building democratically controlled public institutions that are centrally focused upon providing products and services on a needs basis, arguing that the poor should instead agree to leave it all to the private sector in future (albeit a 'Grameenized' private sector, as he says). Yet, as I have emphasized at various times in this book, if the last one hundred years of history have shown the poor one thing above all others, it is that the most important poverty-reducing advances they have secured have virtually all arisen because of some form of state intervention and collective provision. From public pensions, public employment opportunities, state healthcare provision, health and safety regulations, job security measures, state education, unemployment insurance, through to a whole range of other public services provided by local and central government according to need rather than wealth or income, we find the democratic state right at the very heart of genuine poverty reduction success. Nor has securing these hugely important gains been easy. It required long popular struggles against the economic and political elites, extensive social mobilization and, eventually, democratic politics. It is also why historically economic and political elites have been so hysterically against all forms of state intervention and social programmes that genuinely empower the poor (for example, the New Deal in the USA in the 1930s).

But if Yunus's professed dream of transferring important state structures into private hands comes to pass, and profitability, or even just financial self-sustainability, becomes the sole motivating force behind these new privatized institutions, the poor will eventually be thoroughly disadvantaged. They will have lost control of the very institutional vehicle that in recent history has been most responsible for helping them escape poverty.

Moreover, even if we leave aside what history and theory suggest to us concerning the impact of privatization, we can always examine instead what has been the recent experience of just the sort of privatization projects called for by Yunus. And here the evidence is pretty damning, to put it mildly. Even a cursory glance in this direction would show Yunus that privatized structures have been almost universally bad news for the poor.[13] The pioneer in terms of privatization was undoubtedly the UK in the 1980s. Massimo Florio's careful study concludes that productivity did not improve under private ownership, there were substantial welfare losses for poor consumers (higher prices for energy, gas, water, public transport and telephones) and there were 'substantial regressive effects on the distribution of incomes and wealth'.[14] In the vast majority of developing countries that followed the UK's lead, the general experience of most privatized structures has been equally problematic. Poverty reduction, equality, social welfare provision, employment creation, social justice and sustainable development goals have all been set back considerably.[15] Among other things, this is why a core demand of the growing protest movements in most developing countries (for example, articulated through events such as the World Social Forum) is to *reverse* many of the privatizations inflicted upon them. Even the World Bank has now very publicly committed itself to rebuilding key state institutions and 'free at the point of use' capacities in education and healthcare (but without offering any *mea culpa* for the huge economic and social damage inflicted in developing countries thanks to its previous 'full cost recovery' mantra). Moreover, let us not forget the fact that the drive for such privatized structures as advocated by Yunus has not been supported by the poor, or by any of the main anti-poverty pressure groups and international NGOs, all of which have in fact determinedly mobilized *against* what Yunus has been opining for on their behalf!

Several things become clear, then. Muhammad Yunus does not appear to have ever harboured any of the broadly leftist ambitions that animated many of the popular movements that emerged in the 1800s to challenge or circumvent capitalism and, among other things, began to argue in favour of providing small-scale finance to the poor as one of the ways to do this.[16] Yunus appears to have had very little truck with the counterculture anti-capitalist, environmental and sustainable development movements that emerged in the 1970s in parallel with his own efforts in Bangladesh.[17] On the contrary, Yunus is on record time and again as seeing microfinance as a way of supporting markets and 'bringing capitalism to the poor', not as a way to genuinely empower the poor through changing the social and power relations of capitalism in their favour. While possibly well intentioned, Yunus's most recent work establishing 'social businesses' and 'inclusive' distribution chains involving microenterprises is a 'top-down' arrangement that helps large companies achieve their own long-run strategic business objectives far more than it is meant to reduce poverty and exclusion. Finally, one must return to Yunus's quite explicit and consistent support for the most anti-poor and disempowering aspects of contemporary neoliberal capitalism, particularly his high-level support for the privatization of democratically mandated state institutions. This stance is a very powerful rejoinder indeed to those arguing that Yunus is 'a great friend of the poor'. As John Harriss has very powerfully argued,[18] those who passionately claim to want to help the poor, but who are unwilling to challenge the fundamentally unequal structures of power and wealth that sustain and reproduce poverty – which I would maintain is the case here with Muhammad Yunus – end up on the wrong side of history.

Microfinance is local neoliberalism

The microfinance model that emerged out of the Grameen Bank experience was found valuable by the international development community, among other things, because in even the poorest community it legitimized the simple textbook capitalist wealth-creation mechanism – individual entrepreneurship. In future, it was hoped, the poor would recognize this methodology as their sole route out of poverty. State intervention, collective organization (trade unions and social movements) and wealth redistribution would eventually wither on the vine as alternatives. Through an informal microenterprise, and with the help of microfinance, the poor could be left to individually articulate their own exit out of poverty. From the late 1980s, the microfinance movement was then colonized by neoliberalism. Thereafter, the poor themselves were also expected to pay the full costs of attempting to secure their own escape from poverty. Paying market-based interest rates on microloans, thus ensuring the financial self-sustainability of the MFI, would allow governments and the international donors to end any remaining direct financial support for the poor.

Arun and Hulme are therefore quite right to conclude that microfinance is not about 'promoting alternatives to capitalism'. They are on shaky ground, however, when they go on to add that 'Microfinance today is about drawing the benefits of contemporary capitalism down to those with low incomes.'[19] While bringing many of the basic structures and methodologies of contemporary capitalism down to the poor, the 'new wave' microfinance model that exists today does this, to my mind, the better to ensure that the benefits of capitalism continue going up to the non-poor. The progression of events and interventions within the new world of microfinance simply cannot be explained in any other way.

In this final section, and at the risk of some repetition, let me nevertheless briefly summarize the various ways in which microfinance was clinically separated from any genuinely transformational pro-poor agenda by the dictates of the 'new wave' microfinance model, and co-opted instead into the service of the anti-poor neoliberal political project. This is where we stand with microfinance today. Whether we remain in this position is another thing.

Microfinance is a politically acceptable policy model The microfinance model readily answers to one of the most pervasive and continuing fears among neoliberals: that the poor might opt to use the democratic process or popular pressure to demand the establishment of state, collective and popular institutions and strategies geared up to directly addressing their plight, perhaps through suppressing markets in their favour. Neoliberals saw the usefulness of microfinance as a way to permanently pre-empt such a radical trajectory. Microfinance delegitimizes and helps dismantle all possible 'bottom-up' attempts to propose alternative development policies that might be of direct benefit to the majority, but which would circumscribe the power and freedom of established economic and political elites. A wide range of progressive policies can be safely removed from the public policy agenda. Such progressive policies include wealth and income distribution measures, land ownership reform, robust social welfare programmes, and quality public services accessible to all on the basis of need. The focus upon individual entrepreneurship also helps to marginalize many other, potentially more powerful forms of ownership, such as state, collective and cooperative ownership.

Similarly, microfinance can be seen as buying commitment to the wealth-generation mechanism preferred by the rich: individual asset accumulation.[20] This policy direction exhibits a superficial progressiveness. But because it is actually predicated upon the dismantling of the traditional and highly successful mechanisms used by the poor to improve their position in the past, mechanisms that take advantage of the poor's most important asset – their vast numbers – it ultimately undermines the situation and status of the poor.[21]

Microfinance thus offers to neoliberals a highly visible and 'feel-good' platform upon which they can publicly claim to be addressing the issue of poverty and inequality, but which in fact delivers up no real possibility of this ever happening.

Promoting financial sector liberalization and privatization Microfinance has played an important role in the promotion of global financial liberalization and commercialization. As Heloise Weber has shown,[22] financially self-sufficient MFIs provide working examples of 'efficient' (i.e. subsidy-free) financial institutions, which developing-country governments must aim to reproduce. Most recently, commercial funding of microfinance programmes, including the outright purchase of established MFIs, has increasingly separated the microfinance industry from its roots in the NGO sector. As a part of the global financial complex, microfinance can be portrayed as a humanitarian example of how the global financial sector 'cares' and is directly addressing core societal problems. At least until the Great Recession, it was hoped that this 'public service function' would contribute to obtaining continued government and public support for the ongoing liberalization of the financial sector.

Advancing the 'minimal state' agenda The international development community's mantra in the 1980s, particularly within the World Bank, was for public services to be privatized, or else to support their existence on the basis of 'full cost recovery'. The imposition of privatization and user fees, however, has generally resulted in an awkward decline in the 'client' base of most services restructuring in this manner. Microfinance provides the poor with a way of managing to live with such regressive policies, spreading the cost of user fees into the longer term. Indeed, one might say that microfinance has been consciously positioned as the permanent substitute for social welfare spending and international donor support. Once the poor accept that they are now in control of their individual and family destiny using microfinance, it is much easier for the government to fully absolve itself of continued responsibility for resolving their predicament. For example, Shiva discusses the role of microfinance in the privatization of the water supply industry.[23] She shows how microfinance programmes have been deliberately deployed in order to ensure a less precipitous, and thus less politically damaging, decline in water demand after privatization raises its price to the poor.

Microfinance facilitates lower costs for the state, the business sector and the middle class at the expense of the poor One aspect of microfinance appreciated by neoliberals is its association with lower labour costs. Under conditions of intense poverty-push competition, vast swathes of personal and other services traditionally supplied by local microenterprises, from haircuts to last-minute groceries to fast food, can be supplied even more cheaply. With hyper-competition and self-exploitation on the rise in most microfinance-saturated locations, especially in the growing number of urban slums in developing countries, one result is gradually declining prices for many of the simple goods and services produced. The middle classes in developing countries thus find a source of cheaper goods and services than before. The state can also benefit from lower-cost providers of inputs, which allows it to reduce taxes on the middle classes and business sector.

At the same time, large companies have not shied away from using microfinance in order to help restore or expand their own profitability. Many SMEs and larger enterprises, including MNCs, are increasingly seeking to drop formal sector SME and/or unionized suppliers, and are moving instead to construct supply and distribution chains based upon non-unionized, lower-cost microenterprise suppliers. This allows the large company to reduce its own costs at the expense of rising poverty and informality. Such moves even give a temporary boost to those microenterprises able to obtain contracts taken away from higher-cost SMEs and unionized suppliers. In fact, many microenterprises are given international donor support precisely to facilitate this type of substitution. But, overall, this movement away from the formal and organized sector is typically bad for the community in the longer term and for the chances of poverty reduction.

Microfinance as 'containment' of the poor Perhaps the most important factor of all here is the 'containment' role that microfinance has been allocated within the neoliberal globalization project. It is widely argued by neoliberals that globalization has the potential to provide a major reduction in poverty. Yet in practice neoliberal globalization policies have increasingly concentrated wealth and power into the hands of a small number of countries, regions and corporate elites. As Jeff Faux and Larry Mishel explain,[24] the global economy has seen a growing worldwide population of the unemployed, powerless, marginalized, hyper-exploited and insecure. The Great Recession is naturally making this situation manifestly worse. Just as was feared would be the case right after the Second World War, notably by Robert McNamara during his long stint as president of the World Bank,[25] the world's growing population of 'losers' is increasingly rejecting the outcome assigned to them. Symptomatic of this rejection is the rising social unrest, increased social and gang violence, the explosion in substance abuse, increasing crime and illegal business activity, the huge rise in pseudo-religions and cults, collapsing levels of social capital in the community, and associated violent conflict.[26]

In the potentially explosive situation emerging in many developing and transition countries today, particularly acute in the growing number of 'mega-cities', microfinance therefore provides a crucial 'safety valve'. The logic is well known, and I briefly explored it in Chapter 3 in the context of nineteenth-century England. Those with a few assets or a tiny income flow have at least *something* to keep them busy, and also to lose should they seek to rebel against the dominant social order. The hope is that the microenterprise sector can therefore positively engage these people in their own immediate survival, and dissuade them from otherwise supporting alternatives to neoliberalism and the globalization project.

Conclusion

Many within the microfinance industry have argued that today's microfinance model is the direct descendant of the various forms of small-scale finance that emerged in the early nineteenth century to democratize and challenge the new system of industrial capitalism.[27] More recently, some have seen microfinance as an intrinsic part of the social justice, environmental and anti-globalization movements. The argument began to evolve that Muhammad Yunus conceived of Grameen Bank-style microfinance as the latest and most innovative institution within these progressive traditions. In both cases, I have shown that the opposite is actually more realistic. Both the Grameen Bank model that emerged in the 1980s, and then even more so the 'new wave' microfinance model that began to replace it from the early 1990s onwards, actually represent a quite fundamental schism with the various leftist and community-driven movements supporting microfinance in the past. In fact, the most accurate location for the microfinance model is within the most fundamentalist and anti-poor variant of capitalism: neoliberalism. Microfinance is 'local neoliberalism'.

Because this will provide insights that are important in helping us frame better development policies in future, we certainly need to study the political-ideological origins of an intervention in policy elite circles.[28] Having said that, if such a study shows that the roots of an intervention said to help the poor actually lie in a political philosophy that actively seeks the disempowerment of the poor – as I have argued is the case here with microfinance and its intimate links with neoliberalism – then pro-poor improvement is largely an inoperative concept. We need instead to completely rebuild the local financial system upon genuine pro-poor developmental concepts and foundations. One way to start to do this is to first examine those local financial systems that in history and contemporary practice have been able to make progress towards genuinely empowering the poor, substantively reducing poverty, and ultimately promoting sustainable economic and social development. The next chapter will explore a number of the most interesting local financial models that stand in opposition to both the Grameen Bank model and the later 'new wave' microfinance model.

SEVEN
Alternatives to conventional microfinance

'[R]ecognising institutional diversity should not be confused with the argument that therefore there are no lessons to be learnt [...] It is both possible and instructive to identify some major principles that underlie [...] successful experience, and to try to adapt the policy tools and institutional vehicles that were used to realise those principles in order to fit local conditions elsewhere, and if necessary devise new policy tools and institutions. Indeed, if East Asian governments had themselves believed in the impossibility of such institutional adaptation and innovation and had ignored earlier success stories, it is doubtful whether we would have an East Asian Miracle to discuss.' Akyuz, Chang and Kozul-Wright[1]

The book has argued that the Grameen Bank microfinance model and – even more so – the 'new wave' microfinance model have all the required attributes of an 'anti-development' intervention; an intervention that initially 'feels good' but ultimately undermines economic and social development, and so also largely frustrates the objective of sustainable poverty reduction. Microfinance is, in fact, a 'poverty trap'. An argument ranged against one particular institutional intervention, however, is often said to be incomplete without at least some pointers in the direction of what might be the building blocks of some feasible alternative. By reflecting upon some important cases where the local financial system has played a particularly important role in facilitating sustainable local economic and social development, the purpose of this chapter is to provide some of these local building blocks. While I have stressed elsewhere that economic, political, historical, cultural and geographical context is important, nevertheless hugely important lessons can be obtained from an examination of the experiences of particular local financial systems with a good track record of supporting economic and social development.

A preliminary word on at-risk groups

Before I go on to assess a number of alternatives to the microfinance model, I first need to say a few words about the role of consumption spending. I do this because microfinance is very often said to be at its best when dealing with the most 'at-risk' groups in the local community, who for whatever reason urgently require some cash simply to survive from this day to the next. Particularly in the aftermath of conflict, natural disaster or economic collapse, we find microfinance proposed as the solution for large numbers of 'at-risk' individuals who have been plunged into extreme poverty and privation. Microfinance is considered valuable because it very quickly puts cash into their hands. This allows for the immediate purchase of the basic necessities of life – food, shelter, medicine and so on. This argument has been deployed to justify microfinance programmes in many post-conflict settings – Bosnia, Kosovo, Iraq, Timor-Leste – as well as post-natural disaster settings – post-tsunami Indonesia and Sri Lanka.

In addition, consider also that the very poor hugely value the ability to consistently obtain tiny amounts of cash which they can use to facilitate their precarious modes of survival. The 2009 book by Daryl Collins, Jonathan Morduch, Stuart Rutherford and Orlanda Ruthven, *Portfolios of the Poor*, is a quite superlative account of how the poor use a whole range of lending techniques to manage their money and survive on as little as $2 a day. Individual survival is greatly helped everywhere if the poor are able to quickly and unfussily obtain and repay consumption spending loans.

So, even though I have argued in this book that we should disqualify microfinance as an intervention with regard to promoting sustainable economic and social development, could we not at least allow microfinance a role in terms of quickly and perhaps consistently supporting urgent consumption spending needs?

I think that this is also a problematic option, however. Even if we accept that the overriding aim is to *quickly* provide modest sums of cash to the most 'at-risk' individuals and families, there is still a much better response to microfinance in the shape of the conditional cash transfer (CCT). In return for generally making some small social commitment – for example, one might have to ensure one's children visit the local health clinic or regularly attend school – CCT models provide instant cash support to the most 'at-risk' individuals and families. Rather than immediately loading up such individuals and families with expensive and often unpayable microdebt, then, the CCT model provides a way of instantly resolving extreme poverty without building in longer-term indebtedness. The limited wealth redistribution element involved does not seem to bother many neoliberal policy-makers either, and may even be welcomed by some.[2] As even the World Bank recognizes,[3] 'Transfers generally have been well targeted to poor households, have raised consumption levels, and have reduced poverty – by a substantial amount in some countries.' Brazil's use of targeted social programmes (*Bolsa Familia*) has helped families to cope, and also to avoid having to indulge full time in poorly rewarding and often dangerous micro-enterprise activities. Mexico's *Oportunidades* project has been widely praised because of the many benefits it has generated for the poor. For example, Skoufias reports that it was responsible for a sharp decrease in poverty (around 10 per cent), rising school enrolment, increased expenditure on food and an improvement in adult health.[4] Venezuela is also successfully working with many types of financial support for the local community, comprising *Bolsa Familia*-style basic income programmes for the very poorest. All told, compared to the growing web of microdebt now negatively affecting the 'at-risk' poor in virtually all developing and transition countries today, the CCT option is preferable by some considerable way.

But even if some form of microdebt arrangement is nevertheless still preferred to meet the regular and ongoing demand from the poor for simple consumption loans, then we may *still* not want to involve conventional for-profit 'new wave' microfinance here. The best option instead is to support consumption spending and lending through forms of community-based credit, such as credit unions.

Credit unions are member-owned, not-for-profit local financial institutions with an impressive historical track record of providing good service to the poor. They work by mobilizing savings from members, and then recycling this cash to other members when in need. Sometimes outside capitalization can help to establish a credit union. But generally – if not ideally – they remain locally controlled and locally financed institutions. Everywhere around the world, therefore, credit unions can and do provide quick and affordable microloans to the poor seeking to smooth their consumption. It helps enormously that with no paid executives to support, and with the goal of serving members not shareholders, credit unions are much less costly to operate. In short, credit unions work with a sustainable development and poverty reduction trajectory, rather than against it (or in favour of personal or elite enrichment). While somewhat more organizationally complex than the types of MFI we have discussed so far, credit unions are nevertheless a more equitable financial mechanism for satisfying important longer-term consumption spending needs of the poor.

Assuming that immediate consumption needs can be adequately addressed by credit unions, we need to focus now on the really crucial development issue here – what are the local financial models that have unequivocally shown how to promote sustainable economic and social development, and so are the basic building blocks of an alternative to 'anti-development' microfinance? The rest of this chapter expands upon this critical issue.

Financial sector models associated with local and regional development success

Following the financial chaos of the Great Depression and then the carnage of the Second World War, many financial systems lay in ruins. Many countries and regions were forced to embark on the reconstruction of their domestic financial systems, with a view to promoting sustainable economic and social development. Much success was registered, particularly in the former West Germany, Spain, Italy, France and the Scandinavian countries. Later on, in the 1960s and 1970s, a number of East Asian countries began to examine the most successful of the Western countries and the example of Japan too, and they soon began to develop similar financial sector interventions to kick-start faster economic and social development in order to catch up.

The result was a new raft of high-performing local financial sector models emerging. Indeed, one might argue that these latest examples speak volumes about the power of a suitably configured local financial system to catalyse sustainable economic and social development, given that the countries concerned were all pretty much mired in abject poverty and underdevelopment when they began their experiment. And while much experience is historically, culturally and geographically specific, of course, these examples manifestly point to the fact that many aspects were readily transferable and adaptable to quite different conditions elsewhere. As we shall see, the East Asian experience is crucial testimony to the importance of learning from neighbouring experiences, and then adopting and adapting similar policies, structures and institutional vehicles. As Akyuz, Chang and

Kozul-Wright argue in the citation at the head of this chapter, without the willingness to learn from others, we might not have had an East Asian 'miracle' to even discuss.

Elsewhere in the international development community, and also in many developing countries, however, the most successful financial models in recent history appear to have been ignored. Instead, from the 1980s onwards simple neoliberal textbook models and 'efficient market' theories have been mainly used as the basis for the design of the financial sector, including the *local* financial sector. One important reason for neoliberal policy-makers to take this position, and for the wider international development community to do so too, is a basic aversion to national and local state intervention and forms of planning. As we shall see, central to many of the most success-ful financial sector models are indeed proactive regional and local governments, non-market forms of capital allocation and subsidized interest rates, all features anathematized by neoliberal policy-makers and the microfinance industry. As we shall see in the case of Vietnam in particular, no matter how successful such heterodox financial sector models may be in practice, for purely political and ideological reasons the international development community and the micro-finance industry have to demand that such models be discredited and destroyed.

Anyway, let us now consider the most successful of the post-Second World War local financial models in a little more detail.

Japan quickly recovers from the Second World War While Japan is traditionally seen as an example of large-scale industry export success, it is much less well known that the country's recovery after 1945 was very much predicated upon the construction of a highly successful local financial system. This local financial system was an outcome shaped by extensive local government institution-building activity, and topped off with much central government support. Community development policy through small enterprises prospered, and it was later officially cited by the Japanese government itself as one of the 'two major pillars of Japanese economic development policy since the Second World War' (the other pillar being export policy).[5] The im-mediate need in the aftermath of Japan's defeat in 1945 was to rebuild the local community on fair and equitable lines, to help the most vulnerable individuals (particularly demobilized soldiers) establish new small enterprises, and to restart local industrial development. In post-war communities, however, the impetus of the private financial sector is to support the least risky and most profitable ventures, which usually means working with safe large firms or import financing of some kind. In Japan, local and regional governments therefore had to fill the 'funds gap' for microenterprises and SMEs which quickly became apparent.

Three powerful state banks were quickly established in the aftermath of the Second World War in order to lend to SMEs, microenterprises and to their associations. The Small Business Finance Corporation provided loans to SMEs, the People's Finance Corporation provided loans to microenterprises and the Shoko Chukin Bank provided loans to their associations for on-lending to members.[6] Complementing these central financial institutions, however, was a dense tissue of local and regional (prefectural) state-led institutions. Local and regional governments quickly accepted the challenge of financially supporting local economic development themselves. Through an array of city, regional and long-term credit banks, the microenterprise and SME sectors were offered large volumes of longer-term, affordable credit. The resources for these measures came partly from central government, but also partly from local savings mobilization achieved through the local state-owned banks. It also helped, as Kitayama showed,[7] that local governments were quick to develop a wide array of their own support programmes and 'soft' measures to support the most growth-oriented locally based microenterprises and SMEs. Numerous special loans were also provided based on certain policy measures, such as equipment upgrading or the introduction to the locality of new technologies.

Alongside these local and regional state-led initiatives, the state indirectly pursued its goal through support for large numbers of credit unions, financial cooperatives and other forms of small-scale non-state mutual association that were also re-established after 1945. Two were particularly important to microenterprise development – the mutual (*sogo*) banks and the credit banks (*shinkin*) formed out of the larger pre-war credit unions. By 1980, more than 63 per cent of the credit banks' lending was to microenterprises and 41 per cent of the mutual banks', compared to 'only' just over 12 per cent for the regional banks.[8] Crucially, Girardin and Ping note that oversight by local governments and the central Zenshiren Bank helped establish local trust and ensured minimal fraud and speculative activity associated with depositors' money, a feature that was to underpin the high local savings rates experienced for most of the 1950s and 1960s.[9] As Nishiguchi shows,[10] these non-state local financial institutions became important complementary community-based providers of funds for new-starts and small growing enterprises outside of the state support schemes. David Friedman usefully summed up the situation as one where, overall,[11]

> In effect, the Japanese created an industrial equivalent of the American savings and loan system for the US housing market. In Japan, however, the thrift institutions funded not home ownership but independent factories. This redirection of capital markets toward small firms nurtured the independent expansion of small companies during the high-growth period.

A key aspect of the 'bottom-up' economic development trajectory fashioned by local and regional governments in Japan was the efficient insertion of thousands of new microenterprises and small enterprises into industry-based supply chains. This was achieved by local and regional governments coordinating their financial sector and other policies in order to provide longer-term, affordable financial support to those individuals with the ideas and motivation to enter into small-scale industrial production and services. In addition, locally based officials from the famed MITI (Ministry of International Trade and Industry) were able to use funds from the Fiscal Investment and Loan Plan (FILP) to provide long-term subsidized loans to key SMEs, mainly to allow for the purchase of new technologies. Sourcing its funds from the huge postal savings system, the FILP was an important indicator to the banks that the firms it chose to support were now a much lower risk, and so the banks should provide any additional funding required.[12]

The iconic example of microenterprise development is the Tokyo suburb of Ota, which became a world centre for machine-tool parts production and servicing, overwhelmingly undertaken within microenterprises. As Whittaker's in-depth study of Ota shows,[13] the easy availability of affordable longer-term local finance removed the principal binding constraint that would otherwise have held back the growth of Ota's industry-based microenterprises. With growing subcontracting demands from the large Japanese industrial companies, the locality's microenterprise sector was in a good position to benefit from these new demands. With easily available capital most microenterprises were able to avail themselves of all the latest technologies, innovations and other productivity-raising features in order to remain at the cutting edge of their work.

The essence of the Japanese local financial systems approach, one might say, was to use the market mechanism as the background against which local government was able to identify and then pro-actively promote those microenterprises and SME sectors calculated to generate most long-term benefit to the local economy. Local governments did this because the market largely failed to catalyse into being the required sustainable development trajectory: the market was largely a passive background force. As the Japanese economy began to boom in the 1960s and 1970s, Japan's local financial model was continually adjusted to reflect the growing need for affordable, longer-term capital for key microenterprises and SMEs. Without the existence of such networks of relatively technology-intensive microenterprises and SMEs, many of the sectors Japan was later to almost completely dominate across the globe would simply not have emerged. For example, the development of industrial robotics was strongly predicated on the prior existence of rafts of highly efficient technology-intensive microenterprises and SMEs able to produce inputs to extremely fine tolerances and specifications.[14]

The Basque experience with a community development bank[15] The small town of Mondragón in northern Spain lies at the centre of one of the most spectacular examples of sustainable 'bottom-up' economic and social development. From being one of the poorest regions in Spain and in Europe in the 1950s, beset by economic decline and industrial collapse, political tension and inter-ethnic discord, the Basque region developed rapidly to become one of the EU's best examples of sustainable and equitable local and regional development. Central to Mondragón's success was a community-owned financial institution.

The Mondragón model is a network of industrial cooperatives (now termed the Mondragón Cooperative Corporation, MCC) that in 2006 employed around 80,000 full-time worker-members. In 2006 it was the seventh-largest corporation in Spain with a turnover of around €12 billion. The beginnings of the MCC are traced back to the mid-1950s and the efforts of the local Catholic priest, Father Don José María Arizmendiarrieta, to address the crushing burden of poverty in the region. Cooperative businesses were chosen for support because they contained far higher potential to address the economic, political and cultural needs of the Basque population. This included a general desire for equality, fairness, dignity and democracy at work, plus a wish to support local solidarity and the wider functioning of the local community.

At the core of the Mondragón model lies the Caja Laboral Popular (CLP, Working People's Bank), a bank established to support and provide funding to new and established cooperative business projects. Since its foundation in 1959, the CLP has been very successful in mobilizing large quantities of local savings. Appealing to a sense of local self-sufficiency and patriotism was made necessary by the fact that the political authorities in Madrid were quite unwilling to give any real support to the region, largely on account of its opposition to the Franco government and its wish for greater autonomy, if not full independence, from Spain. The phrase *Libreta o maleta* (Open a savings account or pack your bags) became common currency, deployed by the MCC pioneers to bring home the point that the Basques had to mobilize their own funds to develop their region rather than rely on Madrid, or else local people would have no other option but to emigrate elsewhere to find employment.

It was the supreme ability of the Mondragón model to successfully reinvest local savings into sustainable cooperative businesses, however, which set apart this local financial system from the rest of Spain. The Basques have a long history of thrift, so a high local savings rate was not something completely new. Savings mobilized by local banks in the past, however, had typically been recycled into simple local businesses with little real growth potential, such as retail outlets. This weak local development dynamic was, of course, partly the reason why the region historically remained trapped in poverty.

The CLP was determined to change things, however. It set out to refocus local savings into much more sustainable and growth-oriented small cooperative businesses, businesses that would create quality forms of local employment. Another phrase was widely used by the MCC pioneers to underpin their effort at local development – *Con todos los ahorros que depositas aquí, vamos a crear puesto de trabajo cooperativos aquí* (With all the savings you put here, we are going to create cooperative jobs here). To that end the CLP quickly established the División Empresarial (Entrepreneurial Division). The División Empresarial was decisive in the successful creation and ongoing support of virtually every cooperative within the Mondragón group thereafter. Just one of the indications of this is that since the 1960s only *three* cooperatives supported by the División Empresarial have failed.

The ability of the Mondragón group to patiently initiate, develop and financially support new cooperatives into successful operation was, as David Ellerman remarks,[16] a very successful form of 'social entrepreneurship'.

The Mondragón local financial model is held by many to be the key to the Basque region's massively successful expansion of cooperative employment over the years. It was spectacularly successful both in mobilizing local savings in an initially poor region, and in then carefully reinvesting this bounty in growth-oriented local cooperative businesses. The Mondragón model not only began to spread across the Basque region, creating a regional success story, but it also expanded elsewhere across Spain. Government officials from the (then) equally poor region of Valencia were some of the earliest visitors in the 1970s, taking back with them the core of the Mondragón financial model. The model was then very successfully adapted to local business conditions and business culture in the Valencia region, turning it also into an economic and social success story by the 1990s. In short, lessons from the Mondragón model are important to every region attempting to develop, but especially those attempting to recover from conflict and exclusion.

Northern Italy's local-regional financial model Northern Italy's regional and locally based financial cooperatives and other financial institutions, especially in the region of Emilia-Romagna, played a central role in one of the most impressive post-war reconstruction and development episodes of all time. With regional/locally owned and controlled financial institutions embedded with long-term development goals, the largely destroyed regions of northern Italy were able to successfully grow thanks to burgeoning microenterprise and SME sectors. Key to this success was the ability to identify and support those enterprises with the best possible growth potential, and wherein crucially important externalities (e.g. technology transfer, innovation, export links, collective R&D) could also be reaped for the benefit of the wider network of enterprises. Long-term affordable financial support was crucial to supporting enterprises in the process of rebuilding their financial strength and attempting to reinvest as much as possible in the latest technologies and business practices. Many of the enterprises and networks supported coalesced into the famous 'industrial districts'. From one of the poorest Italian regions in the 1950s, Emilia-Romagna rapidly emerged to become one of the EU's ten richest regions by the 1990s, and its capital, Bologna, became Italy's richest city.

One of the most important of the region's institutions was the cooperative. Long an established feature of the region, after 1945 the newly elected communist-socialist governments now saw cooperatives as institutions that could lead the way towards the 'inclusive' economic and social recovery they desired. As Ammirato shows,[17] with support from sympathetic regional governments in the north the cooperative movement was given a hefty boost. This included the region's financial cooperatives, which were seen as a core component of the overall financial engine that would catalyse the hoped-for 'inclusive' recovery. Another point in favour of financial cooperatives was that they were clearly not going to engage in widespread speculative activities. A wave of speculative activities and elite-sponsored 'get rich quick' schemes would clearly undermine the fragile accommodation that had been reached between the defeated Fascists and their wealthy business supporters, on the one hand, and the victorious partisans and the working classes, on the other. Allowing such processes of illegality to continue unchecked in the northern Italian regions ran the risk of blowing apart the nascent recovery. This was an outcome that was eventually to transpire in the southern part of Italy, as Robert Putnam notably pointed out.[18]

After 1945, the financial cooperatives immediately began to mobilize savings as best they could. This cash was then carefully invested in traditional investor-driven businesses with obvious growth potential, but also, as in the case of Mondragón, as much as possible in cooperative enterprises. The main cooperative bank in Emilia-Romagna, Cooperbanca, had branches right across the region, and it quickly became a mainstay of enterprise lending. The smaller cooperative banks in northern Italy were also helped to recover and were quickly able to provide additional support to both cooperatives and important microenterprises. Also operating alongside the financial cooperatives were, from 1947 onwards, networks of Artisan Funds. These Artisan Funds were established and capitalized by the central government in Rome, but largely managed and accessed regionally. Linda Weiss brilliantly recounts how these Artisan Funds were quite pivotal to the recovery and development of the local enterprise sector thanks to their provision of long-term (ten-year) low-interest loans for machinery purchase and workshop modernization.[19]

From 1947 onwards, the northern Italian regions also greatly benefited from a network of full and part publicly owned Istituti di Credito Speciale or Special Credit Institutes (SCIs).[20] The most important SCIs were established right across Italy at the regional level (*Mediocrediti Regionali*), and were meant to focus on providing low-cost medium- to longer-term credit to small and medium industrial, and especially to relatively technology-intensive, enterprises. Their 'localness' helped ensure that they worked close to their clients, thus building up trust and reputation, and they could also assess their clients better by being near to them. The SCIs established in the region of Emilia-Romagna, for example, turned out to be particularly proactive, transparent and well managed. The result was that a disproportionate share of the central funding available was channelled to the SME sector in this one region, leading to Emilia-Romagna becoming one of the most developed and richest regions in Europe by the 1980s.

All told, the northern Italian regions hugely benefited from a local financial system that could drive forward the process of 'inclusive' development through enterprise development. As in Mondragón, it was crucially important to savings mobilization that most local financial institutions were willing and able to commit to sustainable local development, as opposed to maximizing the returns to be enjoyed by their external shareholders or, worse, their more visible directors and senior managers. It was not lost on the cooperative movement at this time that the local private commercial banks much preferred to concentrate their funds on supporting the highly lucrative post-war consumption goods import trade. With a firm financial base, the financial system was then able to begin to identify and support the most sustainable business propositions. Microenterprises were supported where they could insert themselves into non-local supply chains through the famous *impannatori*, individuals at the head of long supply chains and 'putting out' networks. Noteworthy in Emilia-Romagna was its ability to find residual value in the previously robust military-industrial sector based in the region. With help from the local financial system, many of the ideas, technologies, products, processes and contacts were successfully parlayed into new, relatively technology-intensive microenterprises and SMEs. Overall, as Guiso, Sapienza and Zingales show,[21] the much deeper and more long-term-focused local financial system found in northern Italy accounts for both the continual supply of new-start SMEs, and their subsequent growth being much higher compared to other Italian regions.

As already noted, many cooperatives were supported because they had obvious advantages in terms of a higher level of fairness, equality and better working conditions. One result of the subsequent strength of the cooperative sector was that it attracted new financial interventions. After 1992, the Italian regions added to their financial support for the cooperative sector with the Coop Fund initiative (*il fonde mutualistico*). This new fund was financed thanks to a new law which stipulated that all cooperatives – many now very successful and financially strong – must contribute 3 per cent of their profit into developing new and expanding existing cooperatives. By all accounts, such Coop Funds have succeeded in patiently developing new sustainable cooperative businesses. The cooperatives' own membership body, LegaCoop, also decided to establish its own version of the Coop Fund with fourteen regional offices to utilize these new mandated funds to support the cooperative sector. Between 1994 and 2001, the LegaCoop-affiliated Coop Fund supported 109 new cooperatives into operation using $48 million of equity funding and $17 million of loans, in the process creating 4,640 new jobs. Similar support provided to existing cooperatives with growth potential deployed $52 million of funding to create 2,690 new jobs.[22]

Overall, the cooperative-based financial system that emerged in an economically devastated northern Italy after 1945 was crucial to its rapid recovery and development. Initially mobilizing both state and non-state funds (i.e. savings), the financial system was to prove adept at parlaying this advantage into a sustainable local development trajectory based on growth-oriented enterprises, especially cooperative enterprises. Crucially, the regional authorities and local governments realized that they needed to drive forward the enterprise development process based on sound economic principles, particularly the need for scaled-up, interconnected (horizontally and vertically) and relatively technology-intensive enterprises.

Taiwan and South Korea The rise of the so-called East Asian 'Tiger' economies is particularly associated with the stunning success of two previously extremely poor countries – Taiwan and South Korea. Superior economic performance in these countries has been largely attributed to the varied activities of central state institutions, rather than to local financial institutions. In South Korea it was government's strategic support for big business (the Chaebols), while in Taiwan state support for agriculture and then a thriving SME sector made all the difference.[23] It remains the case, however, that a suitable *initial* foundation for rapid economic growth and development in these two countries was built upon successful rural transformation, and especially small-scale economic development activities, both of which developments were a product of very proactive regional, local and village-level-based financial institutions.

In the 1950s, South Korea was one of the world's poorest countries. Following a military coup, in the 1960s South Korea embarked on a new policy of achieving rapid economic and social development. This new direction involved major changes to the financial system, including at the local level. After 1960, the local township and village administrations were quick to support local farmers' credit unions to get started. Alongside quality extension services for farmers and potential rural entrepreneurs, this important initiative greatly helped to kick-start rural development and facilitate agricultural self-sufficiency.[24] It was important, too, that from the 1960s onwards the decentralized units of the major state banks were able to offer low-cost credit to local microenterprises. The aim was to promote rural industrialization, especially utilizing the high skills of many of the refugees from North Korea who moved south after the conclusion of the Korean War. Allowing local entrepreneurs to bypass the traditionally usurious private lenders (the state bank loaned at 25 per cent per annum compared to the 60–70 per cent offered by the private lenders) meant rural industrial projects could bring in new and second-hand machinery from the major urban centres.[25] Overall, South Korea was able to construct a solid and equitable rural-based economic and social development trajectory that neatly complemented the Chaebol-based industrial development effort under way at the national level. In 1997, after South Korea was caught up in the Asian financial crisis, the Korean government was once more able to embark on a new credit-driven policy approach; this time supporting SMEs as the engine of growth. Special venture capital funds and credit availability were increased with regard to SME investments in technology and innovation. Korea's banks were instructed to restructure their loan portfolios away from the Chaebols and towards potentially high-growth SMEs.[26] In this way, South Korea built up a remarkably resilient SME sector, one that provided new jobs and strong support for the restructuring Chaebols.

Taiwan took far more seriously than South Korea the task of constructing a small enterprise-based economic model through appropriate forms of local financial intermediation. As in South Korea, however, the Taiwan government was first interested in improving rural agricultural productivity in order to create food self-sufficiency, before switching in the 1960s to a more export-based development strategy. Township and village state bodies initially began to offer support to basic local farmers' associations, which were able to help peasants pool their savings and thereafter offer low-cost credit for irrigation and new agricultural technologies. Thorbecke notes that local and village administrations soon became competent at establishing more sophisticated rural funds and credit cooperatives that were able to aid the savings mobilization and local investment cycle, thereby underpinning the required industrialization drive in the countryside.[27] As Fei, Ranis and Kuo sum up,[28]

> The farmers' associations and credit cooperatives, set up by the Japanese to facilitate agricultural extension programs and rice procurement, were top-down institutions dominated by landlords and non-farmers. As a result, most farmers did not directly benefit from them. In 1952 government consolidated those institutions in multipurpose farmers' associations restricted to farmers and serving their interests. In addition to the original function of agricultural extension, the activities of farmers' associations expanded to include a credit department, which accepted deposits from farmers and made loans to them, and to provide facilities for purchasing, marketing, warehousing, and processing. The associations thus became clearinghouses for farmers, who controlled and maintained them and viewed them as their own creatures.

It greatly helped that the number of agricultural extension services workers in Taiwan provided by local and village administrative units was far and away above that in other East Asian countries.[29] Agricultural-sector-related SMEs also benefited from many special bank programmes aimed at creating efficient agricultural supply chains concerned with the processing of export items, such as canned mushrooms and pineapples.

In terms of the wider industry-based microenterprise and SME sector, Wade points to two main sources of funding that prevailed early on.[30] First, Taiwan enjoyed a set of banks (e.g. an SME Bank) and bank programmes providing discounted credit to SMEs operating in priority development areas. Second, a centrally and locally well-regulated curb market provided large sums of capital at interest rates freely determined between supplier and demander. Foreign banks were kept out of Taiwan until well into the 1970s, and thereafter for a long time allowed only into areas of business (e.g. savings mobilization) the government considered would not undermine its overall development goals. Taiwan's huge economic success, however, is largely based upon the expansion of its now very technologically sophisticated SME sector. It is here that the most innovative financial institutions were to prove crucial in establishing and then nurturing the SME sector. Taiwan very quickly developed a comprehensive financial structure able to support technology activity. A wide variety of special financial support programmes were provided through the government-owned banks to help SMEs obtain new technology and develop new technology processes. This financial sector component was a key part of the overall technology support structure, described by Lall as 'perhaps the developing world's most advanced system of technology support for small and medium enterprises'.[31] It also helped that larger companies receiving special discounted loans had, in return, to proactively support subcontracting and other forms of efficiency-enhancing integration within the local SME sector.

Overall, both South Korea and Taiwan were extremely proactive and innovative in developing local and regional financial systems that could help them achieve their strategic development and poverty reduction goals. Initially, the proactive financial sector programmes undertaken by township and village administrations in both countries led to the efficient and equitable reconstitution of the local community as a self-sufficient agricultural unit. Success here then underpinned the wider efforts to transform the local economy into an efficient rural-industrial entity. This was then the ideal platform for the later large-scale industrial policy interventions in South Korea, and technology-based SME development interventions in Taiwan, that catapulted both countries towards rapid growth and ultimately major economic success.

Local finance crucial to China's rise to power The Chinese economic miracle stands as the most impressive economic development and poverty reduction episode of the last forty years, possibly of all time. What is often forgotten, however, is that the foundation for China's rapid development was established at the local level, in the shape of rafts of highly efficient, largely production-based Township and Village Enterprises (TVEs). The TVE experiment began in the southern coastal regions of China. TVEs were largely local-government-owned enterprises. Despite their ownership structure, TVEs were nevertheless strongly profit-seeking, operated under hard budget constraints and according to strict performance targets. The number of TVEs grew very rapidly, and by 1996 nearly 7.6 million industrial TVEs were operating.[32] Initially, the profits and taxes generated by the TVEs enabled highly proactive local governments to finance a range of increasingly sophisticated business infrastructures, such as industrial parks, incubators and, a little later on, modern facilities geared to foreign investors. Foreign investors began to hear about the TVEs, and from the early 1990s FDI began to arrive to partner up with those TVEs capable of producing low-cost goods and services in demand by Western consumers. This positive association with FDI was crucial in helping China to deepen and sustain its growth trajectory well into the 1990s. Even though by the late 1990s many of the TVEs were being privatized or closed down, in line with internal and external pressure on the Chinese government to move much more rapidly towards a neoliberal policy orientation, China's experience in this specific period remains a hugely important pointer to other countries seeking successful rural industrialization and growth.

Even less well known is the fact that two key local financial institutions essentially stood behind the TVE experiment. First, there was the Rural Credit Cooperative (RCC) model. The RCCs first emerged in the 1950s as carefully controlled local units of the Agricultural Bank of China (ABC), but became powerful local institutions in their own right after reforms began in 1979. RCCs were mainly owned by farmers through equity stock. They collected deposits from rural households and some TVEs. Initially providing loans to individuals, from the early 1990s onwards they mainly provided loans to TVEs.[33] Second, there were the Urban Credit Cooperatives (UCCs). The first UCC was established in Luhae County in Hebei Province in 1979, but by 1986 there were 1,114 UCCs throughout China.[34] The UCCs had a combination of owners, including private businesses and private individuals, but substantial ownership by the local authorities and local state banks was generally the norm. This was important in incorporating the UCCs into local development plans, and to ensure the confidence necessary to mobilize local savings.

The importance of the RCC and UCC experiment is evident in a number of ways. First, RCCs and UCCs were well equipped to mobilize local savings. Even in China's poorest communities this proved to be possible. Crucially, by demonstrating that most (50–60 per cent) of local savings would be reinvested locally in the TVEs, and so (hopefully) new quality local jobs would be created and sustained, both the RCCs and UCCs were able to build trust in their operations and in their vision of community development. (It also helped that many farmers feared that their savings would be lost or wasted if deposited in the large state banks, many of which were then heavily engaged in supporting the declining heavy industries in the north of the country.) Second, because local governments owned the TVEs, and so stood to lose out financially if any of them failed, the process of identifying which TVEs to establish or expand was apparently quite quick and efficient. Highly profitable and generously local taxpaying TVEs were a real bonus to local government officials seeking higher office. By the same token, a local government official forced to petition the higher authorities for financial assistance in the event of losses in some TVE project often meant the end of any promotion chances. Third, local governments in China realized that there was no point in establishing some new TVE with less than the required scale or with inappropriate technology. It therefore helped that large and affordable enough loans were made available for local TVEs. As O'Connor remarked, this enabled 'new [TVEs] [...] to start up on a larger scale than otherwise (and than private enterprises), with a higher degree of mechanization and more modern technology'.[35] Initially, with Hong Kong nicely placed as the entrepôt port, most TVEs sought financial support to produce simple manufactured goods destined for export. Later, in the early 1990s, when the Chinese economy began to grow very rapidly and to entice in large amounts of FDI, the RCCs and UCCs were able to direct funds towards those industrial TVEs best placed to make a productive local supply chain link with a foreign company.

The TVE experiment reached its peak in the late 1990s. In line with the turn to neoliberalism in China in the 1990s, however, the local financial system began to come under pressure to reform in the approved neoliberal direction. Predictably, the RCCs began to come under pressure to privatize, often from incumbent managers simply seeking personal gain. The pressure began to build for the RCCs to be converted into full profit-maximizing shareholder/manager-owned financial entities. In parallel, many of the much larger UCCs were merged to become even larger city-based commercial banks. Some

UCCs were also privatized, and subsequently lost their development mandate as they too were forced to go in search of maximum profits for their new local owners, most of whom were previously their directors and senior managers, now wealthy players in the new market-driven financial system.

Most recently, with Chinese economic policy-makers now increasingly in thrall to the neoliberal policy model, the Chinese government has begun to downplay the interventionist RCC and UCC experiment as the initial source of China's great economic success. It is now better not to mention that such community-driven institutions were vital to China's success. One reason for this is that otherwise there might be some comment as to why the UCCs and RCCs were then privatized and passed almost for free over to their former directors and senior managers. Largely for the same ideological reasons – the need to suppress the fact of positive performance by community-driven financial institutions – the international development community has welcomed the direction of this reassessment by the Chinese government. As one stick to beat the UCCs and RCCs, microfinance advocates have taken to pointing out the often sizeable losses incurred in many of them.[36]

This is quite an unfair assessment. Among other things, it ignores the fact that the risks taken supporting many potentially fast-growing TVEs, and so the inevitable losses incurred when some of these projects went bad (as in any Silicon Valley venture capital outfit, for example), are actually swamped by the upside registered by those TVEs that succeeded. In fact, one might say that on a simple cost–benefit analysis, the UCCs and RCCs have been nothing short of a staggering economic development success, given the TVEs' role as the foundation stone upon which China's economic miracle was actually built. Nevertheless, the Chinese government is now being solemnly told by the international development community that its future microenterprise and SME growth should ideally come through rafts of 'new wave' MFIs, the creation of which has become one of the international development community's new strategic policy goals in its engagement with Chinese policy-makers.

In spite of some operational difficulties, it remains the case that the community-based RCCs and UCCs that emerged in the early 1980s were the primary financial institutions behind the TVE movement, which was in turn the engine behind China's spectacular period of rural industrialization and growth. Both forms of community-based financial institution very successfully mobilized savings in poor rural and urban communities. These savings were then judiciously invested back in sustainable TVEs, an enterprise format that offered real payback to the local community in the form of secure jobs, rising incomes for the community, high local taxes and local technology transfer. The RCCs and UCCs therefore offer a number of important lessons to other developing countries also seeking to mobilize and judiciously invest scarce local capital in order to promote rapid rural industrialization, sustainable job creation and poverty reduction.

India's Kerala model of development India's Kerala State has long been famous in the international development community for its achievement of very high levels of human development in spite of persistently low levels of GDP growth per capita. Many are appreciative of the enormous social progress made in the state, and have contributed to the effort to tease out the precise factors responsible for such an important outcome.[37] Some attribute much of the progress to Kerala's proportionately quite large share of India's huge remittance income flow.[38] Others, notably Amartya Sen, while generally applauding the Kerala model, also seek to understand why per capita growth has been lower in Kerala than in many other states in India.[39] Higher wages, good working conditions and generous social provision in Kerala are obvious deterrents to profit-maximizing mobile national and multinational investment, which accounts for the fact that few big companies have indeed chosen to locate in the state. Still others see the issue of low growth per capita and high social development as separate issues. What is important, as Parayil believes,[40] is that in spite of its low growth per capita Kerala was able to achieve by far the best social development indicators in all of India.

Less well known about Kerala is the fact that it has pioneered its own quite distinct microfinance model. The motivation was, at least partly, to develop new endogenous economic activities that would answer those critics just noted, who applaud the social development progress in Kerala but point to its weak economic growth experience. As in other parts of India, individuals in Kerala are encouraged to form self-help groups (SHGs) and neighbourhood help groups (NHGs) which then obtain 'soft' loans from the local cooperative banks to match their own savings. Unlike in other states in India, the SHGs and NHGs in Kerala come under much more pressure to formulate and put forward only what are seen as sustainable projects, which are then financed by the local cooperative banks. In addition, village councils consider any project within the context of the local plan that is arrived at through popular participation. As Thomas Isaac and Franke describe it, 'Kerala microcredit projects [are] better than the existing Grameen Bank counterparts' because, among other things, great efforts are made to ensure that individual loans 'maximise interconnections and [...] avoid overinvestment in any particular activity'.[41] The projects funded in Kerala are then, 'in theory at least – connected to an overall village development plan in which the outcomes of the loans in terms of the products have an immediate local market'.[42] This shows a sophisticated understanding of two fundamental flaws in the microfinance model that I have already highlighted – that is, the lack of 'connectivity' and the 'fallacy of composition' issues. Initially inspired by the broad outlines of the Grameen Bank, the Kerala model has introduced many such fundamental modifications to try to avoid the Grameen Bank's fundamental flaws.

Kerala's own brand of SHG and NHG financing of cooperatives has to date played a quite decisive role in the economic and social (especially solidarity-building) success of the Kerala model. Special efforts are made to encourage and financially underpin cooperatives wherever possible. This is because Kerala's microfinance model is based on emphasizing 'the solidarity of the SHGs to undertake production together rather than simply using social pressure to compel individuals to repay loans'. This collective effort and planning differentiate the direction (if not the outcome) of the Kerala SHG model from other SHG models in India, including the large SHG movement in Andhra Pradesh.[43] The Kerala SHG model is about moving women away from involvement in SHGs solely in order to access microloans for simple 'no-growth' individual projects, much as they would do if working with any mainstream MFI (though interest rates are considerably less via the SHG route than in commercial MFIs). Instead, the aim is to foster collective activity that can reap some simple economies of scale and scope, thus improving the chances of eventual success in creating forms of sustainable employment.

By the same token, the financial sector and SHG movement in Kerala treat the informal sector somewhat differently than elsewhere in India. Informal sector operations are strongly encouraged to formalize into cooperatives whenever possible, in order to improve the chances of empowering individuals and reducing poverty. Notably, the largest cooperative in Kerala (and one of the largest in India) is located in traditionally one of the weakest and most exploitative of individual microenterprise activities – making bidis, or traditional cigarettes. With upwards of 32,000 members, the bidi cooperative ensures that those involved have some power over their lives and working conditions and, crucially, enjoy a much higher percentage share of the eventual financial returns than is typical across the industry. More widely still, the Kerala microfinance model attempts to eradicate exploitative informal sector labour through trade union mobilization, rather than contributing towards its legitimization and expansion as elsewhere in India (and in developing countries in general). Kerala stands out as one of the few locations in developing countries that makes a deliberate effort to encourage informal sector workers to organize and to unionize.

At least in intent, if not (yet) in terms of widespread and sustainable outcomes, the Kerala microfinance model represents a very important departure from the Grameen Bank microfinance model. Many of the serious flaws in the Grameen Bank model have been identified and, at least partially, corrected in Kerala. Key *genuine* empowering trajectories involving the poor are offered support – such as cooperatives, unionized workplaces, 'connectivity' between otherwise weak individual enterprises, the use of planning to avoid local overcapacity arising, and so on. Engagement with the informal sector is accepted, but only on condition that the long-term goal is to formalize the informal sector as much as possible. It remains to be seen whether Kerala's unique microfinance model, as well as the entire Kerala development model, can succeed into the longer term. But there are certainly optimistic portents to suggest that what has been achieved so far for the poor might be a firm enough foundation for its evolution into bigger and better things.

Venezuela's popular economy experiment Starting around 2000, one by one the countries of Latin America have cast off the neo-liberal economic policy framework imposed upon them by the major development institutions (i.e. the World Bank and the IMF) acting in concert with the US government. Years of steadily rising poverty, inequality, unemployment and deprivation have convinced them that there must be an alternative. Microfinance programmes have been a mainstay of the attempt to reduce poverty and promote 'bottom-up' development in Latin America à la Hernando de Soto's vision, but such programmes appear to have achieved very little indeed. One result is that disillusion with microfinance has turned into a flowering of new local financial sector developments, such as in Bolivia (the BDP experiment) and in Mexico, Brazil and Argentina (CCTs). One country, Venezuela, stands out, however, for having charted a very positive development trajectory – so far – thanks to a radically new set of pro-poor local financial institutions and innovations. Reflexively demonized by much of the Western media as 'too interventionist', in truth Venezuela is simply responding to a failed neoliberal development model that produced nothing but stratospheric levels of poverty, inequality and suffering – all this in a country that since the 1920s has enjoyed huge revenues from its oil and gas industry. At the core of the new Venezuelan model is an explosion of 'bottom-up' social and community-driven development programmes, mostly financed by higher oil industry revenues. Notably influential in the initial design of this new system was the 1993 work of Osvaldo Sunkel, who proposed a more human-centred 'bottom-up' version of the old import-substitution policy framework.[44] Particular emphasis has been placed on establishing networks of agricultural, marketing and worker cooperatives through Sunacoop, the National Superintendency of Cooperatives. As the Venezuelan government argues, cooperatives are viewed as a central component of 'an economic model with a rationality centered towards collective well-being rather than capital accumulation'.[45]

This preference culminated most recently (2004) in an ambitious plan to buy out failing, and even successful, large private enterprises for conversion into worker and community cooperatives. There are major programmes of support for the creation of cooperatives involving individual microenterprises as the core members, in order that they might better reap collective economies of scale and scope (as well as enjoy equality and solidarity). There is also a major shift towards pro-poor public purchasing and contracting policies, such as favouring the award of public contracts to businesses owned by minorities or else those located in the very poorest communities. A decree was issued that Venezuela's state companies should all attempt to increase the local content of their outputs through subcontracting with local SMEs and microenterprises, and especially through working with cooperatives. Part of the influence here was the obvious 'bottom-up' development success of Brazilian public procurement programmes in establishing sustainable clusters and cooperatives involving many production-related small firms.[46] Crucially, 'connectivity programmes' in Venezuela are most often facilitated by finance made available at low interest rates and long repayment periods (sometimes also 'grace periods'), significant free training opportunities and free technical assistance for microenterprises.

Small-scale finance is one of the core instruments through which this new social development trajectory is meant to be realized in Venezuela. Three microcredit banks were established to provide the important financing needs of local businesses. These are the Banco del Pueblo (People's Bank), Banco de la Mujer (Women's Bank) and FONDEMI (Fund for Microenterprise Development).[47] In addition, FONDEMI has been granted significant resources to underpin the rafts of communal banks in Venezuela that finance small-scale projects with the potential to develop and grow. These three core MFIs provide a range of subsidized microcredits to appropriate business projects. A key institution here is also the Ministerio para la Economía Popular, MINEP (People's Economy Ministry), which has been described by some analysts as a popular version of the US Small Business Administration.[48] MINEP financially supports microenterprises, cooperatives and other productive units that are in line with the sustainable human-centred development strategy enunciated by the Venezuelan government. MINEP has provided major programmes of finance for start-up worker cooperatives, typically with fewer than ten founder-members. The financial conditions are extremely favourable, with low interest rates and long maturities the standard offer. The MINEP cooperative training and financing programme was established in 2004, and by 2005 more than 45,000 cooperative enterprises were functioning.

Individual microenterprises receive substantial funding in Venezuela through the MFIs established by the state. In contradistinction to the 'new wave' microfinance model, in Venezuela financial support is provided mainly on condition that an individual microenterprise can somehow integrate into larger business networks in order to reap collective economies of scale. It is widely accepted in MINEP, as well as more widely still,[49] that it is very often *isolation* which undermines a microenterprise, and not its own efficiency or the lack of motivation to escape poverty of those involved. One other reason for such inter-enterprise networking, it is hoped, is that it will also help to identify real, not perceived, local demand gaps. Adding unwanted local supply to already overcrowded local market sectors can therefore be avoided. This is specific recognition that for microenterprise development to be successful it must graduate away from the 'no-growth' and income-destroying informal sector microenterprise ghettos familiar to Venezuela in the past, and still common in most other Latin American countries today.

As noted, the Venezuelan government appears to recognize the dangers of wrongly inflating even further already 'saturated' local market sectors. Banco de la Mujer is particularly aware of this perennial problem. It therefore aims to help its women microfinance clients within a very supportive framework that identifies and targets only genuinely sustainable businesses within the community. Unlike in virtually all other conventional microfinance programmes, such a 'hands-on' approach is specific recognition that, in their own words, simply providing the poor with access to finance is not a solution to poverty. Rather, if vital links between microenterprises and sustainable forms of industrial and consumer demand are not part of the deal, it is an abdication of responsibility towards the poor.[50] With support from Banco de la Mujer, those receiving microcredits to date (1,280 cooperatives and 11,540 microenterprises) have also been given encouragement to set up their own support networks, or Popular Networks. These associations of women are designed to provide women with greater 'voice' in the community, but also to help them to identify for themselves new sustainable project areas that are likely to be of most benefit to women.[51]

Venezuela-style microfinance is thus radically different from both the Grameen Bank model and the latest 'new wave' microfinance model. It is much more akin, in fact, to the hugely successful 'comprehensive' microfinance support programmes pioneered in post-1945 Japan and northern Italy. Most noticeably, as in the northern Italy case, much of the funding for microenterprises is actually targeted at supporting cooperative enterprises. As in Japan, access to microfinance is also made conditional upon a reasonable level of sophistication (not just simple trade activities, for example), and that the receiving microenterprise or cooperative possesses the ability to integrate into supplier networks of some sort. These and other microloan conditions have been established in order to best fulfil Venezuela's planned goal of promoting 'endogenous development', which, according to Wilpert,[52] is based on five key development principles: using existing local capacities and addressing existing needs; enhancing community participation and local planning (for example, through cooperatives); promoting 'bottom-up' forms of development rather than 'top-down'; promoting solidarity and cooperation more than competition; and, finally, using modern technology without compromising the ecological equilibrium.

While it has been only a few years in operation, the early results of Venezuela's 'bottom-up' financial sector experiment are nevertheless impressive. At least partly thanks to the extremely supportive local financial system, and the resulting 'bottom-up' development trajectory thereby established, unemployment has decreased from nearly 15 per cent in 1999 to just under 8 per cent in 2008. Interestingly, employment in the informal sector – the traditional destination of most micro-entrepreneurs – has actually *fallen* over this time period, to just over 6 per cent of the total labour force. The level of poverty has also fallen, with the number in poverty falling from over 50 per cent in 1998 to just over 33 per cent in 2007, while extreme poverty has halved, from 20 per cent of the population to just under 10 per cent.[53] While these advances cannot all be laid at the door of the new local financial system, the evidence nevertheless does show that it has been of crucial importance in helping secure the poverty reduction, solidarity-building and sustainable job generation progress achieved.

Vietnam – a special case of 'progress with the wrong model'

Since the early 1990s, Vietnam has used its financial sector to promote a 'bottom-up' economic and social development trajectory. The result is that Vietnam is now universally recognized as having brought about one of the most successful developing-country poverty reduction episodes of the last twenty years. Poverty dramatically fell across all categories in the period 1993–2004. As measured by per capita consumption, the poverty rate fell from just over 58 per cent in 1993 to just under 20 per cent in 2004, representing a fall of almost 40 per cent in just eleven years. In the context of the UN's Millennium Development Goal of halving extreme poverty in the period 1990–2015, Vietnam's progress in reducing the poverty rate by 2004 to one third of its 1993 level is simply astonishing.[54] At least partly, this progress has been achieved by ensuring a very pro-poor economic policy – the Gini coefficient rose only from 0.34 in 1993 to 0.36 in 2006[55] – so that poor people have really shared in the benefits of the Vietnamese economy's growth and development. Duncan Green, head of research for the UK aid agency Oxfam GB, for example, describes Vietnam as the international development community's new 'poster child',[56] an object lesson to other poor developing countries in the way to begin to escape poverty and underdevelopment.

Crucially, Vietnam's stunning progress is intimately connected to the operation of a number of financial sector innovations and community-based financial institutions, alongside many coordinated supporting policy interventions. In fact, a wide variety of small-scale finance institutions have been established since the early 1990s, all of which have proved to be important in catalysing an extremely productive and sustainable enterprise development trajectory into existence. But what is even more intriguing here is the fact that Vietnam's financial sector has been modelled on core principles consistently anathematized by the microfinance industry for many years. Following study visits to the Grameen Bank in Bangladesh in the early 1990s, the Vietnamese rejected the Grameen Bank model in favour of a more proactive and developmental microfinance model similar to the Chinese model of UCCs and RCCs just noted above. By all accounts, if the key claims made by the microfinance industry and its supporters since the early 1990s are to be believed, the resulting heterodox and supposedly 'inefficient' microfinance system in Vietnam should have achieved very little in terms of development and sustainably reducing poverty. Yet, to their obvious discomfort, as we shall see below, the exact opposite has transpired.

Major reforms to the Vietnamese economic system began in 1986 in the shape of the policy of *doi moi* (renovation). Among other things, *doi moi* involved an increased emphasis upon independent small-scale family farms and private non-farm entrepreneurial activities. Along with better-managed state enterprises, these renewed private entities were slated to re-energize the local economy. Three core financial institutions were established to massively increase the flow of small-scale finance into these new private sector areas and into poor communities. First, there is the Vietnam Bank for Agriculture and Rural Development (VBARD). VBARD is the largest bank in Vietnam, with a network of more than two thousand branches. Its clientele are nearly 70 per cent rural households. Its loan portfolio in 2008 comprised loans for fisheries and livestock (40 per cent of portfolio), investment and working capital loans for annual and perennial crops, principally rice, rubber, tea, coffee (32 per cent) and handicrafts and trade (10 per cent), with the remainder going into rural infrastructure.[57] Average loan size in 2004 was $1,320, a good indication that the bank's primary focus is on small enterprises and family farms, rather than survivalist microenterprises or consumption lending.[58] VBARD provides both savings and microlending services mainly to the informal microenterprise sector. By the end of 2005, VBARD had nearly seven million savings accounts holding deposits of $7.5 billion.[59]

Second, there is the Vietnam Bank for Social Policy (VBSP) (formerly the Vietnam Bank for the Poor, VBP), which mainly provides subsidized microloans to the poor. The VBSP previously worked through the VBARD branch network, but in 2002 it established its own branch network. The VBSP continues the policy and directed lending programmes previously managed by the VBP and a number of state-owned commercial banks. Interest rates on VBSP loans are even lower than in VBARD, as are the loan sizes.

Third, there are the People's Credit Funds (PCFs), which were established from 1993 onwards as the replacement for hundreds of credit cooperatives that failed in the 1980s.[60] Established by the State Bank of Vietnam (SBV), the country's central bank, the PCFs are commune-based rural credit institutions based on the *Caisse Populaire* system successfully used in Quebec, Canada. By 2008, there were more than one thousand PCFs operating in fifty-six of Vietnam's sixty-four provinces, with more than 1.2 million members and total assets of nearly $900 million. Membership has also grown, from an average of just over 250 members per PCF in the mid-1990s to nearly 1,200 per PCF today. The PCFs mobilize a quite substantial amount of savings in the rural areas, rising to nearly $600 million in 2007. The average deposit balance per PCF rose from $28,000 in 1994 to nearly $600,000 in 2007. Average loan size has gone up too, from just $169 in 1997 to $931 in 2007, indicating that PCFs work at the higher end of the microenterprise market.[61] The apex organization standing above the PCFs is the Central People's Credit Fund (CCF). The PCFs are member-owned, while the CCF has been majority-owned by the SBV since its inception, with the PCFs and four state banks owning the remainder. SBV's share in the CCF increased in 2008 from 73 to 96 per cent, however, a move made prior to the CCF's planned conversion into a commercial bank.

Alongside these three main MFIs are a host of other organizations, including both state- and non-state-driven institutions, which work to provide low-cost (subsidized) credit to the poor as part of local development and poverty reduction programmes. Specifically addressing the needs of women in Vietnam, for instance, is the Women's Savings Group (WSG) system. Begun in 1991, this programme created self-managing revolving funds at the commune level. It is able to provide both a savings mechanism for women and a subsidized loan fund to be accessed for important consumption spending needs. By 2004, the WSG system was covering 98 per cent of Vietnam's communes. The WSGs also successfully disburse national government loan funds.

All told, in a relatively short time the Vietnamese government has succeeded in constructing a comprehensive and sophisticated framework of financial support for the vast bulk of the poor in the country. In other words, Vietnam's local financial system seems to have succeeded admirably in extending outreach. A report contracted by the UK's DfID aid arm found that the largely state-driven supply of small-scale finance was more than adequate for the country prior to the new millennium,[62] noting that 'The government seems [...] to be meeting much of the demand from credit-worthy households, even at low interest rates. The increased share of government loans in total household borrowing between 1992–98 [...] supports this conclusion.' Later on, a major two-volume report prepared for the World Bank also backed up this conclusion, describing the situation as one where[63]

> The quantitative outreach of microfinance (financial depth) in Vietnam is impressive, and very few people indeed are fully excluded from access to some form of financial service. There are under-served niche markets of very poor people in remote and under-served areas (ethnic minority communities) but the biggest market segment for microfinance in Vietnam are the 24% poor and low-income households that by and large already have access to some financial services. Contrary to perceptions, the 'unmet demand' in Vietnam is very small, especially within the traditional microfinance market.

Crucially, the quite dramatic poverty reduction trajectory in Vietnam very closely correlates to the significant volume of financial support disbursed through Vietnam's pro-poor local microfinance structure. Several factors are important here. Development of the agricultural sector has hugely benefited from the easy availability of small-scale capital on affordable terms and maturities. Far more than in other developing countries, small family farmers have been able to access affordable credit in order to deploy high-yield seed varieties, upgrade their own irrigation facilities, introduce new forms of mechanization and construct (often in partnership with neighbouring farms) important forms of storage and small-scale processing. Entirely new comparative advantages have been explored and underpinned through affordable loans, such as in the coffee sector and in certain types of fisheries. Pivotally, reinvestment rates are also high, because low interest rates help the farmers to retain a much larger share of the returns from agriculture. This is particularly so in rice farming. This is why most rice farmers have been able to effect an escape from the traditional Asian rice sector 'poverty trap', whereby high interest payments mean that the farmer remains just as poor as in the previous year (for example, neighbouring Cambodia is hugely held back by such problems[64]). With most Vietnamese households both consuming and producing rice, the programmed local increase in output first displaced the significant amount of rice imports. Food consumption and security improved markedly. Next, the growing surplus emerging from the most productive family farms was directed into the export trade. By the mid-1990s, Vietnam was the world's third-largest rice exporter (after the USA and Thailand).

More recently, Vietnam has made great strides in supporting rural light industrial businesses, both microenterprises and, particularly, growth-oriented SMEs. ASMED (the Agency for Small and Medium Enterprise Development) reports that more than 160,000 new enterprises were formally registered between 2000 and 2005, a significant increase on the previous decade. Perhaps more importantly, the capitalization of this new raft of enterprises is significantly higher than that of the previous generation. Private firms are also significantly reinvesting in their businesses. Aggregate investment by private firms as a percentage of the overall investment has risen from just under 23 per cent in 2000 to more than 32 per cent in 2005.[65] In addition, it is the exports of Vietnam's SMEs which account for much of the positive economic impact made nationally.

All told, Vietnam's microfinance model is a thoroughly heterodox model in a number of ways, but it works spectacularly well. Summing up some of the key differences from the 'new wave' microfinance model, these would include:[66]

- Vietnam's MFIs are not privately owned, but typically public or semi-public entities.
- They have much lower administrative expenses, partly because they eschew large salaries and bonuses to employees, and partly because they are subsidized by some outside bodies and the state.
- They do not borrow to fund their activities, but rely on equity, donations and savings.
- They are mainly policy-based lenders, pushed to focus on sectors

and geographic regions calculated to register most positive impact in terms of longer-term development and poverty reduction. For example, this accounts for why loans to petty trade-based micro-enterprises are very much lower than in other developing-country MFIs.

• They charge much lower interest rates that elsewhere in the world (in 2008 between 8 and 13 per cent), partly because they have much lower expenses than 'new wave' MFIs, and partly because the state sees no problem investing in (subsidizing) their activities because of the hugely important development outcomes realized to date.

But this success is hugely resented by the microfinance industry Given such dramatic success in both agriculture and industry, and without the need for the Compartamos-style exploitation deemed necessary in developing countries to extend outreach, one might be forgiven for assuming that the international development community would be driven to reflect a little more on the obvious benefits of such a heterodox microfinance model. Not a chance. In fact, from the mid-1990s up to the present day, the international development community has been quite rigid in its insistence that the Vietnamese simply must adhere to the standard 'new wave' microfinance model. As they were doing everywhere else, microfinance advocates operating in Vietnam first tried in the early 1990s to get the 'new wave' microfinance model accepted as the basic foundation for microfinance sector develop-ment in the country. When this effort failed, and the Vietnamese government embarked instead on its own 'home-grown' microfinance model, a rearguard action was mounted to try to reverse the decision. Driven on by key allies in the US government and the World Bank, the microfinance industry has not let up in its campaign against the Vietnamese government's heterodox local financial model.

The issue of the extensive use of subsidies in Vietnam's MFIs has naturally been one of the microfinance industry's core grievances. Right from the start, CGAP argued against Vietnam's decision to eschew the 'new wave' microfinance model, refusing to provide tech-nical support and funds as punishment for its decision.[67] Others soon joined in the assault. Leading 'new wave' microfinance advocate from as far back as the early Harvard Institute of International Develop-ment (HIID) days, Marguerite Robinson has been a particularly scathing critic of Vietnam's heterdox use of microfinance.[68] Regularly predicting it would end in disaster, while failing to even mention the great success achieved with Vietnam's 'home-grown' local financial model in the meantime, Robinson seems to believe that poverty reduction success can be recognized and tolerated only if it involves the right (neoliberal) ideological model.

Even today, when the evidence of significant progress is undeniable, the effort to get the Vietnamese government to backtrack on its choice of microfinance model continues unabated. Notably, the World Bank and CGAP doggedly continue to make the case for the 'new wave' microfinance model. Further pressure was forthcoming in 2004, for example, when the World Bank produced a comprehensively critical study of the VBSP.[69] This was then backed up by a contracted-out two-volume report prepared in 2007 by a group of dedicated microfinance specialists, which – as required – gave Vietnam's microfinance sector a good kicking.[70] The 2007 consultants' report remains adamant that 'the gradual elimination of subsidized credit mechanisms and other distortions in the sector is crucial to the development of sound microfinance'.[71] No real analysis of the manifestly positive development impact of Vietnam's local financial system to date is provided. It is simply taken as given that converting to the 'new wave' model will bring significant benefits for Vietnam's economy and people. The consultants' report also expressed its upset at the fact that non-state MFIs were being held back by the subsidized competition provided by the state-driven MFIs, which was seen, without any real explanation as to why, to be a very bad thing for Vietnam's poor. Perhaps the problem is, as the report tellingly concludes, the fact that 'There is still a widespread tendency for some in the Government to see microfinance as a social tool to combat poverty.'[72] How silly of them.

Finally, local institutions in Vietnam have also been generously funded (by such as the Ford Foundation) in order that they can mount a lobbying blitz on behalf of the 'new wave' microfinance model. The main international donor channel for some time was the Vietnam Microfinance Working Group. With international donor support in 2009 it converted itself into a formal association, the Vietnam Microfinance Association (VMA), the better to lobby for 'needed changes'. The explicitly political mission of the VMA is made abundantly clear, however, in its vision statement, which notes that it aims to bring about[73] 'a large and dynamic microfinance industry of professional, sustainable and efficient institutions that offer un-subsidized, high-quality, and demand-responsive financial services to a growing portion of the poor and low-income population of Viet Nam, enabling the Government of Viet Nam to gradually phase out policy lending'.

Backing up this effort is a new programme unrolled in late 2009 by the Asian Development Bank (ADB) which aims to bring a number of informal MFIs into the formal sector, among other things by training them in the concept of 'market-based microfinance'. Now ignoring the conclusions of previous reports praising the Vietnamese local financial system for its effective coverage (such as the 2007 two-volume DFC report cited above), the rationale is that the current largely state-driven MFIs have, on the contrary, 'struggled to meet the real financial needs of the poor, and offer limited services'.[74]

In spite of massive success with its own local microfinance model to date, it really does seem that – by hook or by crook – Vietnam will somehow be made to fit in with what the international development community considers to be 'best practice'.[75] The microfinance model pioneered in Vietnam clearly represents to the microfinance industry and its supporters in the international development community 'the threat of a good example'.[76] It needs to be repeated that Vietnam's heterodox local financial model was principally designed to promote small-scale enterprises (not so much microenterprises) and scaled-up small-farm projects (not so much subsistence farms), both of which the government felt had a better chance of promoting productivity growth and sustainable local economic and social development. And, as we have seen, it has been an extremely successful financial model in terms of attaining these original development goals. Of course, there has been a financial cost to this success. Some local financial institutions are not fully self-sustaining, and require regular govern-ment subsidies. But this is seen as perfectly acceptable in view of the very impressive economic and social development results that can be, and were, achieved. Nowhere is the corrosive influence of neoliberal politics and ideology within the microfinance industry more apparent than in the resistance to Vietnam's heterodox local financial model.

Conclusion

Even a cursory glance at recent (post-1945) economic history reveals that there are many local financial system alternatives to micro-finance. Crucially, once one distils the key lessons from all of these experiences, one finds the building blocks for a very sophisticated and proactive local financial system model – a financial model unlike anything associated with the Grameen Bank experiment, and with even less in common with the 'new wave' microfinance model that dominates today. While some of these experiences relate to already advanced economies, which some might argue precludes any lessons as regards what developing countries might be able to achieve, the fact that many developing countries have achieved enormous success with virtually the same model (of course, updated to take account of today's different business environment) indicates that it is broadly transferable to other contexts.

These earlier and ongoing financial models differ from today's microfinance model in a number of areas: the routine willingness to use subsidies (let us perhaps use the less ideologically charged word 'investment' instead); the use of sectoral targeting lending methodologies; a preference for longer-term loan maturities; a drive to integrate microenterprises into supply chains as production-based units; public and community ownership of financial institutions; and attempts to incorporate microenterprise and SME development into local strategic planning processes. All of these key aspects of the financial models described above are anathema to the microfinance model, yet they have been made to work very well in practice. Moreover, a clue as to why such patently good experience has been carefully incorporated into successive financial models in some geographical regions (East Asia) but not in most others – that is, those countries under the sway of the Washington DC-based international financial institutions – comes from the microfinance industry's almost hysterical reaction to the success of Vietnam's heterodox local financial model. The microfinance industry and, particularly, the Washington DC-based international development community institutions, appear to be determined to promote poverty reduction only so long as the policies chosen are in full agreement with the approved ideology (neoliberalism), and almost irrespective of whether such policies actually work or not.

This chapter has, among other things, given the lie to the oft-repeated claim made by the microfinance industry that there are no (or *no longer*) any meaningful alternatives to microfinance. Rather, I would claim that there have always been, and still are, manifestly far better strategic policy interventions than microfinance. The financial support channelled through MFIs into microenterprises is not the only use for these funds. As many of the above countries found, it pays handsomely to try to redirect finance into more sustainable and developmental uses. Moreover, as the East Asian countries have sometimes brilliantly shown, and as many European countries also demonstrated in the nineteenth and early twentieth century,[77] a country can easily learn from the experiments and successes of its neighbours, and then turn towards fashioning its own financial sector policies geared to its own contemporary economic, political and social reality. It remains to be seen for how much longer the international development community will continue to disallow developing and transition economies similar leeway.

EIGHT
Conclusion: the need for a new beginning

'A true revolution of values will soon cause us to question the fairness and justice of many of our past and present policies. [...] True compassion is more than flinging a coin to a beggar. It comes to see that an edifice which produces beggars needs restructuring.' Dr Martin Luther King, Jr[1]

'Markets are not magic: Debt is not freedom: The Gods have failed: It is time to live without them.' Larry Elliot and Dan Atkinson[2]

Over the last thirty years microfinance has become one of the most important international development policy interventions in the field of poverty alleviation and development. Huge amounts of international development aid, philanthropic investment and commercial funding have been committed in its direction. Most of all, the savings of ordinary people, especially including poor people, have increasingly been intermediated through MFIs. The intentions appeared to be just and the ambitions were bold. It all looked so optimistic at the start. The initial progress looked even better. Reports began to emerge from the pioneering MFIs that they were creating and sustaining large numbers of jobs and income flows, local women were being empowered as never before, and a 'bottom-up' development process was emerging that would soon see the typical local economy finally shake itself free of poverty and underdevelopment. Bangladesh was held up as leading the way in perfecting this economic miracle cure, a cure that Muhammad Yunus confidently said would see global poverty completely eliminated in a generation. Under the international development community's wise guidance and with its financial aid, other developing countries soon began to follow the path marked out by the Grameen Bank and Bangladesh. Bolivia, (southern) India, Bosnia, Peru, Cambodia, Nicaragua, Mexico, Uganda, Mongolia – all these countries expected to register similar important economic and social gains thanks to having fairly quickly achieved microfinance 'saturation'. And with increasingly large amounts of cash being channelled since 2000 into the global expansion of microfinance, just about every developing and transition country began to eagerly look forward to similar benefits.

The aim of this book, however, has been to show how seriously wrong this uplifting picture actually is in practice. In truth, microfinance represents an *anti-development* policy – a development policy that largely works *against* the establishment of sustainable economic and social development trajectories, and so also against sustainable poverty reduction. For the majority of people in developing and transition countries, their country's diversion into microfinance has actually undermined previous and ongoing efforts to reduce poverty, unemployment, inequality and underdevelopment. In many ways microfinance represents a wrong turning similar to the former Soviet Union's plan-driven channelling of its own scarce resources into inefficient giant factories, huge collectivized state farms and a bloated military-industrial complex. Microfinance is the mirror image of Soviet-style central planning, and just as misguided and ultimately ineffective. Supremely emblematic of the many problems I have recounted in this book is the sad fate that has befallen Jobra, the famed village in Bangladesh where Muhammad Yunus effectively began the microfinance revolution back in the late 1970s: unfortunately, after thirty or so years of unparalleled easy access to microfinance, its hapless inhabitants still remain trapped in extreme poverty and deprivation.[3]

Let me briefly summarize the main themes and findings of the book as follows.

1 Microfinance has, in a roundabout way, been present for a long time. Movements to provide forms of small-scale finance to help the poor began to flourish in the late eighteenth century, gathering speed as the negative impacts of industrial capitalism began to emerge. The result was that the nineteenth century became a century of reformist and radical leftist experiments using forms of what we would now call microfinance. From the 1960s onwards, a new generation of reformers, radicals and anti-capitalists emerged and began to argue against 'faceless' corporate capitalism (and against centrally planned communism too), and they suggested that modern society needed to move towards a more 'human-centred' and environmentally sustain-

able economic system based on smaller units, democratic principles and using local finance. Neither of these two important traditions, however, had much influence on Muhammad Yunus, who, picking up from earlier microcredit experiments pioneered by Akhtar Hameed Khan, began to promote his own version of microcredit in Bangladesh in the mid-1970s. Muhammad Yunus's contribution was to be seen as the first to really popularize the microfinance concept as a contemporary development intervention. He did this, however, by pitching the concept to those on the right of the political spectrum. Yunus's ideals were firmly based on validating individual entrepreneurship and self-help and promoting the financial responsibility of the poor. The international development community took note. Rather than fight collectively through the state or trade unions or social movements and other forms of social mobilization, or argue for land reform or wealth redistribution, or vote in a pro-poor government (if you had the opportunity), it was hoped that the poor could now be encouraged to settle for informal microenterprise activity instead, supported by microfinance. Thereafter, the poor could be left to themselves to 'get on with it'. The very few lucky 'winners' in the informal sector could naturally be picked out, applauded and publicized. Meanwhile, the far larger number of outright losers could simply be forgotten about, or even blamed for their own poverty status (for example, they were lazy or they made poor asset portfolio choices). The opportunity was all that mattered. So, Yunus's idea and ideals were never about seriously challenging capitalism, but essentially about bringing capitalism down to the poor in order to legitimize and strengthen it.

2 As the neoliberal political project gathered steam in the 1980s, however, it soon became clear that Yunus's original Grameen Bank model would not survive intact. Poverty lending was interesting only so far as it could be financially self-sustaining. The poor simply had to pay for their own escape from poverty. The neoliberal policy-making establishment began to build support for its commercialized replacement, one that would overturn most of the principles Yunus had incorporated into the Grameen Bank as fundamental to its operation. We saw how key neoliberal-oriented institutions pushed in this commercializing direction, especially USAID and the World Bank (particularly through CGAP). Through USAID the US government took the lead in offering generous financial support to those US-based organizations willing to push the commercialization idea forward. The challenge was notably taken up by the NGO ACCIÓN and the

Harvard Institute for International Development (HIID), both of which became central to the development of the neoliberal counter-offensive in favour of commercialized microfinance, and in providing important working examples too (respectively Bancosol and BRI). The result by the early 1990s was the 'new wave' microfinance model, a financial model premised upon an MFI aggressively pursuing profit and financially incentivizing its own staff and supporters as never before. At a time when Wall Street began to hold the world in awe of its supposed accomplishments and efficiency, it seemed perfectly appropriate for these US-based institutions to want to inject Wall Street's 'best practice' methodologies, values and ambitions right into the heart of microfinance. Within a short period of time the 'new wave' microfinance model emerged to become the dominant microfinance model. Muhammad Yunus was encouraged to remain the 'friendly face' of microfinance, and subsequently showered with awards, but his original Grameen Bank model was sidelined. Microfinance was instead effectively colonized by neoliberalism, a political creed that even its key architects willingly and openly admit is premised upon the effective disempowerment of the poor in favour of 'more productive' economic and political elites. Microfinance thus became the preferred local strand of neoliberalism. That is, microfinance became *local neoliberalism*.

3 More than ever before, a sophisticated public narrative was required to shield developing-country governments and the wider public from the political and ideological aims and, increasingly, personal greed now driving forward microfinance. A public narrative gradually evolved based upon a set of interwoven myths that would project economic development, poverty reduction, empowerment and social-capital-building at the heart of microfinance, while centrally stressing that it 'came at no cost to donor governments or to tax-payers' thanks to market-based interest rates. In fact, an 'absurd gap' now exists between the reality of microfinance and the heady rhetoric. Almost all of the main foundations of microfinance are based on carefully crafted and deliberately maintained myths. The current public narrative surrounding microfinance is as close to actual reality as the Walt Disney film *The Lion King* is to daily events in the Serengeti National Park. Going farther with the jungle metaphor, I pointed out that the main current 'elephant in the room' so far as microfinance is concerned is that a very large and growing percentage of microfinance (estimates range from between 50 and 90 per cent)

is now channelled into simple consumption spending. Few in the microfinance industry wish to publicly acknowledge that this is in fact the case, however. Having established microfinance on the basis that it helps a poor person start a microenterprise – the overwhelmingly dominant image any ordinary member of the public has about microfinance – the reality that this is an increasingly rare occurrence cannot now be exposed for fear of destroying the entire edifice of microfinance.

4 Most important of all, I pointed out that we do not find that the basic Grameen Bank microfinance model made anywhere near the positive contribution to poverty reduction and development its supporters claim that it did and does. One core reason for the 'absurd gap' between the myth and the reality is that impact assessments are specifically designed to avoid discussion of two key downside factors: displacement and client exit. In terms of the first factor, we saw that Muhammad Yunus founded his Grameen Bank microfinance model on a misunderstanding of the 'fallacy of composition'. Yunus wrongly believed that a local version of Say's law existed – that an unlimited number of microenterprises could be productively floated into the worst recesses of local poverty and deprivation, starting in Bangladesh. The local supply of the products and services produced by this rush of new local microenterprises would always and automatically create the local demand to secure their purchase. This fundamental error was quickly exposed in Bangladesh, but it was largely kept quiet in order not to undermine the validity of the Grameen Bank's claims to be pioneering individual entrepreneurship and self-help among the poor as the solution to poverty. Promoting the required ideology of self-help was far more important to the international development community than whether or not microfinance actually worked for the poor (or even just better than other possible policy options). In terms of the second factor – client exit – we know from many country experiences that this factor signally undermines the longer-run success of any microfinance programme. But, again, this important downside to microfinance was, and is, largely ignored for fear of how deep it might actually go.

5 Not least because impact assessments contain some very fundamental flaws, then, we assessed the microfinance model's real contribution to economic development in terms of the effect upon the key development 'triggers' that we pretty much know underpin sustainable local economic and social development. The key global finding is

that with regard to almost all the core 'triggers' of importance, the microfinance model makes a quite negative impact. Some minor positive impact in some areas – such as providing important immediate help for 'at-risk' individuals recovering from conflict, natural disaster or economic collapse – cannot make up for the significant downsides registered elsewhere in the local economy over the long term. The industrial and agricultural base of many developing countries – a base often put together at huge cost and long-term sacrifice – has been largely undermined by the microfinance sector's failure to appreciate the importance of scale, connectivity, formalization, technology and innovation. The local economy has been helped to become import dependent. Valuable reserves of social capital have been plundered and destroyed by the microfinance sector simply in order to ensure high repayment levels, thereby to secure an MFI's financial survival. Increasingly, too, the objective is to maximize profits, thereby to inflate salaries and bonuses for MFI staff, as well as dividends for shareholders.

6 Importantly, the most valuable local enterprises in the SME sector have, not coincidentally, been starved of the appropriate funds necessary to get started and to upgrade. Indeed, all those countries at the forefront of the microfinance revolution have extreme difficulty in mobilizing financial support with which to develop their crucially important SME sectors. With microfinance such a well-regarded financial intervention, and then later on such a hugely profitable one too, there is no sense at all for a market-driven privately owned local financial system to work with the SME sector. The gradual and inexorable primitivization and weakening of the typical local economy in microfinance-'saturated' countries, regions and localities, as microfinance is prioritized over all forms of SME finance, is therefore almost inevitable. This may even be called an 'Iron Law of Microfinance'.

7 As if the above development problems were not enough, analysis of the current 'new wave' microfinance model, and the specific economic and social trajectories it has set in motion, reveals an even more depressing picture. As a commercially oriented institution, the typical MFI may indeed be able to 'pay its own way', but it does so only by abandoning the few recognizable benefits generated by 'old paradigm' microfinance of the Grameen Bank kind. Ideologically driven and, increasingly, greed-driven 'new wave' microfinance deepens the microfinance 'poverty trap'. It increasingly sucks up resources from the poor (from the bottom of the pyramid) in order to benefit

two groups: first, institutional investors, many based in rich countries; and, second, key employees/owners of an MFI itself, among other things helping create the new antisocial phenomenon I denoted as the 'microfinance millionaires'. Once the institutional shareholders and the managers and directors have taken their cut, the scope for poverty reduction is minimal. Importantly, no matter what the poor might say they want, high interest rates must be maintained as much as possible in order to keep the tribute flowing up to both these groups, and also to avoid any possibility of tribute flowing from the wealthy down to the poor in order to keep an MFI in operation. In addition, the profit-driven expansion of an individual MFI inevitably risks giving rise to an over-accumulation of capacity overall, which brings us to the growing problem of 'microcredit bubbles'. The bursting of these 'microcredit bubbles', whether gradual or instant, results in a major economic reversal and havoc within the poorest communities.

8 It is increasingly coming to be accepted that there is no concrete evidence to support the widespread and long-standing claims that microfinance is positively associated with sustainable economic development and poverty reduction impacts. This is in spite of more than thirty years in which, for obvious reasons, the microfinance industry has been desperately trying to locate just such important evidence. In fact, virtually the only achievement 'new wave' microfinance can legitimately lay claim to is that it can increasingly 'pay its own way'. This claim means little, however. Many of the very best public interventions require investment or subsidies (if you will), but cost–benefit analysis proves beyond a doubt that the investment/subsidy was worthwhile. Moreover, one is also naturally tempted to say, the tobacco industry can also pay its own way, yet most sensible people still realize that the expansion of 'big tobacco' over the last fifty years has been nothing short of a monumental disaster for humankind. In both cases – microfinance and tobacco – financial self-sustainability achieved thanks to a powerful addiction to a well-marketed product tells us absolutely nothing about the real long-term value of that product to the individual or the local community. I concluded that the Pandora's box that is commercialization has been opened, and it cannot now be easily closed. Wall Street-style antisocial trajectories are now the norm. The 'new wave' microfinance model's claims to be a poverty reduction tool are now dead in the water.

9 All of the above problems naturally pose the question as to why the international development community willingly supported, and

continues to support, microfinance. I briefly explored this conundrum in Chapter 6. Initially, the microfinance concept was publicly 'sold' to the international development community by Muhammad Yunus on the hope that meaningful amounts of jobs and income would result. The real initial attraction to the international development community, however, was that microfinance would help validate the notion that individual entrepreneurship through informal sector activity could be projected as the only legitimate way for the poor to attempt to escape their poverty. Fighting against all manner of state-driven and collective responses to poverty, especially against communist-socialist movements in developing countries, the rich developing countries saw in the Grameen Bank a practical way forward. Here was a highly visible and 'feel-good' way of appearing to support the poor in developing countries, while in reality greatly limiting their current and future options to make substantive pro-poor changes to their own society, changes that had to be resisted because they would inevitably disadvantage economic and political elites. As the neoliberal revolution got into full swing from the mid-1980s onwards, the poor themselves were then given the added burden of actually covering the cost of the microfinance revolution under way. The drive to remove subsidy and to promote dependence upon market interest rates instead was a global imperative of neoliberalism. Its application within the world of microfinance was to be expected at some stage, no matter the impact upon the poor.

10 An important overarching hope in neoliberal policy elite circles is that, with microfinance to hand, the poor will in future present much less of a challenge to capitalism, and therefore to the power and privilege enjoyed by economic and political elites. The hope is that the poor will come to see their individual salvation solely through the lens of petty market interaction. We know, however, that poverty is essentially a function of a lack of power and political organization. I therefore pointed out that the poor will achieve little if they accept their newly assigned role as 'micro-entrepreneurs', and so, as they are meant to do, increasingly shy away from challenging the fundamental structures of power and privilege. The poor in the past have achieved many important pro-poor gains and material improvements. But, except for a tiny few cases, these gains have *not* come about through individual entrepreneurial action, but through democratic politics, social movements, pressure groups, trade unions and the like. To use Amartya Sen's construction,[4] the poor have been able to obtain the

important 'collective capabilities' that best help ensure that development and growth are firmly *pro-poor*. Job security legislation, a public health service, the minimum wage, public employment, state pensions, state education and training services, and so on and so forth, have all played their crucial part in meeting the needs of the poor in society for a more secure and dignified working life. But those promoting microfinance, starting with Muhammad Yunus, have consistently avoided addressing the key issues of power and politics. Even the much-vaunted 'solidarity groups' that are an outgrowth of many microfinance programmes are very largely designed to support and remain within the orbit of existing power and political structures, not to fundamentally challenge such structures on behalf of the poor. On this reading, therefore, other than giving the surface appearance of activity, effort and concern, microfinance is preordained to achieve almost nothing for the poor. To use the parlance made famous on the 2008 US presidential election campaign trail, microfinance is no more than 'lipstick on the pig'.

11 Finally, I outlined a number of important heterodox experiments with local finance. In contrast to both Grameen Bank-style microfinance and the 'new wave' microfinance model that followed, these local financial models have over time incontrovertibly produced positive impacts for the poor, and for local society in general. I showed that these local financial models provide the fundamental building blocks of a far more developmental and pro-poor local financial model than the two microfinance models considered here. The suggestion was that there is much to learn from these important examples. Indeed, if the dominant 'new wave' microfinance model is to be phased out, here is where developing and transition countries should start to look in order to find the building blocks for its replacement. Some indication of why learning from such financial models remains difficult today, however, is provided by the very final example, that of Vietnam. In spite of overwhelming evidence that Vietnam has achieved important poverty reduction gains thanks to its heterodox microfinance model, the international development community has mounted a long and, at times, hysterical campaign to get Vietnam to abandon it and adopt the 'new wave' model in its place. If this is the reaction to very obvious success with a particular local financial system, but one unacceptably built around non-neoliberal principles, then this clearly shows what is *really* driving certain sections of the international development community and the microfinance industry.

What appears to count much more here is the politics and the ideology, and not whether the poor are really being helped to improve their lives. This is a profoundly disturbing final observation to make on the activities and objectives of the key international development organizations and the main supporters of microfinance today.

Concluding thoughts

For those with an interest in seeing sustainable economic and social development in developing countries and elsewhere, certainly including myself, it is thoroughly discomforting to have to conclude that microfinance does not work. Would that it were otherwise. It hurts even more to realize that the microfinance model not only does not work, it is also *known* not to be working. To a large extent, microfinance has been supported and protected on account of its supreme serviceability to the international development community's preferred societal model of neoliberal capitalism. What counts here is not so much achieving genuinely sustainable development and poverty reduction (though it would help!), but ensuring the unquestioned application of market forces, fiscal discipline and personal financial responsibility, all to be vectored through private individual entrepreneurship. Even though it is through exercising their *collective capabilities* that the poor have in the past registered the most social progress and the greatest improvement in their material living standards, it is hoped that in future they will nevertheless come to accept the abandonment of such a strategy.

Progress for the poor, if any, is henceforth to be secured on an *individual* basis through petty individual entrepreneurship, and based upon their own meagre resources topped up with a little microfinance. Safe in the knowledge that their own power and privileges can now no longer be challenged by collective effort and social mobilization, economic and political elites in the developed countries can rest easy. The poor can be left everywhere to fight it out among themselves as to who might emerge with a tolerable life. Of course, a few individual 'success stories' will be identified and carefully promoted in order to maintain the impression that much progress is being achieved by, and on behalf of, the poor. All the time, however, it is apparent that the poor are really being forced back into their historic isolation and powerlessness, which portends little real advancement in reality. This is a profoundly depressing scenario, but it most accurately explains the international development community's rationale and strong support for microfinance during the last thirty years or so better than any other explanation.

In a very real sense, then, the microfinance model represents one more example of the 'kicking away the ladder' approach vividly described by Cambridge economist Ha-Joon Chang in his award-winning book of the same name.[5] As Chang describes it, history shows that the developed countries achieved their great success through many varied forms of state intervention allied to social mobilization strategies (for example, powerful trade unions, as in Scandinavia). History also shows, however, that the rich developed countries have routinely acted to dissuade the developing countries from using these same policies and interventions. One of the most basic reasons is, as Chang maintains, that 'Already established countries do not want more competitors emerging through nationalistic policies they themselves used in the past.'[6] Extensive state intervention helped a small group of countries to develop and become rich, but then these same now-rich countries had a very powerful reason to promote free markets and non-interventionist policies in developing countries in order to keep their *own* position of wealth and strength intact. Essentially, by denying to developing countries the chance to use their own resources to build their own industries and agricultural sectors in the way the rich developed countries had done in the past, and still do, it is possible to maintain the existing highly unequal global economic and social order.

Seen in this context, then, it is quite clearly *not* the case that the poor in developing and transition countries have been generously and selflessly offered the microfinance model to better their lot. Instead, microfinance is simply one more strand in the ongoing attempt to impose neoliberal policies around the globe, policies that are designed to work − first and foremost − in favour of economic and political elites in the developed economies. Put simply, the poor need to be encouraged to focus their energies and commitment on individual petty entrepreneurship aided by microfinance. They will then be more likely to eschew the radical pro-poor policies, democratically elected pro-poor governments and progressive social movements that history shows can greatly help their cause, but which will end up jeopardizing the business and political interests of the developed Western countries.

So, finally, to the hugely important question: Where do we need to look to find the local financial models that can replace the underachieving and politically suspect microfinance model? As just noted, Chapter 7 briefly summarized a range of local financial policies and microfinance programmes with obvious potential to serve the poor far better than either the Grameen Bank model or its 'new wave' replacement. Through the auspices of proactive state and non-state community-based institutions, local finance can become instead a powerful tool that can *really* help build and underpin sustainable local economic and social development, and so bring about sustainable poverty reduction. In the aftermath of the effective collapse of the neoliberal policy model in late 2008 following the bankruptcy of Lehman Brothers, and in the context of the 'Great Recession' that this historic event quickly precipitated, such community-driven local financial models are now a good deal more realistic than they have been for some considerable time. And as probably never before in recent history, unfortunately, they are certainly required.

Notes

1 Introduction

1 The original term was actually microcredit, but this was subsumed into the broader term microfinance in the early 1990s. The world largely knows the phenomenon as 'microfinance' so I will largely use this term as the generic descriptor in this book.

2 For example, see 'The future of capitalism', an excellent two-month series of major articles and think-pieces, web-based discussions and video presentations produced by the *Financial Times* starting in April 2009.

3 See 'The Great Stabilisation', *The Economist*, 19 December 2009.

4 Already the attempt by economic and political elites to ensure 'business as usual' has started, including unprecedented amounts of cash flowing into lobbying bodies working on behalf of Wall Street's remaining financial institutions. See 'Wall Street steps up political donations, lobbying', *Wall Street Journal*, 23 October 2009.

2 The rise of microfinance

1 Remarks from Dr Muhammad Yunus's acceptance speech given on the occasion of his receiving the Help for Self-help Prize of the Stromme Foundation, 26 September 1997, in Oslo, Norway. See *Newsletter of the Microcredit Summit Campaign*, 1(2), November/December 1997.

2 As Hulme and Moore suggest, microfinance is perhaps the sole development policy that the 'average person in the street' might know a little about. See Hulme and Moore (2006).

3 For example, see Yunus (2007), Yunus with Jolis (1998); see also Counts (2008); Dowla and Barua (2006); Hulme (2008). As I write, a film version of the life of Yunus is in preparation.

4 See Nasim Yousaf, 'Dr Akhtar Hameed Khan – the pioneer of microcredit', *The Frontier Post* (Pakistan), 10 September 2007, www. thefrontierpost.com/News.aspx? ncat=bn&nid=36&ad=09-10-2007.

5 The standard text on the 'Comilla Model' is Raper (1970).

6 For example, see Yunus (1989: 159).

7 A key text expounding this view is Von Pischke et al. (1983).

8 This is when the moneylender takes on a particular client with the express purpose of eventually taking over their land. The practice has been called 'debt farming' by Roth (1983). See also the discussion in Robinson (2001: 178–80).

9 For example, see Yunus (2007: 35).

10 See Yunus (ibid.: 46).

11 For example, see the illuminating discussion in Rutherford et al. (2003: 15–16).

12 See Counts (2008: 66).

13 For an excellent discussion of the SHG concept and, in particular, the similarities to and differences from the Grameen Bank model, see Harper (2002).

14 See Levitsky (1989).

15 See Seibel (2005). In practice, however, the terms microfinance, microcredit and microloans are all pretty much interchangeable.

16 See Morduch (1999).

17 A typical example would be Jackelen (1989).

18 Personal communication with Malcolm Harper.

19 Quoted by Daniel Pearl and Michael Phillips in their article published in the *Wall Street Journal*, 27 November 2001.

20 For example, see Adams et al. (1984). While ideologically bang on target, however, David Hulme and Paul Mosley reported that much of the beating doled out by the Ohio School was quite seriously misplaced – see Hulme and Mosley (1996: vol. 1, ch. 1). For a more recent and very effective rebuttal of many of the key Ohio School ideas, see Chang (2009).

21 It was somewhat ironic, as Naomi Klein points out, that HIID ran into its own financial scandal typical of the extensively deregulated 'grab what you can' business environment that it was promoting on ideological (neoliberal) grounds. Some of HIID's US staff working in Russia on its privatization programme were found to be using their inside knowledge to make stock market investments through their wives and girlfriends. The US government sued Harvard University. This effectively forced HIID to close down in June 2000, and Harvard University was then subject to the largest ever US government fine levied against a US academic institution ($26.5 million). See Klein (2007: 235).

22 Sachs has famously abandoned his earlier neoliberal posture, and now strongly promotes much greater state and international donor community intervention, as well as subsidies for many pro-poor services. For example, see Sachs (2005). This conversion has not always been accepted uncritically. For example, development economist Erik Reinert refers to Sachs as now mainly involved in 'palliative economics', which Rienert describes as the desperate attempt by Sachs to fix the many problems directly caused by his earlier neoliberal policy advice. See Reinert (2007).

23 See Robinson (1995).

24 In November 2003, however, 30 per cent of BRI's shares were sold to the public through an IPO.

25 See Drake and Rhyne (2002: ch. 2).

26 In August 2009 Maria Otero was appointed US Under-Secretary of State for Democracy and Global Affairs in the administration of President Barack Obama.

27 Quoted in 'Millions for millions', *New Yorker*, 30 October 2006.

28 See Otero and Rhyne (1994).

29 Personal communication with Tom Dichter.

30 See Donors' Working Group on Financial Sector Development and the Committee of Donor Agencies for Small Enterprise Development at the World Bank (1995).

31 The 'Pink Book' also had a companion volume – the 'Blue Book' (see Committee of Donor Agencies

for Small Enterprise Development 2001) – which regulated the establishment and operation of Business Development Services (BDS) institutions. Produced by almost the exact same institutions (and even some of the same individuals) as the 'Pink Book', the 'Blue Book' pretty much set out the very same commercialization guidelines for the approved establishment and operation of BDS providers. It is germane to the present analysis of commercialized MFIs to note that the results of commercialized BDS provision were very poor indeed almost everywhere. In eastern Europe, for example, a major evaluation of EU-financed SME programmes in the 1990s (see EU 2000) found that most of the EU-financed commercialized BDS institutions soon arrived at one of three outcomes: they closed down because poor clients could not afford to pay for their commercial services; they shifted into unrelated, but typically more lucrative, areas of consulting work (such as work for MNCs, governments and for the international development agencies themselves); or, finally, they opportunistically converted into an RDA to be funded in future by the EU. See also Bateman (2000).

32 For example, see Otero and Rhyne (1994); Ledgerwood (1999).

33 For example, see Armendáriz de Aghion and Morduch (2005: ch. 9).

34 See Rutherford et al. (2006: 2).

35 The story of Grameen II is comprehensively dealt with by Dowla and Barua (2006).

36 Withdrawal of this savings amount is possible after the three years are up, but savers must still keep a minimum balance of 2,000 taka, or the withdrawal must be no more than one half of the amount in the account, whichever is larger. For an explanation and examples of how such obligatory savings schemes work in practice to significantly raise interest rates, see Mitra (2009).

37 See Counts (2008: 66).

38 This account was also initially capitalized with 2.5 per cent of any microloan provided, but withdrawal is thereafter possible unless the client is on a bridge loan or flexible loan product.

39 See Rutherford et al. (2006: 12).

40 See Collins et al. (2009: 172).

41 See Rutherford et al. (2006: 39).

42 See Yunus (2007: xi). When it became apparent that poverty was not being reduced as much as had been claimed it would be, and when in many places poverty was actually becoming even worse, 'moving the goalposts' in this manner became a very common fallback feature right across the microfinance industry.

43 See Hulme (2008: 9).

44 For example, the ILO now defines microfinance to be '… the provision of financial services to the poor *on a sustainable basis*' (my italics). See p. 1 of the ILO Circular 246: *Organization: Microfinance for decent work: organization and responsibilities of the Social Finance Programme (SFP)*, 31 January 2007.

45 See Smith and Furman (2007).

46 As David Roodman reported, however, it turned out that there was a serious element of deception involved in the way that Kiva raised funds for the microfinance movement. See 'Kiva is not quite what it seems', *David Roodman's*

Microfinance Open Book Blog,
2 October 2009, blogs.cgdev.org/
open_book). See also 'Confusion
on where money lent via Kiva goes',
New York Times, 8 November 2009.
  47 See Leleux and Constantinou
(2007).
  48 An initial public offering is
the first sale of shares by a company
to the general public and investors.
The IPO provides capital for the
company to expand and develop.
  49 See Karlan and Zinman
(2009); Banerjee, Duflo, Glennerster
and Kinnan (2009).
  50 See Roodman and Morduch
(2009).
  51 See M. Davis (2006).

3 Microfinance myths and realities

  1 The famed *New York Times*
journalist Ron Suskind is interview-
ing a White House aide about the
policies of George W. Bush. See
'Faith, certainty and the presidency
of George W. Bush', *New York
Times*, 17 October 2004.
  2 See Galbraith (1976 [1958]:
128).
  3 See Hospes and Lont (2004: 3).
  4 For example, see Gulli (1998);
Morduch (2000).
  5 See Dichter (2007).
  6 See Rahman (1999: 106).
  7 See Goldin Institute (2007: 5).
  8 See Collins et al. (2009, esp.
ch. 6).
  9 See 'Microcredit: why India is
failing', *Forbes*, 10 November 2006.
  10 Finscope is an initiative of the
FinMark Trust and is the most comprehensive national household survey
focused on financial services needs
and usage across the entire South
and southern African population.

  11 FinMark Trust, press release,
December 2006.
  12 Rutherford is quoted in
'Microcredit loans "used to buy
food"', *Financial Times*, 4 June
2009.
  13 See De Soto (1989).
  14 See Polanyi (1944).
  15 See Mayhew (1985 [1851]).
  16 Interestingly, as Tom Dichter
points out, 150 years before the
UN Year of Microcredit, Henry
Mayhew himself was behind an
initiative to set up a 'loan office
for the poor'. This initiative was
designed to give the poor grants and
soft loans to help them do better
in the netherworld of survivalist
microenterprises that Mayhew so
eloquently documented. See Dichter
(2007: 185).
  17 The term lumpenproletariat is
first defined in a book by Karl Marx
and Friedrich Engels completed in
1845 but first published in 1932 – see
Marx and Engels (1932 [1845]).
  18 See Harvey (2006, esp. ch. 2).
  19 For example, see Blanchflower
and Freeman (1993).
  20 For example, see Breman
(2003, 2009); Breman and Das
(2000); Roy and Alsayyad (2004).
  21 See Karlan and Goldberg
(2007).
  22 See Ellerman (2007: 155).
  23 As we now know with awful
clarity (for example, see Kansas
2009), because the main ratings
agencies were keen to pick up as
much work as possible from Wall
Street's investment banks, they were
very easily influenced into declaring
an AAA rating on huge amounts of
worthless investment instruments
(e.g. sub-prime mortgage-backed
assets).

24 See UN-Habitat (2003).

25 See M. Davis (2006: 183).

26 See MFI Solutions and La Colmena Milenaria (2008: 19).

27 See News Release no. 2009/240/PREM, World Bank, 11 March 2009.

28 See World Bank (2009).

29 Ibid.: 39.

30 For example, see Agarwal (1990).

31 See Getubig et al. (2000: 5).

32 See World Bank (2001).

33 US economist Paul Krugman shows that the US government's New Deal in the 1930s was quite decisive in creating a middle class in America – see Krugman (2007). Larry Elliot and Dan Atkinson point out that Britain's welfare state did the same for the UK after 1945 – see Elliot and Atkinson (2008: 75).

34 For example, Graham Wright ludicrously conflates the socially constructed demand for microfinance with a wise rejection by the poor of class politics and social mobilization. As he argues on their behalf, 'it is hard to escape the conclusion that "class struggle" is not the best way of empowering the poor, and that the poor themselves have found much more effective, non-confrontational ways of achieving the same ends' – see Wright (2000: 4).

35 See De Soto (1989).

36 For example, see World Bank (2003).

37 See High-Level Commission on the Legal Empowerment of the Poor (2005).

38 See Pait (2009: 17).

39 See Kagawa (2001: 14).

40 See Calderon (2004); Field and Torero (2006).

41 See Gilbert (2001: 9–11).

42 See Manji (2006) and Nyamu-Musembi (2006).

43 See Durand-Lasserve and Selod (2007).

44 See Hulme and Mosley (1996).

45 See Hulme (2008: 8–9).

46 For example, see Barua (2006: 7–15).

47 Ibid.: 9.

48 Released 13 October 2006, Oslo.

49 For a range of documents, go to www.genfinance.info/Micro CreditSummit.html.

50 See 'Women's work', *Time*, 24 March 2008.

51 See Standing (1999); Ehrenreich (2001).

52 See Antonopoulos (2008).

53 See Toynbee (2003).

54 See Goetz and Sen Gupta (1996).

55 See Goldin Institute (2007: 3).

56 See Rahman (1999).

57 See Karim (2008).

58 See Gill (2000).

59 See Pupavac (2005).

60 The level of gender equality and extent of participative and gender-sensitive social services structures in the former Yugoslavia's system of 'worker self-management' was one of its most positive characteristics – for example, see Seibel and Damachi (1982).

61 See Mayoux (2002: 80).

62 Ibid.: 80.

63 See Manji (2006: ch. 6).

64 See World Bank (2003).

65 For example, see Doran et al. (2009).

66 Ibid.: 124.

67 See Rankin (2002).

68 See 'Grameen Bank, which pioneered loans for the poor, has

hit a repayment snag', *Wall Street Journal*, 27 November 2001.

69 See Dyal-Chand (2007).

70 See Williams (2007).

71 See Kabeer (2001: 64).

72 See Harvey (2006: 178–9).

73 See Gates (1998).

74 See Robinson (1995: n. 5).

75 See Yunus with Jolis (1998).

76 For example, see Langer (2008).

77 See CGAP (2008).

78 See Wright (2001).

79 See *MicroBanking Bulletin*, April 2001, p. 37.

80 See Balkenhol (2007: 225).

81 See 'The poor in debt: Oikocredit's concern in microfinance', Oikocredit press release, 8 December 2009.

82 See Duquet (2007).

83 See Centre for the Study of Financial Innovation (2008).

84 Ibid.: 8.

85 See Galbraith (1976 [1958]).

86 Sub-prime loans were extended with very little concern for eventual repayment because the banks made their money from immediately securitizing and selling mortgage-backed securities on to other parties, who in turn sold them on to yet other parties. An excellent description of the way that things got out of hand is by the *Financial Times* journalist Gillian Tett – see Tett (2009).

87 For example, see CARE (2005a, 2005b).

88 See Otero (1994: 102–3).

89 See 'A global surge in tiny loans spurs credit bubble in a slum', *Wall Street Journal*, 13 August 2009.

90 Some researchers have shown that the rate of return on tiny projects can often be quite high,
so that high interest rates need not always be a problem. For example, see De Mel et al. (2008).

91 Reported in 'Death by microcredit', *Times of India*, 16 September 2006.

92 See Karlan and Zinman (2006).

93 See Mayoux (2001: 257).

94 In Mexico, for example, the huge Bank Azteca chain actually went to court rather than comply with a new law requiring banks to inform clients of the total financing costs and real interest rates they were being charged for microcredit. Bank Azteca sought a protective order, which was granted by a federal judge – see 'The ugly side of Mexican microlending', *Business Week*, 13 December 2007.

95 See Brett (2006).

96 See 'The dark side of microcredit', *New Age Extra*, 28 August– 3 September 2009.

97 See Mathew (2006).

98 See Newman (2006: 3).

99 See Allen (2007).

100 See Manos and Yaron (2008).

101 See Stiglitz (2003).

4 Microfinance as poverty trap

1 See Yunus (1989: 156).

2 See Roodman and Morduch (2009: 4).

3 See World Bank (2009: 33).

4 See Ellerman (2007: 159).

5 See Balkenhol (2006: 2).

6 See Pitt and Khandker (1998); also Khandker (1998).

7 See Morduch (1998).

8 See Khandker (2001, 2005).

9 See AIMS (2000).

10 See Copestake et al. (2005).

11 See Khalily (2004).

12 See Goldberg (2005).

13 Ibid.: 46.

14 For example, see 'Small change – billions of dollars and a Nobel Prize later, it looks like "microlending" doesn't actually do much to fight poverty', *Boston Globe*, 20 September 2009.

15 See World Bank (2008: 104).

16 See Roodman and Morduch (2009).

17 See ibid.: 1–2.

18 See Johnson (1998).

19 See Schumpeter (1996 [1942]).

20 One should remember that for the non-producers, of course, the declining prices on locally produced goods and services are actually a benefit. See Tschach (2003).

21 For some illustrations of how the 'fallacy of composition' operating at the global level also seriously undermines international development strategies, see Mayer (2003).

22 Launched in 1982, the EAS was a small monthly cash grant set at just above the value of the unemployment benefit forgone. Those claiming the EAS allowance had to prove they had an additional £1,000 ($1,530 in 1983) of their own to invest in their microenterprise. Starting with just 2,500 EAS microenterprise entrants in the period 1982–83, the number of entrants rose quickly, peaking in 1986–87 when in that period alone more than 100,000 individuals were encouraged to set up their own microenterprise with EAS support – see Storey (1994: 278).

23 Employment specialist Chris Hasluck (1990) reported that displacement effects were very high indeed, effectively meaning almost no net jobs were being created. In some sub-sectors, such as 'hairdressing and beauty', Hasluck found that the rate of displacement was approaching 100 per cent – that is, for every new EAS-supported microenterprise an equivalent reduction in employment was registered in a non-EAS microenterprise in the same locality. Even worse, incumbent non-EAS microenterprises generally registered a noticeable decline in their turnover, income and profits, thus serving to undermine the existing microenterprise base. Storey and Johnson (1987) and then Storey and Strange (1992) reported that displacement effects were most striking in those regions marked out by the highest levels of unemployment and poverty (e.g. the Midlands, north-east England), which suggested that in a situation of deep poverty and severe economic problems a microenterprise-led policy had very limited applicability as either enterprise development or poverty reduction policy.

24 Ahmad and Hossain (1984).

25 Ibid.: 19.

26 Ibid.: 21.

27 See Quasem (1991: 131), quoted in Hulme and Mosley (1996: vol. 1, p. 119).

28 See Osmani (1989).

29 See Seabrook (1996: 35–7).

30 See INSEAD (2004).

31 See Cohen (2001: 5).

32 See INSEAD (2004: 1).

33 See Counts (2008: 78).

34 See 'Unplanned obsolescence', *Fast Company*, 118, September 2007.

35 Ibid.

36 See Yunus (2007: 93).

37 Such 'telephone ladies' are

now a ubiquitous feature in most developing countries, with similar minimal employment and income creation impacts for the poor being registered compared to the huge benefits garnered by the savvy telecommunications companies involved. Mexico and Colombia are good examples.

38 Report and quotes contained in *Fast Company* magazine, 118, September 2007.

39 See Popli (2008).

40 'Even in the industrial powerhouse city of Puebla', Tilly and Kennedy note, '[the] head of the union of vendors at the informal Hidalgo Market reports that unemployed job seekers have increased the group's ranks by ten percent in the last year alone.' See Tilly and Kennedy (2007).

41 See Popli (2008).

42 International Press Service (IPS), Mexico City, 2 September 2003.

43 See CSID (2009).

44 See 'Give them a better life', *The Economist*, 24 May 2008.

45 Significant intra-community violence was also seen in Kenya in 2008 and 2009, for example. As Charles Njoroge reported, this development was predictable, since 'Creating millions of jobs through hawking and trading is a mirage and a source of sustained conflict in urban areas.' See *Business Daily* (Nairobi), 29 April 2008.

46 See 'Violence spreads around Johannesburg', *International Herald Tribune*, 21 May 2008; 'Thousands flee as hatred spreads', *Guardian*, 24 May 2008.

47 See Birks Sinclair and Associates Ltd (2003).

48 See ILO (2004, 2008a).

49 See 'No cushion to fall back on: the global economic crisis and informal workers', www.inclusivecities.org.

50 See M. Davis (2006: 182).

51 Even today, in the context of the global recession, many current and former World Bank and IMF labour market economists still optimistically look to the informal economy to easily absorb a sizeable proportion of those recently made unemployed – see 'The rise of the underground', *Wall Street Journal*, 14 March 2009. The ILO seems to have more of a grasp on reality here, reporting that expansion of the informal sector is inadvisable as well as unfair, since 'As was the case in previous crises, this could generate substantial downward pressure on informal-economy wages, which before the current crisis were already declining' – see ILO (2009: 8).

52 Some researchers are willing to accept that it is a serious omission, however. For example, summarizing a vast amount of impact data, researchers Sebstad and Cohen right away point out that 'One limitation of the field study data is that the researchers did not interview or otherwise include significant numbers of the program dropouts, or former clients, of the MFI programs' (see Sebstad and Cohen 2000: 17). Nonetheless, I can find no major research project or impact assessment that has gone on to examine what this might ultimately mean in terms of the long-run sustainable development impact of microfinance.

53 See Storey (1993: 2).

54 See Davis et al. (1998).

55 See Shane (2008).

56 See Johnson and Loveman (1995). The foreword to the book was provided by Jeffrey Sachs.

57 Moreover, a quite significant percentage of those designated as 'self-employed' were actually individuals who had been summarily fired from their formal position and invited to continue as a self-employed contractor. This was principally undertaken so that the company could save on taxes and social contributions, and also – sadly, in the home of the iconic Solidarity trade union – in order to expel trade unions from the workplace and so reduce any pressure for higher wages and better working conditions. This arrangement continued to be a major economic and social (and statistical) problem for the Polish government right into the 2000s. For example, see 'Poland's informal economy: a false self-employment scandal', ICFTU Online, 003/120104, 12 January 2004.

58 See Heinegg et al. (2007).

59 It was only with Poland's accession to the EU in 2004 that the dramatic rise in rural poverty and unemployment (which reached almost 20 per cent in 2002) was finally brought under some sort of control. Among other things, the prospect of EU accession in the early 2000s meant the arrival of significant EU 'pre-accession' structural funds, while accession itself in 2004 unlocked even more structural funds. In addition, accession opened up the immediate possibility for almost two million Poles to move to work in western Europe (mainly going to the UK and Ireland). Even *after* Poland's accession to the EU, for some time

the country stood out as the sole new entrant continuing to experience *rising* poverty.

60 See Hulme and Mosley (1996: vol. 1, pp. 120–21).

61 Ibid.: 122.

62 See P. Davis (2007: 8).

63 See Alexander-Tedeschi and Karlan (2006).

64 For example, see Mishan (1981).

65 An excellent analysis can be found in Jomo and Fine (2006).

66 For example, see 'With all its talent, India wonders why innovation is elusive', *International Herald Tribune*, 10 December 2009.

67 See Intellecap (2007).

68 See Karnarni (2007a: 39).

69 Press release announcing the award of the $1.5-million Conrad N. Hilton Humanitarian Prize for 2008 to BRAC.

70 See Pretty (1999).

71 See Pretty (2005).

72 See Norberg-Hodge et al. (2002: 75).

73 Obvious examples here include the commercially successful large-scale vineyards and wineries in parts of South Africa, which is also the location for the highest concentration of poverty in the country (see Du Toit 2004), and Kenya's horticultural export sector, which is fantastically successful for its mainly European owners, yet the local workforce receives poverty-level wages (see Pollin et al. 2008).

74 This is the famous 'adverse selection' concept articulated by Joseph Stiglitz and Andrew Weiss in their seminal 1981 paper – see Stiglitz and Weiss (1981).

75 See Posani (2009: 21).

76 See Chang (2009).

77 See Tata Institute of Social Sciences (2005: 3).

78 See Ghate (2007: 156).

79 Reported in 'Can financial inclusion drive a rural recovery?', *Wall Street Journal*, 25 September 2009.

80 See Kumar and Golait (2009: 137).

81 See Posani (2009: 32).

82 See Shiva (2002).

83 See 'Death by microcredit', *Times of India*, 16 September 2006.

84 See Patel (2007: 32).

85 See 'Why poor farmers in Mexico go hungry', *International Herald Tribune*, 4 March 2003.

86 See World Bank (2004a: 174).

87 Farmers possessing large farms near the US border, with access to large loans and with solid supply links, actually did very well in the 1990s, producing large quantities of fresh vegetables and fruit for sale in US markets. See Patel (2007: 48).

88 See 'Microfinancing gains pace in Africa', *New York Times*, 2 May 2007.

89 See 'By disregarding Western advice, Malawi becomes a breadbasket', *International Herald Tribune*, 3 December 2007.

90 See *Business Daily* (Nairobi), 29 April 2008.

91 See Ehigiamusoe (2008).

92 See World Bank (2007: 20).

93 See WM Global Partners (2003).

94 Ibid.: 45–6.

95 See Agripolicy (2005: 23).

96 Ibid.: 5.

97 See Bateman and Sinković (2007).

98 For example, see Agripolicy (2006).

99 See Bosnić (2007).

100 See Christoplos (2007: 15).

101 For example, see IFAD (2006: 16–20); Doran et al. (2009: 4).

102 See Harper (2007: 93).

103 See Schmitz (1999).

104 See Dichter (2006: 4).

105 See 'The hidden dangers of the informal economy', *McKinsey-Quarterly*, August 2004.

106 For example, see ILO (2008b).

107 See Rainnie (1989).

108 See M. Davis (2006: 185).

109 Ibid.: 185.

110 An excellent summary can be found in Guha-Khasnobis et al. (2007).

111 See Reinert (2007).

112 For the example of Baden-Würtemberg, see Cooke and Morgan (1998: ch. 4).

113 See Braun (1990).

114 Reported in 'Free-for-all on trade will harm everyone, says UN', *Guardian*, 3 October 2003. The document referred to is UNCTAD (2003).

115 See Ellerman (2005).

116 For example, see Baumol (1990).

117 See Moyo (2009).

118 Asked by a magazine interviewer to respond to the fact that 'there has been much criticism of microfinance of late', her reply was, if nothing else, succinct – 'Has there?' See 'Interview with Jeff Chu', *Fast Company* magazine, 1 April 2009.

119 Moyo makes the important claim for Grameen that its microloans are taken out 'mainly for power tillers, irrigation pumps, motor vehicles, and river craft for transportation and fishing' (Moyo 2009: 127), which gives the

strong impression that Grameen Bank is mainly engaged in local productive investment projects. This sentence used by Moyo is actually taken from a paper by the Grameen Foundation's development director, Lamiya Morshed, presented to the MicroCredit Summit in 2006 (see Morshed 2006: 6), which also refers in the same sentence to the 'More than 933,000 micro-enterprise loans amounting to US$316 million'. If we divide $316 million by 933,000, however, we get an average loan figure of just $338, which would suggest that not very much serious investment in capital assets has taken place, and that the microloans associated with the mechanized equipment noted above are probably outlier examples. A more representative figure of what Grameen does is the average loan size in the whole of Grameen Bank's operations, which, according to the Mix Market survey in 2007, was less than $100 (see www. mixmarket.org/mfi/grameen-bank/ data). This $100 figure is in line with evidence from elsewhere that most of Grameen's lending today is really for consumption purposes, and not for income-generating activities, still less for motor vehicles, river craft, and so on.

120 See Hulme (1999).

121 In 2008 it was reported that household debt (household microloans) in South Africa had quadrupled in just five years. As many as 300,000 South African households are now classified as 'over-indebted' after having accessed a household microloan for consumption spending or a simple income-generating project. These unfortunate individuals are part of the larger total of 1 million South Africans the government has now classified as 'debt-stressed', forcing the National Credit Regulator to urgently register an additional 360 debt counsellors to try to cope with the accumulating misery. See *Business Day* newspaper, 22 May 2008.

122 See Bond (2007a).

123 See UN-Habitat (2003: 103).

124 See 'Benin microfinance sector: from prosperity to crisis', Corinne Riquet, CGAP Microfinance Blog, 29 June 2009.

125 See *Business Daily* (Nairobi), 29 April 2008.

126 Moyo (2009: 124–5).

127 See Gelb and Bienen (1988: 255).

128 See Isola (2005).

129 See Anyanwu (2004).

130 In 2005 the Nigerian government launched a new policy measure aimed at massively *increasing* the amount of formal microcredit as a share of the total amount of credit disbursed by the financial system. The plan is to increase the share of formal microcredit as a percentage of total formal credit from its then around 1 per cent total to at least 20 per cent by 2020, and, second, to increase the share of microcredit as a percentage of GDP from 0.2 per cent to at least 5 per cent by 2020. See Central Bank of Nigeria (2005).

131 See 'South Africa in danger of deindustrialization', Bloomberg, 8 September 2009.

132 See Levy (2007).

133 See Woodruff (2001).

134 See Dos Santos (2008: 2).

135 See Levy (2007).

136 Quoted in *IPS NewsNet*, 2 September 2003.

137 Of course, this is not to say

that development strategies other than microfinance are not making a difference in Cambodia; they are. But where Cambodia has indeed successfully developed of late – as in construction, textiles and tourism – this has required large amounts of investment going into longer-term-focused projects, often mobilized by members of the Cambodian business and political elite on the international capital market. In other words, what little development *has* taken place can generally be accounted for by factors *other* than microfinance.

138 See Clark (2006).

139 In December 2009, the huge Jardine Matheson Group acquired a 12.5 per cent stake in ACLEDA – see 'Jardine Matheson Group acquires 12.25% stake in ACLEDA Bank Plc', *FMO News*, 17 December 2009, www.fmo.nl.

140 See Bateman (2003). Note that with three out of five Cambodian families depending on their land and rice farming for a living, a major opportunity to support these people would be through accelerated development of the rice processing sector, particularly through investments in milling (where much of the value-added is made).

141 A survey in 2003 by the World Bank's Mekong Private Sector Development Facility (MPDF) found almost no loans in SME capacities, and a grand total of just *eleven* medium- to longer-term loans advanced across the twelve banks interviewed. See MPDF (2003).

142 Plus in 2009 it was reported that rising numbers of MFI clients in Cambodia are being forced to sell their land and farms in order to try to repay their microloan, thus making them much poorer than ever before. See 'Cambodia joins microloan clean-up', *Asia Times Online*, 14 August 2009.

143 Leszek Balcerowicz, the main architect of the 'shock therapy' programme in Poland, argued strongly against any forms of state intervention to support SMEs. His view was that stabilization, privatization and liberalization were all that were required in Poland to establish a sustainable small and medium enterprise development trajectory. See Balcerowicz (1995: 246).

144 Haudeville, Dabic and Gorynia remark upon the high level of technologies, skills and innovation activity in Poland prior to 1990 and note that, unlike in some other transition economies, almost none of this valuable inheritance was utilized or built upon in Poland after 1990 – see Haudeville et al. 2002.

145 Of the more than 54,000 loans disbursed by Fundusz Mikro between 1994 and 1 March 2003, amounting to over $100 million in total, 56 per cent of the loans went to traders, 35 per cent to small-scale services and 9 per cent to production (data accessed at www.funduszmikro.pl).

146 See Hardy and Rainnie (1996: 252).

147 For example, the international community refused to allow plans to go forward for an SME Development Bank. This was a plan advanced by some of Bosnia's best economists and which would use part of the revenues from the privatization process to stimulate new industry-based SME projects

and technology transfer. See Bateman (2003).

148 See Bateman (2008).

149 See UNDP (2002).

150 See Piore and Sabel (1984).

151 Of course, many of the original insights behind the 'industrial district' model can be traced back to the great English economist Alfred Marshall. See Marshall (1919).

152 Key publications, associated with the International Institute for Labour Studies, include Pyke et al. (1990); Pyke and Sengenberger (1992); Pyke (1994).

153 See Gereffi and Wyman (1990).

154 See Becattini (1990).

155 See Nishiguchi (1994).

156 See Weiss (1988).

157 See SAPRIN (2001: 5).

158 See Andor and Summers (1998: 109).

159 See Bateman (2008).

160 See Putnam et al. (1993).

161 See Rankin (2002).

162 See Leys (2001).

163 See Bateman (2004).

164 See Rahman (1999).

165 See Karim (2008).

166 See Holman (2006: 27).

167 See Kaffu and Mutesasira (2003: 10).

168 See Hulme and Mosley (1996: vol. 1, p. 153).

169 See M. Davis (2006).

5 Commercialization: the death of microfinance

1 See North (1990: 9).

2 See Klein (2007: 235).

3 Such as local government ownership, mixed public and private ownership and cooperative ownership.

4 See Chang and Grabel (2004: ch. 8).

5 For example, see Florio (2004).

6 See Elliot and Atkinson (2008: ch. 2).

7 See Aliaga and Mosley (2007: 122).

8 See Vik (2007).

9 See Mosley (1999).

10 See Schreiner (2004).

11 For example, see Brett (2006).

12 See Weisbrot and Sandoval (2006).

13 This was an inheritance associated with Latin America's Import Substitution Industrialization (ISI) concept of development, an idea developed within the Economic Commission for Latin America (ECLA) and most associated with its director, the Argentinian economist Raul Prebisch.

14 Notably John Brett – see Brett (2006).

15 The proportion of clients taking loans from multiple institutions increased from 13 per cent in 1996 to 24 per cent in 2000. See Vogelgesang (2001: 30).

16 See Rhyne (2001).

17 See Loehrer (2008).

18 It also needs to be remembered that most formal bank credit has been traditionally appropriated by the tiny handful (only fifty to sixty) of farming families owning 90 per cent of Bolivia's cultivable land, and a few large export-oriented agro-businesses – see *Bolivia: Two years of 'post-neoliberal' Indigenous nationalism – a balance sheet*, www.bilaterals.org, accessed 8 August 2009.

19 Discussion with Carlos Marcelo Diaz Quevedo, director of BDP, at the KfW Microbanking seminar held at the Frankfurt School

of Finance and Management, Frankfurt, 10 July 2009.

20 See Rhyne (2001).

21 The indications are that the level of poverty in Bolivia has been coming down quite rapidly since 2006 – see ECLAC (2008: 11).

22 See Prahalad (2004).

23 For example, see Karnarni (2007b); Crabtree (2007).

24 See 'Devinder Sharma's negative assessment of microfinance institutions', *India Microfinance*, 27 November 2009, indiamicrofinance.com/blog/microfinance/microfinance-articles/devinder-sharmas-negative-assessment-of-microfinance-institutions.html.

25 See Arun and Hulme (2008: 5).

26 See Wenner (2008: 3).

27 See UNDP (2008).

28 For example, see Chopra and Meindl (2006).

29 A number of other issues added even more to the general feeling of unease over what the social business concept was actually demonstrating with this example. First, GrameenPhone was levied a $60 million fine for non-payment of local taxes on some of its services, a somewhat curious oversight for a company supposedly operating in the interests of the poor (see 'Noble laureate's VIOP controversy', www.weeklyblitz.net, accessed 24 July 2009). Second, in 2008 Danish TV researchers revealed that many local suppliers to GrameenPhone were working under pretty horrendous conditions, with routine use of child labour. Some analysts argued that because they were hidden from the public view, whereas the famous telephone ladies were in full view of the media, there was little concern for these suppliers and their working conditions. See 'Telenor, Peace Prize winner caught in labour scandal', *Aftenposten*, 14 May 2008.

30 See Ghalib and Hossain (2008).

31 See 'Saving the world with a cup of yogurt', Fortune-CNN, 15 March 2007.

32 In early 2009 French television reported on many of the disgruntled sellers involved in the scheme, as well as on the aggressive loan officers charged with recovering the microloans in default – see 'The crushing burden of microcredit', *France 24*, 8 April 2009.

33 'Operation Flood' was an Indian government programme that ran from 1970 to 1996. It successfully created a national dairy industry integrating India's small farmers – most of whom were women – into an efficient network of village dairy cooperatives, commercial dairy processors and distributors, all backed up with new technologies to ensure quality and efficiency. In little more than a decade, India was converted from a major milk-importing country into a major dairy producer and global dairy exporter. Meanwhile, the small-scale farmers involved through their cooperatives (in 1984 72 per cent of the farmers operated less than five hectares of land) have been able to build a successful farming operation, with many escaping the poverty and insecurity that hitherto plagued their lives. See IFPRI (2009: ch. 17).

34 In Europe Danone is coming under serious pressure to retract the health claims it has long made for its so-called 'probiotic' milk drink,

because there is simply no independent scientific foundation to back these claims up. Danone maintains that its own in-house scientists have produced evidence suggesting positive health benefits, but this evidence has not been verified by any outside independent body. The matter eventually went to the European Food Safety Authority (EFSA). The UK's *Guardian* reported that 'EFSA has published five opinions on probiotics' claims [and] all five opinions on probiotics published so far have been negative'. The lack of any independent support to back up its claims notwithstanding, Danone has in the meantime used its huge marketing power to create significant demand for probiotic milk on the basis of its *presumed* health benefits, and it has established an efficient supply chain to distribute the product across Europe, allowing it to forge a dominant market position in Europe in an ultra-high-profit niche product line. Yet, the *Guardian* report concluded, 'the fact is, nearly a decade after they achieved mass consumption, we are still waiting to hear whether EFSA's scientists think they work or not'. See 'Are probiotics really that good for your health?', Special Report, *Guardian*, 25 July 2009.

35 See Robin Ratcliffe, Presentation to the 12th MFC Conference of Microfinance Institutions, 25–27 May 2009, Belgrade.

36 Quoted in *Stanford Social Innovation Review*, 9 June 2008.

37 Quoted in 'Setting standards for microfinance', *Business Week*, 28 July 2008.

38 See www.mftransparency.com, accessed 13 June 2009.

39 Either directly or through proxies, the tobacco, pharmaceutical, fast-food and alcohol industries are famed for getting involved in programmes designed to control or regulate the consumption of their products, the self-serving aim being to as far as possible block such measures, or at least to dilute and shape them to their own advantage.

40 See Ghate (2007).

41 Ibid.: 166.

42 See Rozas (2009).

43 A special workshop held in March 2009 reported that in the state of Tamil Nadu 'Debt exists in the case of most families in Tamil Nadu economic and social life, numerous surveys have shown that 90% of these families are indebted, and that in more than 40% of cases, outstanding debts exceed annual income.' Among the key themes of the workshop were 'over-lending', 'taking out a loan in order to repay a loan' and 'over-confidence in the joint guarantee' (www.ifpindia.org/Workshop-on-Overindebtedness-and-its-effect-on-village-economy-of-Pazhaverkadu-region.html, accessed 17 June 2009).

44 See Ghate (2007).

45 See Shylendra (2006).

46 See Commission on Farmers' Welfare (2004: i).

47 Ibid.: ii–iii.

48 See Aggarwal (2006).

49 See Ghate (2007: 168).

50 See Sirtaine and Skamnelos (2007: 16).

51 See Chen and Chivakul (2008: 3).

52 See Kraft (2007).

53 See *Baltic Economies Weekly*, 116, 13 July 2006.

54 See Dos Santos (2008: 2).

55 See 'Microcredit: why India is failing', *Forbes*, 10 November 2006.

56 Reported in *The Times of India*, 16 September 2006.

57 See Dos Santos (2008: 2).

58 See IMF (2008).

59 Reported in *Stratfor Global Intelligence*, 12 May 2009.

60 See Beck et al. (2008).

61 See Hulme and Moore (2008).

62 See DfID (2008: 2–3).

63 See www.procreditbank.rs/about_mission, accessed 13 June 2009.

64 Graphic descriptions of the damage done to the poor by payday lenders in the USA (for example, see Parrish and King 2009) suggest similarities with the local dynamics we find in developing countries today, but dynamics that are effectively *sanctioned* by the international donor community. As even one radical free market supporter felt impelled to ask, 'Why is giving high-interest loans to the inner-city poor considered exploitative in the United States but wonderful and compassionate in Bangladesh?' – see Tucker (2006).

65 See Turner (2008).

66 See *Financial Times*, 29 July 2008.

67 For example, see Gehlich-Shillabeer (2008).

68 See 'A global surge in tiny loans spurs credit bubble in a slum', *Wall Street Journal*, 13 August 2009; also 'For global investors, "microfinance" funds pay off – so far', *Wall Street Journal*, 13 August 2009.

69 See Bateman (2003, 2007a).

70 See Demirgüç-Kunt et al. (2007: 17).

71 See 'Microfinance meltdown in Bosnia: could we have averted the crisis?' SEEP Network, report on track session at the MFC Conference, 4 November 2009, Belgrade.

72 See 'Balkan loan guarantors struggle to pay others' debts', Reuters RPT-FEATURE, 17 August 2009.

73 See 'Increasing risks in microfinance: a case study of Bolivia', BlueOrchard.com, www.blueorchard.org/.../blueorchard/.../08_Increasing%20Risks%20in%20Microfinance, 2008.

74 'In 1999, Compartamos teamed up with investor/partner ACCIÓN to apply for an innovations grant from USAID. The US $2 million grant was disbursed through ACCIÓN in three parts: $800,000 purchased equity in Compartamos, $1 million was lent to Compartamos by ACCIÓN as subordinated debt, and $200,000 was extended as a technical assistance grant.' See CGAP (2005: 2).

75 See Waterfield (2007). See also CGAP (2005).

76 Much of this information is from CGAP (2007).

77 Remarks by Muhammad Yunus, *Microcredit E-News*, 5(1), 2007.

78 Comments reported in the *New York Times*, 5 April 2008.

79 Quoted in 'In Mexico, the success of microfinancing presents big problems', *International Herald Tribune*, 4 April 2008.

80 Quoted in *The Times* of London, 14 July 2008.

81 See CGAP (2007: 20).

82 See Duggan and Goodwin-Groen (2005: 3).

83 See ACCIÓN (2007).

84 See comments by Richard Rosenberg at finance.groups.yahoo.

com/group/MicrofinancePractice/
message/7275.

85 As I write, however, a major
$2 million social impact evaluation
of Compartamos is under way by a
team led by Professor Dean Karlan
of Yale University. The first results
are expected in 2011.

86 ACCIÓN has publicly stated
that the huge financial windfall it
made at the IPO ($300 million) plus
the regular dividend payments it
receives on the shares it kept at the
time of the IPO (in 2008 around
$1.8 million) will all be invested in
extending microfinance to other
poor individuals across the globe.

87 See CGAP (2007: 15),
www.cgap.org/p/site/c/template.
rc/1.9.2440.

88 Comments by Carolina
Velazco, Manager of Strategic Plan-
ning at Compartamos, reported in
Dow Jones Newswires, 1 June 2007.

89 See posting by Dave Richardson, 24 July 2007, www.microfin.
com/dfnpostings4.

90 Comments by Dave
Richardson under the heading
'Compartamos IPO issues – nagging
questions – part 2', DFN website,
13 July 2007.

91 See the Compartamos IPO
document, 6 April 2007, p. 22.

92 See posting by Dave
Richardson, 'Dividends paid to
shareholders', DFN Discussion,
14 July 2007.

93 See posting by Dave
Richardson, 'Compartamos results
in Mexico', DFN Discussion,
21 October 2009.

94 On many of the discussion
websites for microfinance in recent
years it is perhaps not coincidental
that there has been a marked rise in

enquiries from individuals wanting
to set up their own MFI, and with
no attempt to hide the fact that very
clear personal financial enrichment
goals are in mind.

6 The politics of microfinance

1 See Yunus with Jolis (1998:
214).

2 See *San Francisco Chronicle*,
5 June 2005.

3 See North (1990).

4 See Heydemann (2008: 32).

5 See Scott (1992).

6 In an interview with an
Indian-based magazine in 2009 in
the context of the global economic
meltdown and rapidly rising poverty in developing countries, Yunus
expressed deep despair with global
capitalism, and he wondered aloud
whether it could ever genuinely
allow poverty to be meaningfully
addressed. See *Microfinance Focus*,
April 2009.

7 See Sen (1992).

8 See Friedman and Friedman
(1980).

9 See Gilder (1981).

10 For example, Yunus accepted
an approach from the Monsanto
Corporation of the USA to jointly
promote biotechnology products
in Bangladesh, such as GM seeds.
International and local NGOs and
environmental activists (notably
Vandana Shiva) were shocked at
such a tie-up, given that it was very
widely felt that Monsanto's products
were already inflicting serious
damage on poor rural communities
and destroying biodiversity (see Patel
2007: 153–63). Without comment
Yunus abandoned the project soon
afterwards – see *New International-
ist*, 334, July 1999.

11 For example, see Bond (2007b).

12 See Chowdhury (2007).

13 See Leys (2001); Elliot and Atkinson (2008).

14 See Florio (2004: 343).

15 See Shiva (2002); Stiglitz (2002: esp. 54–9); Chang and Grabel (2004).

16 For example, see Birchall (1997).

17 For example, see Schumacher (1973); De Sousa Santos (2006).

18 See Harriss (2002: 13).

19 See Arun and Hulme (2008: 3).

20 The work of Michael Sherraden in the USA has been extremely important in popularizing this methodology of individual advancement. See Sherraden (1991).

21 For example, see Ellerman (2007).

22 See Weber (2002).

23 See Shiva (2002).

24 See Faux and Mishel (2000).

25 See George and Sabelli (1994: ch. II).

26 For example, see Putnam et al. (1993); Chua (2003); Collier (2007).

27 For example, see Seibel (2003).

28 See Hossain and Moore (2002).

7 Alternatives to conventional microfinance

1 See Akyuz et al. (1999: 33).

2 CCT is in the tradition of 'targeted' social policy that can in the long run make it more difficult to instal a universal welfare state. Thanks to Ha-Joon Chang for pointing this out to me. See also Wood (2009).

3 See World Bank (2009: 2).

4 See Skoufias (2001).

5 See MITI (1980: 14).

6 See Whittaker (1997: 174).

7 See Kitayama (1995).

8 See Whittaker (1997: 174).

9 See Girardin and Ping (1997).

10 See Nishiguchi (1994).

11 See Friedman (1988: 167).

12 See Weiss (1998: 140).

13 See Whittaker (1997).

14 See Porter (1990: 225–38).

15 Much of this section is drawn from a study trip the author made to Mondragón in 2006 under contract to UNDP – see Bateman et al. (2006).

16 See Ellerman (1982).

17 See Ammirato (1996).

18 See Putnam et al. (1993).

19 See Weiss (1988).

20 Recent changes to the banking structure in Italy have removed the SCIs as a separate category of financial institution.

21 See Guiso et al. (2004).

22 See Logue (2006).

23 The seminal texts are Amsden (1989); Wade (1990); and Chang (1994).

24 See Whang (1981).

25 See Han (1997: 215).

26 See Prasad and Gerecke (2009).

27 See Thorbecke (1979: 181–2).

28 See Fei et al. (1979: 37–71, quoted in Das Gupta et al. (2003: 12–13).

29 See Wade (1982, 1983).

30 See Wade (1990: esp. ch. 6).

31 See Lall (1996: 207).

32 See O'Connor (1998).

33 See Girardin and Ping (1997: 38–42).

34 Ibid.: 42–50.

35 See O'Connor (1998: 28).

36 For example, see Robinson (2001: 145).

37 For example, see Parayil (2000); Veron (2001).

38 For example, see Rajan and Zachariah (2007).

39 See Sen (1999: 48).

40 See Parayil (2000).

41 See Thomas Isaac and Franke (2002: 158).

42 Ibid.

43 See EDA (2006). The state-driven SHG operating in Andhra Pradesh, however – Velugu – attempts to promote very similar collective development methodologies to those aimed for in Kerala's SHGs. See 'Promising approaches to engendering development', siteresources.worldbank.org/INT-GENDER/Resources/Velugu.pdf.

44 See Sunkel (1993).

45 Quoted in Piñeiro Harnecker (2005).

46 See Tendler (1997: ch. 5).

47 See Wilpert (2007: 77).

48 See Sugar (2006).

49 See Weiss (1988).

50 See Pearson (2005).

51 See Wynter and McIlroy (2006).

52 See Wilpert (2007: 80).

53 See Albert (2008).

54 See Vietnamese Academy of Social Sciences (2007).

55 Reported in 'From poverty to power: a conversational blog written and edited by Duncan Green', Oxfam International, 15 October 2008.

56 See Green (2008); see also the comments in 'From poverty to power: a conversational blog written and edited by Duncan Green', Oxfam International, 15 October 2008.

57 See Banking with the Poor Network in collaboration with the SEEP Network (2008: 25).

58 See DFC (2007a: 105). Recall from Chapter 5 that average loan size in Bangladesh is well under $100.

59 DFC (2007b: 12).

60 The credit cooperatives failed largely because they were weakly regulated. Among other things, many were 'captured' by inside managers keen to inflate profits through 'pyramid-style' practices, thereby to maximize their own financial rewards – see O'Connor (1998: 29).

61 See Seibel (2009: 12).

62 See McCarty (2001: 9).

63 See DFC (2007b: 14).

64 See Bateman (2007b).

65 See EU (2008).

66 See Banking with the Poor Network in collaboration with the SEEP Network (2008: 23).

67 A typical comment is 'CGAP will not provide capital to microfinancing institutions here [in Vietnam] because the required sustainability and a business plan do not exist', report from a UNDP-sponsored monthly meeting of the donor working group on poverty held on 24 March 1997, quoted in a report by Financial Times Information, 31 March 1997.

68 See Robinson (2001: 71).

69 See World Bank (2004b).

70 See DFC (2007a and b).

71 See DFC (2007b: 10).

72 See DFC (2007a: 7).

73 See Vietnam Microfinance Working Group, *Vietnam Microfinance Bulletin*, 13, July 2009.

74 See 'ADB, Japan help Viet Nam transform, diversify

microfinance services', ADB press release, 6 October 2009.

75 There are, however, some signs of 'push-back' on the part of the Vietnamese government. In September 2009, for example, the government announced the establishment of its own high-profile microfinance advisory body, the 'Working Committee on Microfinance', which will report to the State Bank of Vietnam. See 'Government sets up Working Committee on Micro-Finance', *Vietnam Business Finance News*, 24 September 2009.

76 This is a term Oxfam once famously used in the context of Nicaragua's successful pro-poor economic and social reforms in the early 1980s, reforms that were blocked by the US government for fear that other countries would follow in the same leftist direction. See Chomsky (2002: 33).

77 See Chang (2007).

8 Conclusion: the need for a new beginning

1 'Beyond Vietnam – a time to break silence', Speech delivered at a meeting of Clergy and Laity Concerned, Riverside Church, New York, 4 April 1967.

2 See Elliot and Atkinson (2008: back cover).

3 In celebration of Muhammad Yunus being awarded the Nobel Peace Prize in 2006, one of the main Dhaka newspapers (the *Bhorer Kagaj*) decided to run a major story on the current situation in Jobra. Unfortunately, it turned out that Jobra village has been unable to escape generalized poverty, not least because most of the initial microcredit recipients supported by the Grameen Bank and other MFIs ended up failing in their plans for a microenterprise. This apparently included the very first client of Grameen Bank, Sufiya Begum, who was widely praised by Muhammad Yunus himself for her advice and fortitude (see Yunus 2007: 45–6), but who died in abject poverty in 1998 after all her many income-generating projects came to nothing. The one major structural change of note in Jobra, the newspaper ominously reported, was a growing indebtedness problem. Finally, those Jobra inhabitants who *were* found to have meaningfully escaped poverty were all associated with one or more family members working in the Gulf states. See 'The Jobra of Yunus: poverty there has not found itself in an archive', *Bhorer Kagaj*, 10 March 2007. The original source is Chowdhury (2007: 202–4).

4 See Sen (1999).

5 See Chang (2002).

6 Ibid.: 61.

Bibliography

ACCIÓN (2007) 'The Banco Compartamos initial public offering', *Insight*, 23, June.

Adams, D. W., D. H. Graham and J. D. Von Pischke (1984) (eds) *Undermining Rural Development with Cheap Credit*, Boulder, CO: Westview Press.

Agarwal, B. (1990) 'Social security and the family: coping with seasonality and calamity in rural India', *Journal of Peasant Studies*, 17(3): 341–412.

Aggarwal, R. M. (2006) *Resource-poor Farmers in South India: On the Margins or Frontiers of Globalization?*, UN University Research Paper no. 2006/97, September.

Agripolicy (2005) 'Structure and competitiveness of the milk and dairy supply chains in the new Member states, in the candidate countries and in the countries of the Western Balkans. Project title: Agro economic policy analysis of the new Member states, the candidate states and the countries of the Western Balkans', D12-3, third six-monthly report.

— (2006) 'Structure and competitiveness of the milk and dairy supply chain in Bosnia and Herzegovina', Country report prepared for the CEEC Agripolicy project (513705).

Ahmad, Q. K. and M. Hossain (1984) *An Evaluation of Selected Policies and Programmes for Alleviation of Rural Poverty in Bangladesh*, Dhaka: Bangladesh Institute of Development Studies, September.

AIMS (2000) *Microfinance, Risk Management, and Poverty: A synthesis study submitted to the Office of Microenterprise Development, USAID*, Washington, DC: USAID.

Akyuz, Y., H.-J. Chang and R. Kozul-Wright (1999) 'New perspectives on East Asian development', in Y. Akyuz (ed.), *East Asian Development: New Perspectives*, London: Frank Cass.

Albert, M. (2008) 'Which way Venezuela?', *ZMag*, 24 July, www.zmag.org/znet/viewArticle/18250.

Alexander-Tedeschi, G. and D. Karlan (2006) *Microfinance Impact: Bias from Dropouts*, Financial Access Initiative and Innovations for Poverty Action, January.

Aliaga, I. and P. Mosley (2007) 'Microfinance under crisis conditions: the case of Bolivia', in Dichter and Harper (2007).

Allen, H. (2007) 'Finance begins with savings, not loans', in Dichter and Harper (2007).

Ammirato, P. (1996) *La Lega: The Making of a Successful Cooperative Network*, Dartmouth: Ashgate Publishing.

Amsden, A. (1989) *Asia's Next Giant*, Oxford: Oxford University Press.

234 | Bibliography

Andor, L. and M. Summers (1998) *Market Failure: Eastern Europe's 'Economic Miracle'*, London: Pluto Press.

Antonopoulos, R. (2008) *The Unpaid Care Work–Paid Work Connection*, Working Paper no. 541, Levy Economics Institute.

Anyanwu, C. M. (2004) *Microfinance Institutions in Nigeria: Policy, Practice and Potentials*, Paper presented at the G24 workshop on 'Constraints to growth in sub Saharan Africa', Pretoria, 29–30 November.

Armendáriz de Aghion, B. and J. Morduch (2005) *The Economics of Microfinance*, Cambridge, MA: MIT Press.

Arun, T. and D. Hulme (2008) *Microfinance: A Way Forward*, Brooks World Poverty Institute (BWPI) Working Paper no. 54, BWPI, University of Manchester, October.

Balcerowicz, L. (1995) *Socialism, Capitalism, Transformation*, Budapest: European University Press.

Balkenhol, B. (2006) *The Impact of Microfinance on Employment: What do we know?*, Paper presented to the Global Microcredit Summit, Halifax, Canada, 12–16 November.

— (2007) 'Conclusions', in B. Balkenhol (ed.), *Microfinance and Public Policy: Outreach, Performance and Efficiency*, London: Palgrave Macmillan for the ILO.

Banerjee, A. V., E. Duflo, R. Glennerster and C. Kinnan (2009) *The Miracle of Microfinance? Evidence from a randomized evaluation*, Mimeo.

Banking with the Poor Network in collaboration with the SEEP Network (2008) *Microfinance Industry Report: Vietnam*, Banking with the Poor Network.

Barua, D. C. (2006) *Five Cents a Day: Innovative programs for reaching the destitute with microcredit, no-interest loans and other instruments: the experience of Grameen Bank*, Paper presented to the Global Microcredit Summit, Halifax, Canada, 12–16 November.

Bateman, M. (2000) 'Neo-liberalism, SME development and the role of Business Support Centres in the transition economies of Central and Eastern Europe', *Small Business Economics*, 14(4): 275–98.

— (2003) '"New wave" microfinance institutions in South-East Europe: towards a more realistic assessment of impact', *Small Enterprise Development*, 14(3): 56–65.

— (2004) *Sustainable Local Economic Development in South East Europe and the Role of Social Capital: Disentangling rhetoric from the emerging reality*, Paper presented at the 8th EACES conference, 'EU enlargement: what comes after 2004?', Belgrade, 23–25 September.

— (2007a) 'Deindustrialisation and social disintegration in Bosnia', in Dichter and Harper (2007).

— (2007b) 'Financial co-operatives for sustainable local economic and social development', *Small Enterprise Development*, 18(1): 37–49.

— (2008) 'Borderlands and

microfinance: impacts of "local neoliberalism"', in M. Pugh, N. Cooper and M. Turner (eds), *Whose Peace? Critical Perspectives on the Political Economy of Peacebuilding*, London: Palgrave Macmillan.

Bateman, M., with R. McIntyre and B. Girard (2006) *Promising Practices: An Integrated Cooperative Approach for Sustainable Local Economic and Social Development in the Basque region of Spain (A Report to UNDP of a Study Visit, 7th July)*, New York: UNDP.

Bateman, M. and D. Sinković (2007) *Assessing the Sustainable Impact of Microfinance in Croatia: A new approach and some new tools of analysis*, Paper presented at the European Association for Comparative Economics Studies (EACES) seminar 'The role of microfinance in promoting sustainable development in southeast Europe', Great Brioni Island, Croatia, 5 July.

Baumol, W. (1990) 'Entrepreneurship: productive, unproductive, and destructive', *Journal of Political Economy*, 98(5): 893–921.

Becattini, G. (1990) 'Italy', in W. Sengenberger, G. W. Loveman and M. J. Piore (eds), *The Reemergence of Small Enterprises: Industrial Restructuring in Industrialised Countries*, Geneva: International Institute for Labour Studies, ILO.

Beck, S. and T. Ogden (2007) 'Beware of bad microcredit', *Harvard Business Review*, September.

Beck, T., B. Büyükkarabacak, F. Rioja and N. Valev (2008) *Who Gets the Credit? And Does It Matter? Household vs. Firm Lending across Countries*, Policy Research Working Paper 4661, Washington, DC: World Bank.

Birchall, J. (1997) *The International Co-operative Movement*, Manchester: Manchester University Press.

Birks Sinclair and Associates Ltd (2003) *Baseline Study on Local Socio-Economic and Labour Market Conditions in Four Pilot Areas: Serbia*, Belgrade: DfID.

Blanchflower, D. and R. Freeman (1993) *Did the Thatcher Reforms Change British Labour Market Performance?*, CEP/NIESR conference 'Is the British labour market different?'

Bond, P. (2007a) 'The meaning of the 2006 Nobel Peace Prize: microcredit evangelism, health, and social policy', *International Journal of Health Services*, 37(2): 229–49.

— (2007b) 'Two economies, microcredit and the Accelerated and Shared Growth Initiative for South Africa', *Africanus: Journal of African Development Studies*, 37(2).

Bosnić, Z. (2007) 'Bosnia and Herzegovina: solid economic growth and political unease – par for the course', WIIW Research Reports no. 341, July.

Braun, H.-J. (1990) *The German Economy in the Twentieth Century: The German Reich and the Federal Republic*, London: Routledge.

Breman, J. (2003) *The Labouring Poor: Patterns of Exploitation, Subordination and Exclusion*, Oxford: Oxford University Press.

— (2009) 'Myth of the global safety

net', *New Left Review*, 59, September/October.

Breman, J. and A. Das (2000) *Down and Out: Labouring under global capitalism*, Oxford: Oxford University Press.

Brett, J. A. (2006) '"We sacrifice and eat less": the structural complexities of microfinance participation', *Human Organization*, 65(1): 8–19.

Calderon, J. (2004) 'The formalisation of property in Peru 2001–2002: the case of Lima', *Habitat International*, 28(2): 289–300.

CARE (2005a) 'The dynamics of debt in southeast Bangladesh – a discussion paper', Rural Livelihoods Programme, CARE Bangladesh.

— (2005b) 'Debt and vulnerability in northwest Bangladesh – a discussion paper', Rural Livelihoods Programme, CARE Bangladesh.

Central Bank of Nigeria (2005) *Microfinance Policy, Regulatory and Supervisory Framework for Nigeria*, Abuja: Central Bank of Nigeria.

Centre for the Study of Financial Innovation (2008) *Microfinance Banana Skins 2008: Risk in a booming industry*, London: CSFI.

CGAP (2005) *Donors Succeed by Making Themselves Obsolete: Compartamos Taps Financial Markets in Mexico*, Washington, DC: CGAP.

— (2007) *CGAP Reflections on the Compartamos Initial Public Offering: A Case Study on Microfinance Interest Rates and Profits*, CGAP Focus Note no. 42, Washington, DC: CGAP, June.

— (2008) *Are We Over-estimating Demand for Microloans?*, CGAP Brief, Washington, DC: CGAP, April.

— (2009) *The New Moneylenders: Are the Poor Being Exploited by High Microcredit Interest Rates?*, CGAP Occasional Paper no. 15, Washington, DC: CGAP, February.

Chang, H.-J. (1994) *The Political Economy of Industrial Policy*, London: Macmillan Press.

— (2002) *Kicking away the Ladder: Development Strategy in Historical Perspective*, London: Anthem Press.

— (2007) *Bad Samaritans: Rich nations, poor policies and the threat to the developing world*, London: Random House.

— (2009) 'Rethinking public policy in agriculture – lessons from history, distant and recent', *Journal of Peasant Studies*, 36(3): 477–515.

Chang, H.-J. and I. Grabel (2004) *Reclaiming Development: An Alternative Economic Policy Manual*, London: Zed Books.

Chen, K. C. and M. Chivakul (2008) *What Drives Household Borrowing and Credit Constraints? Evidence from Bosnia and Herzegovina*, IMF Working Paper (European Department), August.

Chomsky, N. (2002) *Pirates and Emperors, Old and New*, London: Pluto Press.

Chopra, S. and P. Meindl (2006) *Supply Chain Management: Strategy, Planning, and Operation*, New York: Prentice Hall.

Chowdhury, O. T. (2007) 'Nobel-man's UN-noble corporate

nexus', in F. Chowdhury (ed.), *Microcredit: Myth Manufactured*, Dhaka: Shrabon Prokashani.

Christoplos, I. (2007) *Agricultural Policies, Programming and the Market in Bosnia and Herzegovina*, HPG Background Paper, London: Overseas Development Institute (ODI), February.

Chua, A. (2003) *World on Fire: How Exporting Free-Market Democracy Breeds Ethnic Hatred and Global Instability*, London: Heinemann.

Clark, H. A. (2006) *When There was No Money: Building ACLEDA Bank in Cambodia's Evolving Financial Sector*, Berlin and Heidelberg: Springer.

Cohen, N. (2001) *What Works: Grameen Telecom's Village Phones*, A Digital Dividend Study by the World Resources Institute, June.

Collier, P. (2007) *The Bottom Billion: Why the poorest countries are failing and what can be done about it*, Oxford: Oxford University Press.

Collins, D., J. Morduch, S. Rutherford and O. Ruthven (2009) *Portfolios of the Poor: How the World's Poor Live on $2 a Day*, Princeton, NJ: Princeton University Press.

Commission on Farmers' Welfare (2004) *Report of the Commission on Farmers' Welfare*, Hyderabad: Government of Andhra Pradesh.

Committee of Donor Agencies for Small Enterprise Development (2001) *Business Development Services for Small Enterprises: Guiding Principles for Donor Intervention*, Washington, DC: Committee of Donor Agencies for Small Enterprise Development, World Bank.

Cooke, P. and K. Morgan (1998) *The Associational Economy: Firms, Regions, and Innovation*, Oxford: Oxford University Press.

Copestake, J., M. Greely, S. Johnson, N. Kabeer and A. Simonowitz (2005) *Money with a Mission: Microfinance and Poverty Reduction*, vol. 1, London: ITDG Publishing.

Counts, A. (2008) *Small Loans, Big Dreams: How Nobel Prize winner Muhammad Yunus and microfinance are changing the world*, Hoboken, NJ: John Wiley and Sons Inc.

Crabtree, A. (2007) *Evaluating 'The Bottom of the Pyramid' from a Fundamental Capabilities Perspective*, CBDS Working Paper Series no. 1.

CSID (Corporate Strategy and Industrial Development) (2009) *From Wall Street Traders to Bree Street Traders: Linkages between the Macroeconomic Environment and Street Trading in Johannesburg*, School of Economic and Business Sciences, University of Witwatersrand.

Das Gupta, M., H. Grandvoinnet and M. Romani (2003) *Fostering Community-driven Development: What Role for the State?*, World Bank Policy Research Working Paper no. 2969, Washington, DC: World Bank.

Davis, M. (2006) *Planet of Slums*, London: Verso.

Davis, P. (2007) *Discussions among the Poor: Exploring poverty dynamics with focus groups* in *Bangladesh*, CPRS Working Papers no. 84, IDPM, University of Manchester, February.

Davis, S., J. C. Haltiwanger and S. Schuh (1998) *Job Creation and Destruction*, Cambridge, MA: MIT Press.

De Mel, S., D. McKenzie and C. Woodruff (2008) *Who are the Microenterprise Owners?: Evidence from Sri Lanka on Tokman v. de Soto*, World Bank Policy Research Paper 4635, Washington, DC: World Bank.

Demirgüç-Kunt, A., L. Klapper and G. A. Panos (2007) *The Origins of Self-Employment*, Washington, DC: Development Research Group, World Bank, February.

De Soto, H. (1989) *The Other Path: The Invisible Revolution in the Third World*, London: I.B.Tauris.

— (2000) *The Mystery of Capital. Why Capitalism Triumphs in the West and Fails Everywhere Else*, London: Black Swan.

De Sousa Santos, B. (2006) (ed.) *Another Production is Possible: Beyond the Capitalist Canon*, London: Verso.

DFC (2007a) *Vietnam: Developing a Comprehensive Strategy to Expand Access [for the Poor] to Microfinance Services. Promoting Outreach, Efficiency and Sustainability*, vol. I: *The Microfinance Landscape in Vietnam*, Hanoi: DFC for the World Bank.

— (2007b) *Vietnam: Developing a Comprehensive Strategy to Expand Access [for the Poor] to Microfinance Services. Promoting Outreach, Efficiency and Sustainability*, vol. II: *Options for a Comprehensive Strategy*, Hanoi: DFC for the World Bank.

DfID (Department for International Development) (2008) *The Road to Prosperity through Growth, Jobs and Skills*, Discussion Paper, Dhaka: DfID Bangladesh.

Dichter, T. (2006) *Hype and Hope: The Worrisome State of the Microcredit Movement*, www.microfinancegateway.org/content/article/detail/31747.

— (2007) *A Second Look at Microfinance: The Sequence of Growth and Credit in Economic History*, Development Policy Briefing Paper no. 1, Center for Global Liberty and Prosperity, CATO Institute.

Dichter, T. and M. Harper (2007) (eds) *What's Wrong with Microfinance?*, London: Practical Action Publishers.

Donors' Working Group on Financial Sector Development and the Committee of Donor Agencies for Small Enterprise Development at the World Bank (1995) *Micro and Small Enterprise Finance: Guiding Principles for Selecting and Supporting Intermediaries*, Washington, DC: CGAP, World Bank.

Doran, A., N. McFadyen and R. C. Vogel (2009) *The Missing Middle in Agricultural Finance: Relieving the capital constraint on smallholder groups and other agricultural SMEs*, Oxfam Research Report, 17 December.

Dos Santos, P. (2008) *The World Bank, the IFC and the Antecedents of the Financial Crisis*, Bretton Woods Project Update, 27 November.

Dowla, A. and D. Barua (2006) *The Poor Always Pay Back: The Grameen II Story*, Bloomfield, CT: Kumarian Press.

Drake, D. and E. Rhyne (2002) *The Commercialization of Microfinance: Balancing Business and Development*, Bloomfield, CT: Kumarian Press.

Duggan, M. and R. Goodwin-Groen (2005) *Donors Succeed by Making Themselves Obsolete: Compartamos Taps Financial Markets in Mexico*, Donor Good Practices no. 19, Washington, DC: CGAP, January.

Duquet, S. (2007) *How Can MFIs Best Work in Competitive and Saturated Markets?*, Paris: PlaNet Finance.

Durand-Lasserve, A. and H. Selod (2007) *The Formalisation of Urban Land Tenure in Developing Countries*, Paper presented at the World Bank's 2007 Urban Research Symposium, Washington, DC, 14–16 May.

Du Toit, A. (2004) '"Social exclusion" discourse and chronic poverty: a South African case study', *Development and Change*, 35(5).

Dyal-Chand, R. (2007) *Reflection in a Distant Mirror: Why the west has misperceived the Grameen Bank's vision of microcredit*, Northeastern Public Law and Theory Faculty Working Paper no. 13-2007, Northeastern University School of Law.

ECLAC (2008) *Social Panorama of Latin America*, Santiago: ECLAC.

EDA (2006) *Self-Help Groups in India: A Study of the Lights and Shades*, Gurgaon: EDA Rural Systems Private Ltd.

Ehigiamusoe, G. (2008) 'Microfinance neglects farmers, African agriculture', African News Network, 26 February, africanagriculture.blogspot.com /2008/02/microfinance-neglects-farmers.html.

Ehrenreich, B. (2001) *Nickel and Dimed: Or (not) getting by in America*, New York: Henry Holt.

Ellerman, D. (1982) *The Socialisation of Entrepreneurship: The Empresarial Division of the Caja Laboral Popular*, Somerville: Industrial Cooperative Association.

— (2005) *Helping People Help Themselves: From the World Bank to an Alternative Philosophy of Development Assistance*, Ann Arbor: University of Michigan Press.

— (2007) 'Microfinance: some conceptual and methodological problems', in Dichter and Harper (2007).

Elliot, L. and D. Atkinson (2008) *The Gods That Failed: How Blind Faith in Markets Has Cost Us Our Future*, New York: Nation Books.

EU (2000) *An Evaluation of PHARE SME Programmes*, Brussels: DG Relex.

— (2008) *Final Evaluation of the Vietnam Private Sector Support Programme (TOR)*, Brussels: Europeaid, EU.

Faux, J. and L. Mishel (2000) 'Inequality and the global economy', in W. Hutton and A. Giddens (eds), *On the Edge: Living with Global Capitalism*, London: Jonathan Cape.

Fei, J. C. H., G. Ranis and S. W. Y. Kuo (1979) *Growth with Equity:*

The Taiwan case, New York: Oxford University Press.

Field, E. and M. Torero (2006) *Do Property Titles Increase Credit Access among the Urban Poor? Evidence from a Nationwide Titling Program*, Mimeo.

Florio, M. (2004) *The Great Divestiture: Evaluating the Welfare Impact of the British Privatizations 1979–1997*, Cambridge, MA: MIT Press.

Fonteyne, W. (2007) *Cooperative Banks in Europe – Policy Issues*, IMF Working Papers no. WP/07/159, Washington, DC: IMF.

Friedman, D. (1988) *The Misunderstood Miracle: Industrial development and political change in Japan*, Ithaca, NY: Cornell University Press.

Friedman, M. and R. Friedman (1980) *Free to Choose*, London: Penguin.

Galbraith, J. K. (1976 [1958]) *The Affluent Society*, New York: New American Library.

Gates, C. (1998) *The Merchant Republic of Lebanon: Rise of an Open Economy*, London: Centre for Lebanese Studies in association with I.B.Tauris.

Gehlich-Shillabeer, M. (2008) 'Poverty alleviation or poverty traps? Microcredits and vulnerability in Bangladesh', *Disaster Prevention and Management*, 7(3): 396–409.

Gelb, A. and H. Bienen (1988) 'Nigeria: from windfall gains to welfare losses?', in A. Gelb and Associates (eds), *Oil Windfalls: Blessing or Curse*, Oxford: Oxford University Press for the World Bank.

George, S. and F. Sabelli (1994) *Faith and Credit: The World Bank's Secular Empire*, London: Penguin.

Gereffi, G. and D. Wyman (eds) (1990) *Manufacturing Miracles: Paths of industrialisation in Latin America and East Asia*, Princeton, NJ: Princeton University Press.

Getubig, M., D. Gibbons and J. Remenyi (2000) 'Financing a revolution', in J. Remenyi and B. Quiñones, Jr (eds), *Microfinance and Poverty Alleviation: Case Studies from Asia and the Pacific*, London and New York: Pinter.

Ghalib, A. K. and F. Hossain (2008) *Social Business Enterprises – Maximising Social Benefits or Maximising Profits? The Case of Grameen-Danone Foods Limited*, BWPI Working Paper 51, BWPI, University of Manchester.

Ghate, P. (2007) *Indian Microfinance: The Challenges of Rapid Growth*, New Delhi: Sage Publications.

Gilbert, A. (2001) *On the Mystery of Capital and the Myths of Hernando De Soto: What difference does legal title make?*, Mimeo, University College London.

Gilder, G. (1981) *Wealth and Poverty*, New York: Basic Books.

Gill, L. (2000) *Teetering on the Rim: Global restructuring, daily life and the armed retreat of the Bolivian state*, New York: Columbia University Press.

Girardin, E. and X. Ping (1997) *Urban Credit Co-operative in China*, OECD Development Centre Technical Paper no. 125, OECD, Paris.

Goetz, A. M. and R. Sen Gupta (1996) 'Who takes the credit? Gender, power, and control over loan use in rural credit programs in Bangladesh', *World Development*, 24(1): 45–63.

Goldberg, N. (2005) *Measuring the Impact of Microfinance: Taking Stock of What We Know*, Washington, DC: Grameen Foundation USA.

Goldin Institute (2007) *Improving Microcredit Programs: Listening to Recipients – a Summary of the Pilot Phase (May–August)*, Chicago, IL: Goldin Institute.

Green, D. (2008) *From Poverty to Power: How Active Citizens and Effective States Can Change the World*, Oxford: Oxfam International.

Guha-Khasnobis, B., R. Kanbur and E. Ostrom (2007) (eds) *Linking the Formal and Informal Economy*, Oxford: Oxford University Press.

Guiso, L., P. Sapienza and L. Zingales (2004) 'Does local financial development matter?', *Quarterly Journal of Economics*, August, pp. 929–69.

Gulli, H. (1998) *Microfinance: Questioning the conventional wisdom*, Washington, DC: Inter-American Development Bank.

Han, S.-B. (1997) 'Local level entrepreneurs in rural Punggi, Korea: economic behaviour and lifestyle', in M. Rutten and C. Upadhya (eds), *Small Business Entrepreneurs in Asia and Europe: Towards a comparative perspective*, New Delhi: Sage Publications.

Hardy, J. and A. Rainnie (1996) *Restructuring Krakow: Desperately Seeking Capitalism*, London: Mansell.

Harper, M. (2002) 'Self-help groups and Grameen Bank groups: what are the differences?', in T. Fisher and M. S. Sriram (2002) (eds), *Beyond Micro-Credit: Putting Development back into Micro-Finance*, New Delhi: Vistaar Publications.

— (2003) *Microfinance: Evolution, Achievements and Challenges*, London: ITDG Publishing.

— (2007) 'Microfinance and farmers: do they fit?', in Dichter and Harper (2007).

Harriss, J. (2002) *Depoliticizing Development: The World Bank and Social Capital*, London: Anthem Press.

Harvey, D. (2006) *A Brief History of Neoliberalism*, Oxford: Oxford University Press.

Hasluck, C. (1990) *The Displacement Effects of the Enterprise Allowance Scheme: A local labour market study*, Coventry: Institute for Employment Research, University of Warwick.

Haudeville, B., M. Dabic and M. Gorynia (2002) 'National differences in technology transfer in East European transition economies', *Mondes en Développement*, 30(12): 75.

Heinegg, A., R. Melzig and R. Sprout (2007) *Labor Markets in Eastern Europe and Eurasia*, Bureau for Europe and Eurasia, USAID.

Heydemann, S. (2008) 'Institutions and economic performance: the use and abuse of culture in New Institutional Economics', *Studies in Comparative International Development*, 43(1): 27–52.

High-Level Commission on the
Legal Empowerment of the Poor
(2005) *Concept Paper: Poverty
Reduction through Improved
Asset Security, Formalisation of
Property Rights and the Rule of
Law*, Washington, DC.

Holman, D. (2006) *What are the
Impacts of Bolivian Microfinance
on Aymara and Quechua
Culture?*, Mimeo, Carlton
College, USA.

Hospes, O. and H. Lont (2004)
'Introduction', in H. Lont and
O. Hospes (eds), *Livelihood and
Microfinance: Anthropological
and Sociological Perspectives on
Savings and Debt*, Delft: Eburon
Academic Publishers.

Hossain, N. and M. Moore (2002)
*Arguing for the Poor: Elites and
poverty in developing countries*,
Institute for Development Studies
Working paper no. 148, IDS,
Sussex.

Hulme, D. (1999) *Client Drop-outs
from East African Microfinance
Institutions*, Kampala:
MicroSave, May.

— (2008) *The Story of the
Grameen Bank: From Subsidised
Microcredit to Market-
based Microfinance*, BWPI
Working Paper 60, Institute
for Development Policy and
Management, University of
Manchester, November.

Hulme, D. and K. Moore (2006)
*Why Has Microfinance been a
Policy Success in Bangladesh
(and Beyond)*, Mimeo, Institute
for Development Policy and
Management, University of
Manchester.

— (2008) 'Assisting the poorest
in Bangladesh: learning

from BRAC's "Targeting the
Ultra-poor" programme', in
A. Barrientos and D. Hulme
(eds), *Social Protection for the
Poor and Poorest: Concepts,
Policies and Practices*, London:
Routledge.

Hulme, D. and P. Mosley (1996)
(eds) *Finance against Poverty*,
2 vols, London: Routledge.

IFAD (2006) *Managing Risks
and Designing Products for
Agricultural Microfinance:
Features of an emerging model*,
Rome: IFAD.

IFPRI (2009) *Millions Fed: Proven
Successes in Agricultural
Development*, Washington,
DC: International Food Policy
Research Institute.

ILO (2004) *Project Brief from the
ILO Social Finance Programme*,
Budapest: ILO.

— (2008a) *Serbia Microcredit Gap
Assessment*, Geneva: Social
Banking Unit, ILO.

— (2008b) *World of Work Report.
Income Inequalities in the Age of
Financial Globalization*, Geneva:
IILS, ILO.

— (2009) *The Financial and
Economic Crisis: A Decent Work
Response*, Geneva: ILO.

IMF (2007) *Mexico: Financial Sector
Assessment Program Update –
Technical Note – Financing of
the private sector*, Washington,
DC: IMF.

— (2008) *Republic of Serbia:
Selected Issues*, IMF Country
Report no. 08/55, Washington,
DC: IMF.

INSEAD (2004) *Telenor in
Bangladesh: The Way Forward*,
Case Study series.

Intellecap (2007) *Inverting the*

Pyramid: The Changing Face of Indian Microfinance, Intellecap.

Isola, W. A. (2005) 'Market reform and de-industrialisation in Nigeria: 1986–2003', in M. Feridun and S. T. Akindele (eds), Nigerian Economy: Essays on Economic Development, Morrisville, NC: Lulu Press Inc.

Jackelen, H. (1989) 'Banking on the informal sector', in Levitsky (1989).

Johnson, S. (1998) 'Programme impact assessments in micro-finance: the need for analysis of real markets, IDS Bulletin, 29(4): 21–30.

Johnson, S. and G. Loveman (1995) Starting Over in Eastern Europe: Entrepreneurship and Economic Renewal, Boston, MA: Harvard Business School Press.

Jomo, K. S. and B. Fine (2006) (eds) The New Development Economics, London: Zed Books.

Kabeer, N. (2001) 'Conflicts over credit: re-evaluating the empower-ment potential of loans to women in rural Bangladesh', World Development, 29(1): 63–84.

Kaffu, E. and L. K. Mutesasira (2003) Competition Working for Customers: The Evolution of the Uganda MicroFinance Sector – a Longitudinal Study from December 2001 to March 2003, Microsave.

Kagawa, A. (2001) Policy Effects and Tenure Security Perceptions of Peruvian Urban Land Tenure Regularisation Policy in the 1990s, Mimeo, Division of Urban Planning and Management, International Institute for Aerospace Survey and Earth Sciences (ITC).

Kansas, D. (2009) The Wall Street Journal Guide to the End of Wall Street as We Know It: What You Need to Know about the Greatest Financial Crisis of Our Time – and How to Survive It, New York: Harper Paperbacks.

Karim, L. (2008) 'Demystifying micro-credit: the Grameen Bank, NGOs, and neoliberalism in Bangladesh', Cultural Dynamics, 20(1): 5–29.

Karlan, D. S. and N. Goldberg (2007) Impact Evaluation for Microfinance: Review of Methodological Issues, Doing Impact Evaluation no. 7, Poverty Reduction and Economic Management (PREM), Washington, DC: World Bank.

Karlan, D. S. and J. Zinman (2006) Credit Elasticities in Less-developed Economies: Implications for Microfinance, Mimeo.

— (2009) Expanding Micro-enterprise Credit Access: Using Randomized Supply Decisions to Estimate the Impacts in Manila, Mimeo.

Karnarni, A. (2007a) 'Microfinance misses its mark', Stanford Social Innovation Review, Summer.

— (2007b) Fortune at the Bottom of the Pyramid: A Mirage, Working Paper, Ross School of Business at the University of Michigan, April.

Khalily, M. A. B. (2004) 'Quantitative approach to impact analysis of microfinance programmes in Bangladesh: what have we learned?', Journal of International Development, 16(3): 331–53.

Khandker, S. (1998) Fighting Poverty

with *Microcredit: Experience in Bangladesh*, New York: Oxford University Press.

— (2001) *Does Micro-finance Really Benefit the Poor? Evidence from Bangladesh*, Paper presented at the Asia and Pacific Forum on 'Poverty: reforming policies and institutions for poverty reduction', Asian Development Bank, Manila, 5–9 February.

— (2005) 'Microfinance and poverty: evidence using panel data from Bangladesh', *World Bank Economic Review*, 19: 263–86.

Kitayama, T. (1995) 'Local government and small and medium-sized enterprises', in H. Kim, M. Muramatsu, T. J. Pempel and K. Yamamura (eds), *The Japanese Civil Service and Economic Development: Catalysts of change*, Oxford: Clarendon Press.

Klein, N. (2007) *The Shock Doctrine: The Rise of Disaster Capitalism*, New York: Metropolitan Books and Henry Holt.

Kraft, E. (2007) 'The boom in household lending in transition countries: a Croatian case study and a cross-country analysis of determinants', *Comparative Economic Studies*, 49: 345–66.

Krugman, P. (2007) *The Conscience of a Liberal*, New York: W. W. Norton.

Kumar, P. and R. Golait (2009) *Bank Penetration and SHG-Bank Linkage Programme: A Critique*, Reserve Bank of India Occasional Papers, 29(3).

Lall, S. (1996) *Learning from the Asian Tigers: Studies in Technology and Industrial Policy*, London: Macmillan Press.

Langer, W. (2008) *The Role of Private Sector Investment in International Microfinance and the Implications of Domestic Regulatory Environments*, Paper available at works.bepress.com/william_langer/2.

Ledgerwood, J. (1999) *Microfinance Handbook: An Institutional and Financial Perspective*, Washington, DC: World Bank.

Leleux, B. and D. Constantinou (eds) (2007) *From Microfinance to Small Business Finance: The Business Case for Private Capital Investments*, London: Palgrave Macmillan.

Levine, R. (2005) 'Finance and growth: theory and evidence', in P. Aghion and S. Durlauf (eds), *Handbook of Economic Growth*, Amsterdam: Elsevier Press.

Levitsky, J. (ed.) (1989) *Micro-enterprises in Developing Countries*, London: Intermediate Technology Publications.

Levy, S. (2007) *Informality, Productivity and Growth in Mexico*, Presentation at the World Bank ABCDE Conference 'Private sector and development', Bled, Slovenia, 17–18 May.

Leys, C. (2001) *Market-driven Politics: Neo-liberal democracy and the public interest*, London: Verso.

Loehrer, J. (2008) 'What does Evo Morales mean for microfinance in Bolivia?', *Stanford Journal of Microfinance*, 1.

Logue, J. (2006) *Economics, Cooperation, and Employee Ownership: The Emilia Romagna model*, dept.kent.edu/oeoc/oeoclibrary/emiliaromagnalong.htm.

Manji, A. (2006) *The Politics of Land Reform in Africa: From Communal Tenure to Free Markets*, London: Zed Books.

Manos, R. and J. Yaron (2008) 'Measuring the performance of microfinance providers: an assessment of past and present practices', *International Journal of Financial Services Management*, 3(2): 171–87.

Marshall, A. (1919) *Industry and Trade*, London: Macmillan.

Marx, K. and F. Engels (1932 [1845]) *The German Ideology,* Moscow: Marx-Engels Institute.

Mathew, E. (2006) *Does Repayment Indicate the Success of Micro-finance Programme?*, Working Paper 172, Institute for Social and Economic Change, Bangalore.

Mayer, J. (2003) *The Fallacy of Composition: A Review of the Literature*, UNCTAD Discussion Paper no. 166, Geneva: UNCTAD, February.

Mayhew, H. (1985 [1851]) *London Labour and the London Poor*, London: Penguin Classics Edition.

Mayoux, L. (2001) 'Women's empowerment versus sustainability? Towards a new paradigm in micro-finance programmes', in B. Lemire, R. Pearson and G. Campbell (eds), *Women and Credit: Researching the Past, Refiguring the Future*, Oxford: Berg.

— (2002) 'Microfinance and women's empowerment: rethinking "best practice"', *Development Bulletin*, 57.

McCarty, A. (2001) *Microfinance in Vietnam: A Survey of Schemes and Issues*, Report prepared for DfID and the State Bank of Vietnam, Mekong Economics Ltd.

MFI Solutions and La Colmena Milenaria (2008) *The Implications of Increased Commercialization of the Microfinance Industry: What can we learn from the discussions that followed the Compartamos IPO?*, MFI Solutions, LLC, USA, and La Colmena Milenaria, AC, Mexico.

Mishan, E. J. (1981) *Introduction to Normative Economics*, Oxford: Oxford University Press.

MITI (1980) *Vision of the Small and Medium Enterprises and Their Policy Direction in the 1980s*, Document B1-43, Tokyo: MITI.

Mitra, S. K. (2009) 'Exploitative microfinance interest rates', *Asian Social Science*, 5(5): 87–93.

Morduch, J. (1998) *Does Microcredit Really Help the Poor? New Evidence from Flagship Programs in Bangladesh*, Unpublished mimeo, Department of Economics and HIID, Harvard University, and Hoover Institution, Stanford University.

— (1999) 'The role of subsidies in microfinance: evidence from the Grameen Bank', *Journal of Development Economics*, 60: 229–48.

— (2000) 'The microfinance schism', *World Development*, 28(4): 617–29.

Morshed, L. (2006) *Lessons Learned in Improving Replicability of Successful Microcredit Programs – How Can the Best Models 'Travel' Better*, Paper presented at the Global Microcredit Summit, 12–15 November, Halifax, Nova Scotia.

Mosley, P. (1999) *Microfinance and Poverty: Bolivia case study*, Paper commissioned by the World Bank as an input into the World Development Report 2000/01.

Moyo, D. (2009) *Dead Aid: Why Aid is Not Working and How There is a Better Way for Africa*, New York: Farrar, Straus and Giroux.

MPDF (2003) *Financing SMEs in Cambodia: Why do banks find it so difficult?*, Private Sector Discussions no. 1, Phnom Phenh: MPDF and IFC-World Bank.

Newman, B. (2006) 'Indian farmer suicides: a lesson for Africa's farmers', *Backgrounder*, 12(4), Oakland, CA: Institute for Food and Development Policy.

Nishiguchi, T. (1994) *Strategic Industrial Sourcing: The Japanese Advantage*, Oxford: Oxford University Press.

Norberg-Hodge, H., T. Merrifield and S. Gorelick (2002) *Bringing the Food Economy Home: Local Alternatives to Global Agribusiness*, London: Zed Books.

North, D. (1990) *Institutions, Institutional Change and Economic Performance*, Cambridge: Cambridge University Press.

Nyamu-Musembi, C. (2006) *Breathing Life into Dead Theories about Property Rights: De Soto and land relations in rural Africa*, IDS Working Paper 272, Institute of Development Studies, University of Sussex.

O'Connor, D. (1998) 'Rural industrial development in Vietnam and China: a study in contrasts', *MOCT-MOST*, 8: 7–43.

OECD (2001) *The New Economy: Beyond the Hype – Final Report on the OECD Growth Project* (Meeting of the Ministerial Council at Ministerial Level), Paris: OECD.

Osmani, S. R. (1989) 'Limits to the alleviation of poverty through non-farm credit', *Bangladesh Development Studies*, 117(4): 1–18.

Otero, M. (1994) 'The evolution of nongovernmental organizations toward financial intermediation', in Otero and Rhyne (1994).

Otero, M. and E. Rhyne (1994) *The New World of Microenterprise Finance: Building Healthy Institutions for the Poor*, London: IT Publications.

Pait, S. (2009) *The Micofinance Sector in Peru: Opportunities, Challenges and Empowerment with Gender Mainstreaming*, Oxfam NOVIB.

Parayil, G. (ed.) (2000) *Kerala – the Development Experience: Reflections on Sustainability and Replicability*, London: Zed Books.

Parrish, L. and U. King (2009) *Phantom Demand*, Center for Responsible Lending, 9 July.

Patel, R. (2007) *Stuffed and Starved*, London: Portobello Books.

Pearson, T. (2005) *Venezuela: This revolution has woken women up*, Green-Left On-line, 9 March, www.greenleft.org.au.

Piñeiro Harnecker, C. (2005) 'The new cooperative movement in Venezuela's Bolivarian process', *Green-Left Review*, 17 December.

Piore, M. and C. Sabel (1984) *The Second Industrial Divide: Possibilities for prosperity*, New York: Basic Books.

Pitt, M. and S. Khandker (1998) 'The impact of group-based credit programs on poor households in Bangladesh: does the gender of participants matter?', *Journal of Political Economy*, 106(5): 958–96.

Polanyi, K. (1944) *The Great Transformation: The Political and Economic Origins of Our Time*, Boston, MA: Beacon Press.

Pollin, R., M. W. Githinji and J. Heintz (2008) *An Employment-targeted Economic Programme for Kenya*, Cheltenham: Edward Elgar.

Popli, G. (2008) *Trade Liberalization and the Self-employed in Mexico*, UNU WIDER Research Paper no. 2008/05.

Porter, M. (1990) *The Competitive Advantage of Nations*, New York: Free Press.

Posani, B. (2009) *Crisis in the Countryside: Farmer suicides and the political economy of agrarian distress in India*, DESTIN Working Paper no. 09-95, London: London School of Economics.

Prahalad, C. K. (2004) *The Fortune at the Bottom of the Pyramid: Eradicating Poverty through Profits*, Pittsburgh, PA: Wharton School Publishing.

Prasad, N. and M. Gerecke (2009) *Employment-oriented Crisis Responses: Lessons from Argentina and the Republic of Korea*, Policy Brief, International Institute for Labour Studies, ILO.

Pretty, J. (1999) *The Living Land: Agriculture, Food and Community Regeneration in the 21st Century*, London: Earthscan.

— (ed.) (2005) *The Earthscan Reader in Sustainable Agriculture*, London: Earthscan.

Pupavac, V. (2005) 'Empowering women? An assessment of international gender policies in Bosnia', *International Peacekeeping*, 12(3): 391–405.

Putnam, R., with R. Leonardi and R. Nanetti (1993) *Making Democracy Work: Civic traditions in modern Italy*, Princeton, NJ: Princeton University Press.

Pyke, F. (1994) *Small Firms, Technical Services and Inter-firm Cooperation*, Geneva: International Institute for Labour Studies, ILO.

Pyke, F. and W. Sengenberger (eds) (1992) *Industrial Districts and Local Economic Regeneration*, Geneva: International Institute for Labour Studies, ILO.

Pyke, F., G. Becattini and W. Sengenberger (eds) (1990) *Industrial Districts and Inter-firm Cooperation in Italy*, Geneva: International Institute for Labour Studies, ILO.

Quasem, M. A. (1991) 'Limits to the alleviation of poverty through non-farm credit: a comment', *Bangladesh Development Studies*, 19(3): 129–32.

Rahman, A. (1999) *Women and Microcredit in Rural Bangladesh: An Anthropological Study of Grameen Bank Lending*, Boulder, CO: Westview Press.

Rainnie, A. (1989) *Industrial Relations in Small Firms*, London: Routledge.

Rajan, S. I. and K. C. Zachariah (2007) *Remittances and Their Impact on the Kerala Economy and Society*, Paper presented at the conference 'International migration, multi-local livelihoods and human security: perspectives from Europe, Asia and Africa', Institute of Social Studies, the Netherlands, 30/31 August 2007.

Rankin, K. (2002) 'Social capital, microfinance, and the politics of development', *Feminist Economics*, 8(1): 1–24.

Raper, A. F. (1970) *Rural Development in Action: The Comprehensive Experiment at Comilla, East Pakistan*, Ithaca, NY: Cornell University Press.

Reinert, E. (2007) *How Rich Countries Became Rich, and Why Poor Countries Stay Poor*, London: Constable.

Rhyne, E. (2001) *Mainstreaming Microfinance: How lending to the poor began, grew, and came of age in Bolivia*, West Hartford, CT: Kumarian Press.

Robinson, M. (1995) *The Paradigm Shift in Microfinance: A perspective from HIID*, Paper presented at the Harvard Institute for International Development (HIID) History Conference, Bermuda, March.

— (2001) *The Microfinance Revolution: Sustainable Finance for the Poor*, Washington, DC: World Bank.

Roodman, D. and J. Morduch (2009) *The Impact of Microcredit on the Poor in Bangladesh: Revisiting the Evidence*, Working Paper no. 174, Center for Global Development, June.

Roth, H.-D. (1983) *Indian Money-lenders at Work: Case Studies of the Traditional Rural Credit Markets in Dhanbad District, Bihar*, New Delhi: Manohar.

Roy, A. and N. Alsayyad (eds) (2004) *Urban Informality, Transnational Perspectives from the Middle East, Latin America, and South Asia*, Lanham, MD: Lexington Books.

Rozas, D. (2009) 'Opinion: is there a microfinance bubble in South India?', *Microfinance Focus*, 17 November.

Rutherford, S., M. Maniruzzaman, S. K. Sinha and Acnabin & Co. (2003) *Grameen II: At the end of 2003 – a 'grounded view' of how Grameen's new initiative is progressing in the villages*, Dhaka: MicroSave.

— (2006) *Grameen II: The First Five Years 2001–2005 – a 'grounded view' of Grameen's new initiative*, Dhaka: MicroSave.

Sachs, J. (2005) *The End of Poverty: Economic Possibilities for Our Time*, London: Penguin.

SAPRIN (Structural Adjustment Participatory Reviews International Network) (2001) *The Policy Roots of Economic Crisis and Poverty*, Washington, DC: SAPRIN.

Schmitz, H. (1999) 'Collective efficiency and increasing returns', *Cambridge Journal of Economics*, 23: 465–83.

Schreiner, M. (2004) *Scoring Drop-out at a Microlender in Bolivia*, Mimeo, Microfinance Risk Management and Center for Social Development, Washington University, St Louis.

Schumacher, E. F. (1973) *Small is Beautiful: A Study of Economics as if People Matter*, London: Blond and Briggs.

Schumpeter, J. (1996 [1942]) *Capitalism, Socialism and*

Democracy, London: Unwin University Books.

Scott, J. C. (1992) *Domination and the Arts of Resistance: Hidden Transcripts*, New Haven, CT: Yale University Press.

Seabrook, J. (1996) *Cities of the South*, London: Verso.

Sebstad, J. and M. Cohen (2000) *Microfinance, Risk Management, and Poverty*, Synthesis Study submitted to Office of Microenterprise Development, USAID, Washington, DC.

Seibel, H. D. (2003) 'History matters in microfinance', *Small Enterprise Development*, 14(2): 10–12.

— (2005) *Does History Matter? The Old and the New World of Microfinance in Europe and Asia*, Paper presented at 'From moneylenders to microfinance: Southeast Asia's credit revolution in institutional, economic and cultural perspective – an interdisciplinary workshop', Asia Research Institute, Department of Economics and Department of Sociology, National University of Singapore, 7/8 October.

— (2009) *The People's Credit Funds of Vietnam*, Asian Development Bank, March.

Seibel, H. D. and U. G. Damachi (1982) *Self-Management in Yugoslavia and the Developing World*, London: Macmillan.

Sen, A. (1992) *Inequality Re-examined*, Cambridge, MA: Harvard University Press.

— (1999) *Development as Freedom*, Oxford: Oxford University Press.

Shane, S. (2008) *The Illusions of Entrepreneurship: The costly myths that entrepreneurs, investors and policy makers live by*, New Haven, CT: Yale University Press.

Sherraden, M. (1991) *Assets and the Poor: A New American Welfare Policy*, Armonk, NY, and London: M. E. Sharpe Inc.

Shiva, V. (2002) *Water Wars: Privatization, Pollution, and Profit*, Cambridge, MA: South End Press.

Shylendra, H. S. (2006) 'Microfinance institutions in Andhra Pradesh: crisis and diagnosis', *Economic and Political Weekly*, 41(1), 7–13 January.

Sirtaine, S. and I. Skamnelos (2007) *Credit Growth in Emerging Europe: A Cause for Stability Concerns?*, Policy Research Working Paper 4281, Washington, DC: World Bank.

Skoufias, E. (2001) *Is PROGRESA working? Summary of the results by an evaluation by International Food Policy Research Institute (IFPRI)*, Discussion Paper no. 118, Food Consumption and Nutrition Division, Washington, DC.

Smith, P. and E. Furman (2007) *A Billion Bootstraps: Microcredit, Barefoot Banking, and the Business Solution for Ending Poverty*, New York: McGraw-Hill.

Standing, G. (1999) 'Global feminization through flexible labor: a theme revisited', *World Development*, 27(3): 583–602.

Stiglitz, J. (2002) *Globalisation and Its Discontents*, London: Allen Lane.

— (2003) *The Roaring Nineties: Seeds of Destruction*, London: Allen Lane.

Stiglitz, J. and A. Weiss (1981) 'Credit rationing in markets with imperfect information', *American Economic Review*, 17(3): 393–410.

Storey, D. J. (1993) *Should We Abandon Support to Start-up Businesses?*, Working Paper no. 11, SME Centre, University of Warwick.

— (1994) *Understanding the Small Business Sector*, London: Routledge.

Storey, D. J. and S. Johnson (1987) *Job Generation and Labour Market Change*, London: Macmillan.

Storey, D. J. and A. Strange (1992) *Entrepreneurship in Cleveland 1979–1989: A Study of the Effects of the Enterprise Culture*, Research Series no. 3, Department of Employment.

Sugar, D. (2006) 'Venezuela and the hackers' revolution', *Synthesis/Regeneration*, 40 (Summer).

Sunkel, O. (ed.) (1993) *Development from Within: Toward a neostructuralist approach for Latin America*, Boulder, CO: Lynne Rienner.

Tata Institute of Social Sciences (2005) *Causes of Farmer Suicides in Maharashtra: An Enquiry* (Final report submitted to the Mumbai High Court), 15 March.

Tendler, J. (1997) *Good Government in the Tropics*, Baltimore, MD: Johns Hopkins University Press.

Tett, G. (2009) *Fool's Gold: How Unrestrained Greed Corrupted a Dream, Shattered Global Markets and Unleashed a Catastrophe*, London: Little, Brown.

Thomas Isaac, T. M. and R. W. Franke (2002) *Local Democracy and Development: The Kerala People's Campaign for Decentralized Planning*, Boston, MA: Rowman and Littlefield.

Thorbecke, E. (1979) 'Agricultural development', in W. Galenson (ed.), *Economic Growth and Structural Change in Taiwan: The post-war experience of the Republic of China*, Ithaca, NY: Cornell University Press.

Tilly, C. and M. Kennedy (2007) 'Up against the *charros* and the *changarros*: Mexico's independent unions confront a wave of lousy jobs', *Dollars & Sense*, September/October.

Toynbee, P. (2003) *Hard Work: Life in low-pay Britain*, London: Bloomsbury.

Tschach, I. (2003) *The Long Term Impact of Microfinance on Income, Wages and the Sectoral Distribution of Economic Activity*, Working Paper Series: Finance and Accounting, no. 105, Johann Wolfgang Goethe-Universitat, Frankfurt am Main.

Tucker, J. (2006) 'Microcredit or macrowelfare: the myth of Grameen', Daily article, Ludwig von Mises Institute, posted 8 November.

Turner, G. (2008) *The Credit Crunch*, London: Pluto Press.

UN-Habitat (2003) *The Challenge of Slums: Global Report on Human Settlements 2003*, London: Earthscan for and on behalf of the United Nations Human Settlement Programme.

UNCTAD (2003) *Annual Report 2003*, Geneva: UNCTAD.

UNDP (2002) *Human Development Report 2002 – Bosnia and Herzegovina*, Sarajevo: UNDP.

— (2008) *Creating Value for All: Strategies for doing business with the poor*, New York: UNDP.

Veron, R. (2001) 'The new Kerala model: lesson for sustainable development', *World Development*, 29: 601–27.

Vietnamese Academy of Social Sciences (2007) *Vietnam Poverty Update Report 2006: Poverty and Poverty Reduction in Vietnam 1993–2004*, Hanoi: National Political Publisher.

Vik, R. E. (2007) *The Social Construction of Success: Policy and practice in a Bolivian microfinance institution*, Oslo: Hovedoppgave sosialantropologi, Sosialantropologisk institutt, University of Oslo.

Vogelgesang, U. (2001) *Microfinance in Times of Crisis: The Effects of Competition, Rising Indebtedness, and Economic Crisis on Repayment Behaviour*, GK Working Paper Series no. 2001-06, University of Mannheim.

Von Pischke, J. D., D. W. Adams and G. Donald (eds) (1983) *Rural Financial Markets in Developing Countries*, Baltimore, MD: Johns Hopkins University Press.

Wade, R. (1982) *Irrigation and Agricultural Politics in South Korea*, Boulder, CO: Westview Press.

— (1983) 'South Korea's agricultural development: the myth of the passive state', *Pacific Viewpoint*, 24(1).

— (1990) *Governing the Market*, Princeton, NJ: Princeton University Press.

Waterfield, C. (2007) *Explanation of Compartamos Interest Rates*, Mimeo, 7 April.

Weber, H. (2002) 'The imposition of a global development architecture: the example of microcredit', *Review of International Studies*, 28: 537–55.

Weisbrot, M. and L. Sandoval (2006) *Bolivia's Challenges*, CEPR Report, Washington, DC: Center for Economic and Policy Research, March.

Weiss, L. (1988) *Creating Capitalism: The State and Small Business since 1945*, Oxford: Blackwell.

— (1998) *The Myth of the Powerless State: Governing the Economy in the Global Era*, Cambridge: Polity Press.

Wenner, M. (2008) *Dealing with Coordination Issues in Rural Development Projects: Game Theory Insights*, RUR-07-06, Washington, DC: Inter-American Development Bank, June.

Whang, I.-J. (1981) *Management of Rural Change in Korea: The Saemaul Undong*, Korean Institute of Social Sciences Series no. 5, Seoul: Seoul National University Press.

Whittaker, D. H. (1997) *Small Firms in the Japanese Economy*, Cambridge: Cambridge University Press.

Williams, S. (2007) 'Commentary: the problem with microlending', *Berkeley Daily Planet*, 26 January.

Wilpert, G. (2007) *Changing Venezuela by Taking Power: The History and Policies of the Chavez Government*, London: Verso.

WM Global Partners (2003) *Evaluation of the Programme for the Return of Refugees and Internally Displaced Persons in Croatia: Final Report*,

Birmingham: WM Global Partners, February.

Wood, T. (2009) 'Latin America tamed?', *New Left Review*, 58 (July/August).

Woodruff, C. (2001) *Firm Finance from the Bottom up: Microenterprises in Mexico*, Working Paper no. 112, Center for Research on Economic Development and Policy Reform, Stanford University, November.

World Bank (2001) *Voices of the Poor*, 3 vols, Washington, DC: World Bank.

— (2003) *Land Policies for Growth and Poverty Reduction*, Oxford: Oxford University Press.

— (2004a) *A Study of Rural Poverty in Mexico*, Washington, DC: World Bank.

— (2004b) *Financial Sector Policy Issues Note: Vietnam Bank for Social Policies*, Washington, DC: World Bank.

— (2007) *Making Finance Work for Africa*, Washington, DC: World Bank.

— (2008) *Finance for All*, Washington, DC: World Bank.

— (2009) *The Moving out of Poverty Study: An Overview*, Washington, DC: World Bank.

Wright, G. A. N. (2000) *Microfinance Systems: Designing Quality Financial Services for the Poor*, London/Dhaka: Zed Books/ University Press.

— (2001) 'Drop-outs and graduates: lessons from Bangladesh', *MicroBanking Bulletin*, 6, April.

Wynter, C. and J. McIlroy (2006) *Celebrating Five Years of the Women's Bank*, Green-Left On-line, 6 October,

Yunus, M. (1989) 'Grameen Bank: organization and operation', in Levitsky (1989).

— (2007) *Creating a World without Poverty: Social Business and the Future of Capitalism*, New York: Public Affairs.

Yunus, M. with A. Jolis (1998) *Banker to the Poor: The Autobiography of Mohammad Yunus*, London: Aurum.

Index

Acceso FFP organization (Chile), 122
ACCIÓN organization (USA),
    16, 22, 132, 142, 143, 144,
    145–6, 203; Campaign for Client
    Protection, 132, 146
accumulation by dispossession, 50,
    151
ACLEDA organization (Cambodia),
    101–2
Africa: development in, 96–9;
    microfinance in, 86
Agency for Small and Medium
    Enterprise Development
    (ASMED) (Vietnam), 195
agriculture, 89, 194; cooperatives,
    105; in Cambodia, 101; kolkoz
    system, 81; role of microfinance
    in, 80–91; state support for, 83;
    subsistence farming, 121 see also
    suicides by farmers
Ahmad, Q. K., 67–8
Akyuz, Yilmaz, 95, 166, 169
Albright, Madeleine, 40
Alexander-Tedeschi, G., 77
Alliance for Fair Microfinance,
    130–1
alternatives to microfinance,
    166–200, 198, 199
Amsden, Alice, 93
Andhra Pradesh state, 186;
    Commission on Farmers'
    Welfare, 134; microcredit bubbles
    in, 140; microfinance crisis,
    132–5; saturation of microfinance
    in, 83
Arizmendiarrieta, José María, 173
Artisan Funds (Italy), 176
Arun, T., 160
Asian Development Bank (ADB), 198

Asian financial crisis, 179
Association for Social Advancement
    (ASA), 44, 48
at-risk groups, 167–9
Atkinson, Dan, 201

Balkenhol, Bernd, 61
Banana Skins report, 53, 54
Banco de Desarrollo Productivo
    (BDP) (Bolivia), 121
Banco de la Mujer (Venezuela), 189,
    190
Banco del Pueblo (Venezuela), 189
BancoSol (Bolivia), 15, 16, 118, 120,
    204
Bangladesh, 2, 3, 6, 24, 53, 67,
    205; land seizures in, 58;
    microenterprise in, 68 (failure of,
    76); microfinance in, 46, 138–9;
    study of, 61–2
Bangladesh Institute of Development
    Studies (BIDS), 61
Bangladesh Rural Advancement
    Committee (BRAC), 11, 138;
    Conrad N. Hilton Humanitarian
    Prize, 80
Bank BRI Unit-Desa (BRI-UD), 15,
    16
Bank Rakyar Indonesia (BRI), 11,
    14–15, 204
barrow traders, 71
Basque region, 190; community
    development bank in, 173–5
Baumol, William, 96
bazaar economy, 119
Benin, microfinance in, 97
bidi cooperative (Kerala), 187
Bill and Melinda Gates Foundation,
    21

Bolivia, 109, 135, 188; debt in, 58; economic crisis in, 120; microcredit bubbles in, 140; microfinance in, 11, 15, 45 (new wave, 118–22)
Bologna, 176
Bolsa Familia (Brazil), 168
Bosnia: consumer microloans in, 137; microenterprise in, 45–6, 102–3; microfinance in, 89 (meltdown of, 140); overindebtedness in, 141
bottom-up development, 99, 188, 190–1
Boulder Institute, 131
Brazil, 168, 188
Brink, Brian, 99
building societies: commercialization of, 114–17; remuneration of managers in, 117

Caisse Populaire (Quebec), 193
Caja Laboral Popular (CLP) (Spain), 174
Cambodia, 195; microfinance in, 101
capabilities of the poor, 209, 210
Central People's Credit Fund (Vietnam), 193
Chaebols (South Korea), 178, 179
Chang, Ha-Joon, 93, 113, 166, 169, 211; Bad Samaritans, 97
changarrization, 100–1, 151–2
child labour, 32
China, 78; local financing in, 181–5
Choudhury, Shafiqual Haque, 11, 48
Christoplos, I., 89
Chu, Michael, 52
client exit/failure, 34–5, 74–7, 119, 205; examination of, 75; in East Africa, 52–3
client poaching, 134
Clinton, Bill, 20
code of conduct of microfinance industry, 131
collateral, elimination of, 40
collective organization, 39, 160, 203

Collins, D. et al., Postfolios of the Poor …, 167
commercialization: of microfinance sector, 2, 14–16, 22, 44, 52, 112–53; (as the death of microfinance, 112–53; background to, 113–14; social mission of, 54–5); of UK building societies, 114–17
Commission on the Legal Empowerment of the Poor, 40
commodity chains, 104
communities, weakening of, 2
Compartamos bank (Mexico), 22–3, 24, 130, 131, 142–52, 196; commercialization of, 112; damaging effects of, 152
conditional cash transfer (CCT), 121–2, 167–8
connectivity, 103–5, 186, 188
Conrad N. Hilton Humanitarian Prize, awarded to BRAC, 80
Consultative Group to Assist the Poor (CGAP), 16–17, 22, 131, 142, 144, 145, 147, 197, 203; criticism of Vietnam, 196; Pink Book, 17
consumer microloans, 29–30, 41, 167, 168, 205, switch to, 135–40
consumption: funding of, 120, 167; smoothing of, 25
contract farming system, 105
cooperatives, 105, 173, 176, 177, 178, 186–7, 188, 190; financial, 176, 180
Cooperbanca (Italy), 176
Counts, Alex, 85
creative destruction, 65
credit unions, 168–9
crime, increasing, 164
crisis, world economic, 3–4, 23, 36, 115
Croatia: consumer microloans in, 137; dairy sector in, 87–8; project evaluation in, 87
cross-border shuttle trading, 97, 105; in Poland, 107

cross-subsidization, 128
crowding out problem, 107
current expenditure, financing of, 134

dairy sector, in Croatia, 87–8
Daley-Harris, Sam, 144
Danel, Carlos, 145, 146
Danone company, 127–9
Davis, Mike, 37, 92–3, 110; *City of Slums*, 72–3
Davis, Peter, 76
Davis, S., 74
debt, 5, 37, 44, 53, 58, 76, 97, 120, 201; as pretext for land seizure, 8–9; in Bosnia, 141; in India, 83–4, 133; of farmers, 134
default on debt, 10, 74, 120
defaulting borrowers, ostracizing of, 108
deindustrialization, 93–6, 102; in Africa, 99; in Mexico, 100–1; in Nigeria, 98
Dell, Michael, 21
demutualization of building societies, 115
Department for Industry and Development (DfID), 138, 139; report on Vietnam, 194
Deutsche Bank, 131
development triggers *see* triggers of development
Dichter, Thomas, 29, 91
disempowerment: of the poor, 31, 32, 39; of women, 49
displacement effects, 34–5, 64–73, 77; damaging, 72; in developing economies, 66–70
distribution chains, non-unionized, 163
dividends, payment of, 150
doi moi policy (Vietnam), 192
drop-outs, 119
dualistic financial structures, 124
Dyal-Chand, Rashmi, 48

East Asian development model, 121, 169, 178
economies of scale, 103, 189
Ehigiamusoe, G., 86
elite capture, 8
Ellerman, David, 34–5, 60, 95, 175
Elliot, Larry, 201; *et al. The Gods that Failed*, 116–17
Emilia-Romagna, 175–8
employee capture, 148–9
employment-generating activity, 26
empowerment, 186; myth of, 31–4; of the poor, 1, 33–4, 158, 160; of women, 25, 31 (myth of, 41–9) *see also* gender empowerment
endogenous development (Venezuela), 190
EnergoInvest organization (Bosnia), 103
Enterprise Allowance Scheme (UK), 66
entrepreneurship: in microfinance sector, 124–5; individual, 210
Estonia, consumer microloans in, 137

failed clients *see* client exit/failure
fairness, in microfinance, 130–2
fallacy of composition, 66, 70, 73, 126, 186, 205
family and friends, borrowing from, 57–8
family assets sold, 58
family farms, 80, 82, 105
farmers' associations, 180
Fei, J. C. H., 180
finance sector, privatization of, 162
FINCA International, 30, 56
Finscope studies, 29
firm size, in India, 79
Fiscal Investment and Loan Plan (FILP) (Japan), 172
flexibilization of labour force, 43, 92
Florio, Massimo, 159
food security, 90, 195
Ford Foundation, 197
Fordism, reaches limits, 103

Franke, R. W., 186
free at the point of use, 159
Friedman, David, 172
Friedman, Milton, 113, 154, 157
full cost recovery, 162
Fund for Microenterprise Development (FONDEMI) (Venezuela), 189
Fundusz Mikro, 102

Galbraith, John Kenneth, 28; *The Affluent Society*, 53
gambling, popularity of, 37
Gates, Carolyn, 51
gender empowerment, 42–9; in Bosnia, 46; used as cover, 46
gender solidarity, 109
Gente Nueva organization, 142
Germany, 93–4
Gilbert, Alan, 41
Gilder, George, 157
Gill, Lesley, 44–5
Goetz, A. M., 43
Goldberg, Nathanael, 62
Goldin Institute, 29
government support, not sought, 13
Grabel, I., 113
grace periods, 37
Grameen II project, 18–19, 42
Grameen Bank, 2, 6, 24, 29, 40, 48–9, 55, 57, 59, 60, 67–8, 80, 108, 110, 123, 138, 139, 157, 164, 166, 201, 203, 208, 209; becomes regular financial institution, 17; client base of, 19; conversion to new wave principles, 42; establishment of, 10; growth of, 11–12; marginalization of, 17–18; marketing of, 19; model of, 26 (flaws in, 187; rejection of, 192, 204); Nobel Prize awarded to, 42; principles of, 7; receipt of subsidies, 13; relation to poverty reduction, 205; struggling members programme, 42; study of, 44

Grameen Danone Foods Ltd, 127–8
Grameen Telecom, 68–9, 127
GrameenPhone, 68–70, 126–7

Halifax Building Society, demutualization of, 116
Haltiwanger, C., 74
Hannan, Mazharul, 69
Hardy, J., 102
Harper, Malcolm, 90, 130
Harriss, John, 160
Harvard Institute for International Development (HIID), 15, 196, 204
Harvey, David, 50; *A Brief History of Neoliberalism*, 33
Hatch, John, 30
health and safety at work, 91
healthcare, 43; of children, 122
Heydemann, Steven, 155
Holman, D., 109
honour and shame, affecting women, 44
Hospes, Otto, 28
Hossain, M., 67–8
Hulme, David, 76, 110, 160
Hungary, consumer microloans in, 137

ICICI Bank, 134; partnership model of, 83
Imp-Act project, 62
impact assessments, 34–6, 61, 75, 77, 110, 205; scepticism about, 63
impannatori, 104, 177
import dependency, 105–8, 206
incentivization of managers, 14
Inclusive Cities project, 72
inclusive supply chains, 125–30, 157, 160
income-generating activities, 1, 8, 9, 26, 29–31
India, 53, 58; consumer microloans in, 137; financing in, 185–7; land seizures in, 58; microcredit bubbles in, 140; microcredit in, 46, 55–6; milk cooperatives in, 128;

missing middle in, 78–9; over-supply of microfinance in, 54
individual asset accumulation, 161
industrial development, process of, 154–5
industrial districts, 103–5
infant industry approach, 17
informal sector, 110; contribution to development, 91; 'discovery' of, 91
informality, threat to social peace, 92
informalization, 91–3
interest rates, 37, 56, 107, 180, 189; cutting of, 135; fluctuations in, 56; high, 22, 24, 49, 51, 59, 84, 85, 86, 95, 133, 134, 142, 207 (damage to clients, 146–8); low, 3, 9, 12, 51, 147, 148, 195, 196; market rates, 14, 18, 160; myths about, 55–7
International Monetary Fund (IMF), 33, 187
International Year of Microcredit, 20
Istituti di Credito Speciale (Italy), 177
Italy: local-regional financial models in, 175–8; microenterprise in, 104

Japan, 190; microenterprise in, 104; recovery from Second World War, 170–3
Jobra village, Bangladesh, 8–9, 202
joint liability, in solidarity circles, 18–19

Kabeer, Naila, 49
Kaffu, E., 110
Karim, Lamia, 44, 109
Karlan, Dean, 56, 77
Karnarni, Aneel, 79
Kendra see solidarity circles
Kenya: microfinance in, 85–6, 97
Kerala State, microfinance in, 185–7
Keynesianism, 4, 156
Khan, Akhtar Hameed, 11, 203; Comilla model, 7–8
Khandker, Shahidur, 61–2, 63

King, Martin Luther, 201
Kiva institution, 21
Klein, Naomi, 112
Kozul-Wright, R., 166, 170
Kuo, S. W. Y., 180
Kupedes microloans, 15

Labarthe, Carlos, 146
land: ownership of, 81; sale of, 82; seized through debt, 8–9; sub-divisions of, 81; titling of, 40–1
Landesbanken, 94
Lebanon, loan structures in, 51
LegaCoop (Italy), 178
Lehman Brothers, 212
Levy, Santiago, 99–100
Leys, Colin, 108
Littlefield, Elizabeth, 145
loan officers, incentivization of, 53
loan use, delinked from loan payment, 90
loans, traditional, 37
local and regional systems, 170, 171, 173, 181; in China, 181–5; in Italy, 175–8
Lont, Hotze, 28
lumpenproletariat, 32–3

Malawi, microfinance in, 85
male hegemony, strengthening of, 44–5
managers, bonuses of, 22
Manji, Ambreena, 85
Marshall Plan, 94
Marx, Karl, 32
Mayhew, Henry, London Labour and the London Poor, 32
Mayoux, Linda, 46–7, 56
McKinsey report, 92
McNamara, Robert, 164
mega-cities, 164
Merrifield, T., 80–1
Mexico: Compartamos affair, 142–52; consumer microloans in, 137; microenterprise in, 70–1, 99–100; microfinance in,

22–3, 84–5; National Survey of
Microenterprises, 100
Mexico Employers Association, 101
microcredit: as human right, 156;
paradox, 91
microcredit bubbles, 3, 140–1, 153,
207
Microcredit Summit Campaign, 20,
42
microenterprise: ghettos of, 189; in
Bangladesh, 68 (failure of, 76);
in Bosnia, 102–3; in India, 79; in
Italy, 104, 177; in Japan, 104, 172;
in Mexico, 70–1; in Poland, 102;
in South Africa, 71
microfinance: addiction to, 36;
alternatives to *see* alternatives to
microfinance; and connectivity,
103–5; and deindustrialization,
93–6; and economies of scale,
78–91; and import dependency,
105–8; and income-generating
activities, 29–31; and
informalization, 91–3; and
poverty reduction, 61; and social
capital, 108–10; antagonistic to
development, 1, 3; as a way of
supporting markets, 159–60; as
anti-development policy, 202;
as containment of the poor,
163–4; as empowering the poor,
31–4; as human right, 52; as
local neoliberalism, 160–4, 204;
as politically acceptable model,
161–2; as poverty trap, 5, 60–111,
121, 154, 166, 206; associated
with lower labour costs,
163; bubbles *see* microcredit
bubbles; case for, 24–6;
coining of term, 12; collapse
of, 120; commercialization
of *see* commercialization of
microfinance; consonant with
neoliberalism, 155–6; demand
for, 51–4; disillusion with, 187;
effect on poverty reduction,
62–3; failure of programmes,
74–7; impact assessments of,
34–6; in Africa, 96–9; in Andhra
Pradesh, crisis, 132–5; lowers
costs for the state, 163; marketing
of, 2; myth of empowerment
of women, 42–9; myth of
helping the poorest, 41–2;
myth of self-sustainability of,
58–9; myth of wanting by the
poor, 36–9; myths and realities
of, 28–59; neoliberalization
of, 14–19; new wave *see* new
wave microfinance; oversupply
of, 122; politics of, 154–65;
programme interventions, 1;
public narrative of, 28, 59, 208;
relation to property titles, 39–41;
rise of, 6–27; undermines poverty
reduction, 120
microfinance millionaires, 123–5, 207
MicroFinance Transparency
organization, 131
micro-insurance, 11
microloans, true costs of, 53
micro-savings, 11
milk cooperatives, in India, 128
Ministerio para la Economía Popular
(MINEP) (Venezuela), 189
Ministry of International Trade and
Industry (MITI) (Japan), 172
mission drift of microfinance
industry, 54–5
Mittelstandpolitik, 94
Mondragón Cooperative
Corporation, 173–5
moneylenders, 24; class of, 8–9;
liberation from, 9–11
Morales, Evo, 119, 121, 122
Morduch, Jonathan, 13, 60, 62, 63
Morgenthau Plan, 93–4, 99, 101
mortgages, 115
Mosley, Paul, 76, 110, 118
Mother Teresa, 142
Moyo, Dambisa, 98; *Dead Aid*, 96–7
Mukherji, Arnab, 54

multinational corporations, 128–30, 157
multiple borrowing, 58
Mutesasita, L. K., 110

Nationwide Building Society, 116
neighbourhood help groups (Kerala), 184–5
neoliberalism, 14, 160–4, 203, 208; collapse of, 212; disenchantment with, 120; failures of, 4
neoliberalization of microfinance, 14–19
new development economics, 78
new wave microfinance, 2–3, 14, 16, 17, 23, 26, 35, 41, 42, 47, 55, 59, 74, 83, 84, 90, 105, 109, 111, 112, 118, 120, 122, 132, 141, 142, 152, 155, 161, 165, 166, 189, 196, 206, 207; as 'best practice', 19–22; in Bolivia, 118–22; myths of, 49–59; problems of, 22–4
Nigeria, deindustrialization in, 98
Nishiguchi, T., 104
non-governmental organizations (NGOs), 12, 16; transformed into commercial banks, 15–16
Norbert-Hodge, H., 80–1
North, D., 112, 154
North American Free Trade Agreement (NAFTA), 84
Northern Rock Building Society, 116–17; taken into public ownership, 117

Ohio State University, 14
Omidyar, Pierre, 21
Osmani, S. R., 68
Ota (Japan), machine-tool production in, 172
Otero, Maria, 16, 145
outreach, 63
Oxfam, 191

Pakistan, 8, 53; land seizures in, 58; microfinance in, 46

Parayil, G., 185
patriarchy, 25, 49
payday lenders, 139
pension plans, 18
People's Credit Funds (PCF) (Vietnam), 193
People's Finance Corporation (Japan), 171
Peru, saturated by microfinance, 40–1
Peru Urban Property Rights Project (PUPRP), 40
petty entrepreneurship, 211
Piore, Michael, with Charles Sabel, The Second Industrial Divide, 103
Pitt, Mark, 61–2, 63
Pocantico Declaration, 131
Poland: cross-border shuttle trading in, 107; microenterprise in, 75–6
Polanyi, Karl, 31
poor, 160, 162, 188, 208; and building societies, 115; containment of, 163–4; effects of interest rates on, 146–8; helping of the poorest, 41–2; invited into capitalism, 156–60; management of money by, 167; organization of, 2; romanticization of, 38; undermining status of, 162; women, creativity of, 8
Poor Law Reform, 31–2
Popular Networks (Venezuela), 190
post-conflict scenarios, 26; microfinance in, 167
poverty, reduction of, 1, 3, 13, 21, 25, 39, 56, 61, 67, 69, 92, 118–19, 120, 122, 129, 130, 135, 151, 154, 159, 186, 201, 210; in Bolivia, 119; in Poland, 75; in Venezuela, 191; in Vietnam, success of, 191–8; state at heart of, 158
poverty-push microenterprise, 70–1
poverty trap, 8; of rural poor, 51 see also microfinance, as poverty trap
power and politics, issues of, 209

Prahalad, C. K., 125; *The Fortune at the Bottom of the Pyramid*, 123
privatization, 14, 45, 113, 151, 158–9, 160, 183; in the UK, 113, 159; of financial sector, 162; of water supply, 162–3
Pro-Credit Bank (Serbia), 139
pro-poor policy, 191, 209, 211
PRODEM organization (Bolivia), 11, 15, 120
profit, maximization of, 206
property titles, formal, 39–41
Pupavac, Vanessa, 45
purdah, 44
Putnam, Robert, 108, 176

Qasem, M. A., 68

Rahman, Aminur, 29, 108; study of Grameen Bank, 44
Rainnie, A., 102
Randomized Control Trials, 35
Ranis, G., 180
redistribution of wealth, 168
regulation of lending programmes, 49
Reinert, Erik, 93
repayment, 37, 53, 84, 89, 120, 206; rates of, 11, 12, 13, 18, 23, 27, 119 (high, 57–8); relation to development, 57; responsibility of women, 44
rice sector, poverty trap, 195
Richardson, David, 148–50
rickshaw sector, in Bangladesh, 68
right to live, 31
Rippey, Paul, 37
Robinson, Marguerite, 196
Roodman, David, 60, 63
rural areas, cut off from financing, 138
Rural Credit Cooperatives (RCC) (China), 182–5
rural jobs, growth of, 90
Rutherford, Stuart, 30

Sachs, Jeffrey, 15
sales territory, issue of, 126
SAPRIN study, 106
savings, 176; emphasis on, 18; local, 152, 172, 174; mobilization of, 148, 177, 181
Say's Law, 73
school attendance, 122
Schuh, S., 74
Schumpeter, Joseph, 65
self-employment, 97; among women, 20, 43; expansion of, 43; promotion of, 33, 66
self-help group (SHG) movement, 11, 60
self-help groups, 83, 132, 134, 135; in India, 79; in Kerala State, 184–5
self-respect of the poor, 38
self-sustainability, 13–14, 27, 207; of microfinance, myth of, 58–9
Sen, Amartya, 156, 185, 208
senior personnel of institutions, enrichment of, 149–51
Serbia: consumer microloans in, 137; microfinance in, 71–2
shakti doi yoghurt product, 127–9
shame associated with debt default, 10
Shane, Scott, 74
SHARE organization (Andhra Pradesh), 135
Sharma, Devinder, 123–4
shinkin banks (Japan), 171
Shiva, Vandana, 162–3
Shoko Chukin Bank, 171
Sinković, Dejan, 88
Small Business Finance Corporation (Japan), 171
social businesses, 157, 160; concept of, 130
social capital, 108–10
social mission: loss of, 130; under commercialization, 54–5
Sociedad Financiera de Objeto Limitado (*sofol*), 143, 149
sogo banks (Japan), 171

solidarity, 2, 25–6, 38, 110
solidarity circles, 10, 11, 25, 108;
   abandonment of, 47–8; and
   gender perspective, 48; issue of
   joint liability, 18–19
Soto, Hernando de, 31, 39, 40, 61,
   73, 93, 187; *The Mystery of
   Capital*, 39–40
South Africa: consumer microloans
   in, 137; microenterprise in, 71
South Korea, 78; financing in,
   178–81
Spandana organization (Andhra
   Pradesh), 135
Speenhamland system, 31
spillover effects, 64, 73
start-up capital, 138
state: intervention by, 188, 211;
   minimal, agenda for, 162–3
Storey, David, 74
street trading, 101, 105–6; in
   Mexico, 99
street vendors, affected by
   displacement effect, 72
sub-prime mortgages, 53, 54
subsidies, problem of, 12–14
subsistence farming, 47
suicides by farmers, in India, 84, 133
Sunacoop (Venezuela), 188
Sunkel, Osvaldo, 188
survivalist activities, 32
survivor bias, 74, 75
Suskind, Ron, 28
sustainable development, 39, 63

Taiwan, 78; financing in, 178–81
Tanzania, microcredit in, 30
taxation: avoidance of, 92; respect
   for, undermined, 91
Telenor company, 68–70, 127
Thomas Isaac, 186
'Tiger' economies of East Asia, 4
Township and Village Enterprises
   (TVE) (China), 181–5
trade unions, 2, 32, 160, 163;
   exclusion of, 43

transparency, in microfinance, 130–2
triggers of development, 78–110,
   205–6

Uganda: microcredit in, 29
   (saturation of, 109–10); petty
   trading in, 97; women in, 56
Ukraine, consumer microloans in,
   137
United Kingdom (UK),
   microenterprise in, 76;
   development policies for, 66–7
United Nations (UN), 20
UN Conference on Trade and
   Development (UNCTAD), 95
UN Development Programme
   (UNDP), 101, 125
UN Millennium Development Goals,
   191
Urban Credit Cooperatives (UCC)
   (China), 182–5
USAID, 16, 34, 203; AIMS project,
   62

Velugu organization (Andhra
   Pradesh), 132
Venezuela: income programmes in,
   168, 187–91
Vietnam: criticisms of, 196–9, 209;
   success in poverty reduction,
   191–8, 209
Vietnam Bank for Agricultural and
   Rural Development (VBARD),
   192–3
Vietnam Bank for Social Policy
   (VBSP), 193, 197
Vietnam Bank for the Poor (VBP),
   193
Vietnam Microfinance Association
   (VMA), 197
Vietnam Microfinance Working
   Group, 197

Wade, Robert, 93
wage employment, 31–2
Waterfield, Chuck, 131, 144

Weiss, Linda, 104, 176
Williams, Sally, 48–9
women, 48; and microcredit, 9, 10, 27, 41; disempowerment of, 43, 45; empowerment of, 25 (myth of, 42–9); farm work of, 47; in self-employment, 20; prioritized as clients, 42; responsibilities shifted to, 46; shaming of, 108–9; telephone ladies, 127–8; unpaid work of, 85
Women's Savings Group (Vietnam), 193–4
Woodruff, C., 100
World Bank, 16–17, 33, 47, 57, 60, 61, 86, 106, 140, 159, 162, 164, 168, 187, 196, 197, 203; doubts on microfinance, 62–3; *Finance for All*, 63; International Finance Corporation (IFC), 143; *Moving Out of Poverty Study*, 37–8; report on Vietnam, 194; study of

consumer credit, 138; *Study of Rural Poverty in Mexico*, 84–5; *Voices of the Poor* study, 38
World Council of Credit Unions (WOCCU), 148, 149
World Social Forum, 159

Yunus, Muhammad, 1, 2, 6–12, 17, 19, 23, 26, 52, 55, 60, 63, 67, 73, 123, 127, 130, 131, 139, 140, 146, 154, 155, 156–60, 164, 201, 202, 203, 204, 208, 209; awarded prizes, 157 (Nobel Peace Prize, 6, 20, 42; US Presidential Medal of Freedom, 6); condemnation of Compartamos, 144; *Creating a World without Poverty*, 157; role as adviser, 20

Zambia, 98
Zenshiren Bank (Japan), 171
Zinman, Jonathan, 56